20TH CENTURY ROCK AND ROLL
HEAVY METAL

Martin Popoff

WATCH FOR THE REST OF THE SERIES

A GUIDE TO THE ARTISTS WHO MADE THE CENTURY'S GREATEST ROCK MUSIC

20th CENTURY ROCK AND ROLL

A COLLECTOR'S GUIDE PUBLISHING SERIES

Psychedelia	ISBN 1-896522-40-8
Alternative Music	ISBN 1-896522-19-X
Progressive Rock	ISBN 1-896522-20-3
Heavy Metal	ISBN 1-896522-47-5
Pop Music	ISBN 1-896522-25-4
Punk Rock	ISBN 1-896522-27-0
Glam Rock	ISBN 1-896522-26-2
Women In Rock	ISBN 1-896522-29-7

For ordering information see our web site at
www.cgpublishing.com

We acknowledge the financial support of the Government of Canada through
the Book Publishing Industry Development Program for our publishing activities.
Published by Collector's Guide Publishing Inc., Box 62034, Burlington, Ontario, Canada, L7R 4K2
Printed and bound in Canada
20th Century Rock and Roll - Heavy Metal
by Martin Popoff
ISBN 1-896522-47-5

20TH CENTURY ROCK AND ROLL

HEAVY METAL

Martin Popoff

Table Of Contents

Table Of Contents

Acknowledgments

The author would like to thank: Angie Aue, The Aylmer Express, Ed Balog, Marco Barbieri, Tracy Barnes, Carl Begai, Mike Bell, Paul Bergeron, Paul Bibeau, Mike Blackburn, Adrian Bromley, Chris Bruni, The Buffalo Bills, Andrew Carter, Century Media, Chart, Dennis Clapp, CMC, Collector's Guide Publishing, Gordon Conrad, Eric Coubard, Neil Cournoyer, Jess Cox, Neil Deas, Marty Dodge, Chuck Eddy, Scott Floman, Ula Gehret, Glass Eye, Bolle Gregmar, Mark Gromen, Alan Grusie, Dan Hanley, Michael Hannon, Ken Harker, Drew Harris, Scott Hefflon, Tim Henderson, Paula Hogan, Andy Hosner, Jaww, Mitch Joel, Jonesy, Kevin Julie, Paul Kennedy, Dan Kieswetter, Hugues Laflamme, Mitch Lafon, John Larocque, Steve Larocque, Lollipop, Magna Carta, Michael Mazur, Metal Blade Records, John Moran, Pete Morticelli, my immediate family (Beth and Trevor!), my family out west (mom, dad, Brad), my family out east (too numerous to mention!), Mark Morton, Nuclear Blast, Brian O'Neill, Sean Palmerston, Jon Paris, Bill Peters, Bryan Reesman, Alex Ristic, Mark Roper, Corey Rotman, Chip Ruggieri, Scrape Records, Jackie Short, Brian Slagel, Rose Slanic, Aaron Small, Erin Smyth, Solus, Wolfgang Spegg, Spitfire Records, Forrest Toop, Kurt Torster, Tom Tremeuth, Tracey Vera, Jeff Wagner, Johnny Walker, Matthew Walker, John Walters and Josh Wood.

Introduction: What Is Influence?

When I was first approached to write the metal book in this series (there are eight similar such diatribes — seek them out), I was looking for a way to elevate the discussion past vague sentiments like "the most important bands in metal," or even more presumptuous and vague "best bands in metal."

So, while still possessing a ring of the sermon on the mount, the idea of influence tweaked my sick, fanatical, librarian-precise mind, while simultaneously providing focus for a task which could potentially result in an exercise worth reading by both the metal novice and serious headbanged student alike.

So down the path I went, delving into the nature of influence and arriving at (through much brain drain) my list of the fifty bands who made the biggest impression on subsequent contributors to the genre (as opposed to those who made the biggest impression on the listeners. See Appendix I for more details.) These are the acts who shaped, reinforced, flavoured, or completely overturned (or down-tuned) metal throughout its first thirty ears-a'-ringing years.

Webster's New World Dictionary, Third College Edition, describes influence as "2 a) the power of persons or things to affect others, seen only in its effects b) the action or effect of such power 3 the ability of a person or group to produce effects indirectly by means of power based on wealth, high position etc. 4 a person or thing that has influence." And further on, "have an effect on the nature, behavior, development, action or though of." But I particularly like its first definition, "I orig. the supposed flowing of an ethereal fluid or power from the stars, thought by astrologers to affect the characters and actions of people."

Webster's New World Thesaurus, by Charlton Laird (he couldn't have actually written the thing, surely?) adds, among others, the following clarifications, "sway, affect, impress, carry weight, count, determine, make oneself felt, bring (pressure) to bear, lead, direct, modify, compel, incite, channel, mold, shape, be recognized, convince, motivate," and finally, "have a finger in the pie" and "lead by the nose"!

So now you know.

Indeed, each of the acts included has painted a broad brush stroke through more than half of the above sentiments and this book has a particular focus on three pretty distinct ideas: a) inspiring; b) jump-starting, invigorating or improving; and c) shifting or shaping. Or, using the catch-all short in deference to Laird, "leading by the nose."

I've broken the book up into three tidy sections — the three decades of metal thus far: the 70's, the 80's and the 90's. Heavy metal has been around for exactly thirty years, exactly three decades. I toyed with the idea of ranking these fifty acts from most influential to least, but decided that the complexities of the influence concept would be clouded through such pompous declarations on the part of one opinionated yapper. I mean, let's face it, picking fifty bands with no hierarchy is presumptuous enough. But bear in mind that fifty is a number large enough to be relatively thorough.

As a concession, however, to the temptation towards bald-faced ranking, I've ordered the bands within each decade from utmost to those of lesser importance. In deference to the mystery of art and the individual relationship of listener to creator, I will leave it to you to decide your own ultimate fifty ranking (or if you give a damn, try to guess mine.)

That said, there's a natural bias within the nature of the concept of influence such that earlier (or conversely longer-running) bands will have the greatest influence. For that reason you can somewhat surmise influence to be greater by sheer accumulation, with acts from the 70's and the early 80's carrying greater weight. There's a multiplier effect that comes with releasing more and more albums. What happens is that the larger body of work allows more inter-album comparisons to be made, and simply provides more musical life over which to pontificate: more press, more criticism and more websited interest; a vicious circle. One final note: the bands were slotted into decades according to which decade contained their most influential golden years, plain and simple.

For those who feel the need to comment, vent, agree or disagree, my e-mail address is martinp@inforamp.net. Snail mailers, go with Martin Popoff, P.O. Box 65208, 358 Danforth Ave., Toronto, Ontario Canada M4K 2Z2.

The Top 50

So without further qualification, hair-splitting and apologetics, here's a look at my take on the 50 Most Influential Bands In Heavy Metal. As with most critical analyses, it's the author's intention that this exercise enhances or otherwise affects, deciphers, identifies, or colours your perception of these bands and the genre in general, ultimately causing you to get more pleasure out of your interaction with the art form. And yes, dude, metal is an art, and art is a life-enhancer, so like, it matters.

Discographical Note: I've included all official studio albums, but only selected hits packs and compilations, the rule being that I've included records by bands not prone to multiple, exploitative "Best Of's" and/or hits collections that are licensed to a label other than the band's official one. With respect to boxed-sets, I've included ones that resemble hits collections as opposed to comprehensive catalogue reissues. So no Aerosmith's BOX OF FIRE, for example. In terms of live albums, we've got only the key, official, non-exploitative records. A further distinction is that most of these are the product of a functioning band, not ones released during break-ups; and again, all are with an official band-sanctioned label, not a licensed situation. So this is by no means a series of complete discographies (I just went through the onerous task of compiling a *Goldmine Heavy Metal Record Price Guide*, so I know discographies!), but it is nothing so lazy as a selected discography either. It's essentially all of the band's core records without the redundancy of regurgitated hits packages or endless stage spoo (this means you, Deep Purple!) And one final note: in terms of record label stated, in most cases I've tried to stay true to documenting the label that the band is on in their home country.

The 70's

⚡ **1** ⚡

Black Sabbath

OK, I'm blowing my promise right away. I will offer one penultimate ranking position. Said I wouldn't, but this one's a fix. Black Sabbath is the number one most influential metal band of all time. But before you check this out, skip forward to Appendix V and read about the pre-history of metal. And then realize how little of all of that has to do with the Sabs, in contrast for example, with how much it has to do with Zeppelin. Uh-huh. That is why Sabbath matters the most. They were a black tide that rolled over every other heavy band, all of which were poncing around with the blues and hippie music.

So again, why the Sabs? For starters, Ozzy Osbourne, Tony Iommi, Geezer Butler and Bill Ward are widely credited with inventing the genre, both in quality and quantity, two hallmarks of intention and thus influence on this count. The witchy debut from early 1970, and PARANOID from late 1970, are considered the first two truly modern "heavy metal proper" albums of all time, with only Deep Purple's IN ROCK arguably matching this claim (see entry.)

Black Sabbath speaks:
Ozzy Osbourne on his role within the band . . .
"That's my job as a front man, to get the crowd going. Ronnie James Dio I think is a fine singer. I've never seen him perform, but he just stands there. The singer has to be a front man. I never professed to be the greatest singer, but I've never had problems with the crowd, you know? There's only one Ozzy. Thank God."

The metal indicators within were many. Both records largely steered clear of previous loud rock conventions like the blues or psychedelia and/or plain ol' 60's garage rock. Lyrically, the band courted the ghoulish, with ghosts, goblins, wizards, evil women and the occult all being fair game, while the band also offered their dark takes on drugs, war, insanity and death.

Musically this was a band all about power chords; dark doomy criminal Birmingham chords, belched out to the steamroller drum rumble of a manic Bill Ward. Ergo, the title track to an entire genre, a song called *Black Sabbath* single-handedly invented both metal and doom (not to mention the everlasting rain motif), while *N.I.B.* (precursor to *Smoke*

On The Water) and *Iron Man* pointed to new compulsive focus on riff. Elsewhere, *Paranoid* (beat out only by Zep's *Communication Breakdown*) struggled forth as a rudimentary type of strafing proto-speed.

> **Black Sabbath speaks:**
>
> *Tony Iommi on influence . . .*
> "Shadows (laughs.) No seriously, we were influenced by all sorts of things. I don't know what makes you come up with that sort of music. The music just formed the way it did. Our roots were the blues, John Mayall, Cream. And we never termed ourselves as heavy metal anyway. It's always been just 'rock'. We just sort of liked it. It just sounded heavy and ominous, and we just liked that type of approach. It just materialized from the stuff we were doing at that time, which was all blues. We were just dabbling around and said, 'oh I like that sound', and it just formed the basis for all those songs. *Wicked World* was the first song we wrote, then *Black Sabbath.*"

As time went on, we got *Sweet Leaf, Children Of The Grave, Sabbath Bloody Sabbath, Hole In The Sky, Symptom Of The Universe* and a host of lesser known monster-liths that have now shown up on a dozen or so tribute albums. These songs demonstrated a band still toiling away when metal could have been deemed old and tired, still looking for ways to reinforce a status that had been assured in the band's productive first year. Furthermore, their catalogue through the rest of the 70's, the 80's and the 90's proved in a deliberate fashion that the early metallic sting was not a happy accident, but a lifelong obsession. The high quality of the output however, may have been deemed a bit of an accident. Many critics cite Sabbath as a band whose writing indeed benefited from the large and wide amount of drugs they were taking. The same thing had been said about Aerosmith. One can never know if this is the case, but we can sense a certain mind-warped desperation to the compositions that couldn't come from mortal concerns, especially come SABOTAGE.

Black Sabbath

So to sum up, in the ultimate act of influence, Black Sabbath had crushed all the spotty bits and fragments offered by other piecemeal inventors in the years leading up to 1970, having as a result, universally been lauded — if we must pick one and one alone — as the crashing first crunch of metal. It's this near unanimous affirmation by serious students of the form that's the biggest proof one could offer for naming the Sabs the reigning grand wizards of metal.

> Black Sabbath speaks:
>
> *Geezer Butler on the band's lyrics . . .*
>
> "I think there are quite a few topics we covered. I think science fiction played a big part, things like *Iron Man*. So science fiction and fantasy and the supernatural, and a lot of politics as well. The one thing we didn't want to do was normal love songs, because everybody in the world was doing them. And our whole band was against all that anyway, everybody talking about splitting up with their girlfriend and stuff. The reason we got together and made our music in the first place because nobody else was doing it. So I just wrote about things that were interesting to me at the time. If I'd read a particularly good book, I'd condense that down to a song. I think when we did the song *Black Sabbath*, we knew we were definitely onto something different. Just by the audience reaction at the pubs we were playing at at the time. We loved the heavier stuff. We were all into Hendrix and Cream and Zeppelin. It just fitted our feeling at the time."

But of course, the Sabs' influence proceeds past this mere instigators notion, eventually covering varied and vast terrain. There is no doubt Sabbath influenced some of the biggest later influences, from the crucially important Judas Priest and Iron Maiden, through the dark thrash of the San Francisco Bay Area sound, and through early doom metallers like Witchfinder General, Candlemass and Trouble. And that just takes us through the mid and late 80's.

> Black Sabbath speaks:
>
> *Bill Ward on the band's sound . . .*
>
> "Well, I know for myself, I knew we were doing something different because everybody hated us. We were thrown out of most places. I felt very alone, along with Tony, Ozzy and Geezer, which created tremendous unison by the way. That was one of our strengths. I felt like it was us against the world, and as a teenager of course, one can feel that way a lot. I knew deep down inside that we were into something that was not a part of anything else I'd been hearing. It was odd. I felt like an oddball. In hindsight I guess one could look back and go, 'Oh my God, we did that and we did this and that got created and fashion came from this', and so much came from hard rock which then turned into metal. But it was different. It was raw. When Led Zeppelin's first album came out, one of the things I was particularly fascinated about was the smoothness of the album. And ours, when I compared it, was so raw and almost punkish, gritty; there's mistakes all over it and I just love it. I saw Deep Purple as a pop band. Again, no disregard to the fellas or anything but I could hear the pop lyrics in the sense that there was that sort of mainline through it. We were singing about shooting heroin and *Hand Of Doom*, *Children Of The Grave*. We were inside a lot of hardcore issues. And I mean, I love Purple, but I saw them as a real solid rock unit but I didn't get the rest of it. And it was the same with Zeppelin, and I love Zeppelin and I totally admire John Bonham as a percussionist. But Robert's lyrics were kind of like love lyrics. And that's not a put-down. But Ozzy was screeching his balls off singing 'What is this that stands before me?' And we were serious about it. It was a very serious band as well as a happy band. But those lyrics meant all the world to us. They did to me and they still do. So I could hear some really good rock units forming, but I always felt we were the odd band out. We'd come in under the gun all the time (laughs) and I just loved it."

Black Sabbath

Into the early 90's, the slow grind of death metal, itself owing much to Sabbath, transformed into a vibrant late doom period, first with ultimate Sabbath tribute bands Cathedral and Solitude Aeturnus, then followed by My Dying Bride and Paradise Lost. Meanwhile stateside, grunge exploded out of Seattle, and although the whole rant, just like punk in 1977, was all about toppling dinosaurs, the enemy was actually the hair bands from California. Coursing stealth-like through the most musically creative of grunge's top tier was, you guessed it, Black Sabbath. So, early on you had the wallow swallow of the Melvins and Dwarves, followed by the Zep / Sab fusion of Soundgarden, followed by an even more Sabbatherian experience called Alice In Chains.

Black Sabbath speaks:

Ozzy Osbourne on the big reunion . . .

"The goal as far as I'm concerned is that it's been on and off for so long that the only way we could make it work is if we do it for real. We toured last year but I may as well have been playing with a different f***ing band. Because as far as I'm concerned, Black Sabbath consists of Bill Ward, Ozzy Osbourne, Geezer Butler, and Tony Iommi. And that's it. I could have Ginger Baker on drums and it wouldn't be Black Sabbath, I could have Phil Collins on drums and it isn't Black Sabbath. So the vibe and the emotion wasn't there. So when we agreed to do the Birmingham shows, it had been so up and down, we just said 'let's record it and see what happens.' We didn't know what it would come to, but not only did it work, it was better than what everybody thought. Everybody was so constipated about playing the music after letting it sit for so long, it was like taking a giant musical shit."

Into the mid and late 90's all of this often subconscious Sabbath study became bow-tied and front-brained. Mopheads from all walks of metal began admitting their unmistakable debt to the mighty Sabs and cover versions, not to mention some of the earliest well-known tribute albums, began popping up. Meanwhile, the Nola sound had its own Sabbath jones through bands like Corrosion Of Conformity, Crowbar, Eyehategod, Acid Bath, Soilent Green and supergroup Down.

Black Sabbath speaks:

Tony Iommi on the band's staying power . . .

"We get it all the time. It's a great honor to know that after all these years we were on the right track. It's funny, I remember an interview with *Melody Maker* in England when we were just three years old. They had said 'isn't it about time that you pack it in and give up? Your music is dying out.' Now over 25 years later, it's as big as ever, if not bigger. It's a great reward for me because I know we were on track with what we did about we believed. A lot of other people have fell by the wayside in their beliefs and I've stayed true. It's great when bands state Sabbath as an inspiration. Some of these bands may not have happened without that initial spark."

As a side note, it's worth mentioning that Sabbath, as it fragmentally existed through the 80's and 90's, was of little influence at all, save for being this thirty year institution that temporally could not be missed. The early Dio years somewhat mattered, but more-so with impact than influence, although *Heaven And Hell* and *Mob Rules* have become a big part of the Dio story. All other eras? They'll probably see their own renaissance, but for now, Tony Martin is a mere footnote.

But Sabbath mania wasn't over with all the overt, often crass commercial gushings of the mid-90's. Black Sabbath's presence continues to be felt through the new doom, stoner rock and psychedelic metals of the late 90's. Practitioners include Fu Manchu, Queens Of The Stone Age (borne of another important stoner rock original Kyuss), Orange Goblin, Sheavy, Terra Firma (again derived from earlier stoner rockers Count Raven and The Obsessed), Roachpowder, Tchort, Spirit Caravan, Spiritual Beggars, Alabama Thunder Pussy, Las Cruces, Archie Bunker, Solace and Atomic Bitchwax.

> **Black Sabbath speaks:**
> *Geezer Butler on the ancient chemistry within the band . . .*
> "There's a long history because Tony and Ozzy were at school together when they were kids (laughs.) I think Tony always intimidated Ozzy at school (laughs), and there's always been a history of that throughout the band. When things happen in childhood, you always think about it. You never quite blow it out of your system. So Ozzy's always had this thing about Tony intimidating him. So they've had a good talk and resolved everything. For now anyway. I wasn't exactly on talking terms with Tony either. I hadn't spoken to him for about two or three years, since the last version of Sabbath. I don't know. I just don't get into many conflicts head on with people. I had butterflies in my stomach for about two weeks before the reunion rehearsals. I hadn't seen Tony for about three years. A lot of bad things were said to each other, things we'd heard through other people. But when I left Ozzy last, it was on good terms, so that was alright. No problem with that. But there was this trepidation about how things would work out. So going into it I was just incredibly nervous. I'd grown up with these guys and now I'm nervous to see them. Really strange. But as soon as I walked in, it was like we'd never been away from each other. Really weird."

Add it all up and that's a Marshall stack of influence.

> **Black Sabbath speaks:**
> *Ozzy Osbourne on the moment when relief set in . . .*
> "Yeah, when I got back from the hotel, I thought f***, we did it. Not only that — It was becoming a f***ing joke. Every time we would get together it would fall apart, then two out of four would go out, then one out of four, then another two out of four. It was such a relief, and I thought, 'is it going to pay off? Are people going to buy this? Are people going to think it's for real? Had we bit off more than we could chew?' We said let's record it in case it never happens again. But we'd suddenly found that we'd missed each other, you know? It wasn't like a band reunion, it was like a family reunion. Emotionally over the years we've had our ups and downs, but we'd still been very close, and not always in a positive way."

Discography
- BLACK SABBATH (Vertigo, 1970)
- PARANOID (Vertigo, 1970)
- MASTER OF REALITY (Vertigo, 1971)
- VOL 4 (Vertigo, 1972)
- SABBATH BLOODY SABBATH (Vertigo, 1973)
- SABOTAGE (Vertigo, 1975)
- WE SOLD OUR SOULS FOR ROCK 'N' ROLL (Vertigo, 1976)
- TECHNICAL ECSTASY (Vertigo, 1976)
- NEVER SAY DIE (Vertigo, 1978)

- ° HEAVEN AND HELL (Vertigo, 1980)
- ° LIVE AT LAST (Nems, 1980)
- ° MOB RULES (Vertigo, 1981)
- ° LIVE EVIL (Vertigo, 1983)
- ° BORN AGAIN (Vertigo, 1983)
- ° SEVENTH STAR (Vertigo, 1986)
- ° THE ETERNAL IDOL (Vertigo, 1987)
- ° HEADLESS CROSS (IRS, 1990)
- ° TYR (IRS, 1991)
- ° DEHUMANIZER (IRS, 1992)
- ° CROSS PURPOSES (IRS, 1994)
- ° FORBIDDEN (IRS, 1995)
- ° REUNION (Sony, 1998)

Led Zeppelin

Alright, alright, so the second most influential band in metal is also a lock-up. You gotta go with Zeppelin. Granted, Zep's origins are more of an embarrassing blend of paisley pasts, reaching into hippy music, past the Stones to plunder the blues, and wrapped in juvenile guitar hero ego struggles and all that British Invasion dreck. Percy and Co. arrived as products of the 60's who crudely and lewdly stole old boogie tunes, buffed them off and turned 'em up. No great formula to speak of, just this vague supergroup status built of Pagey's over-extended studio-bred reputation, plus the fact that Plant the satyr had a fathomless voice and Bonham was a Keith Moon pounder with intelligent tricks. But along the way, Page, Plant, Jones and Bonham cooked up and then patronizingly disowned some filling metal meals. And most importantly, they looked good doing it.

Led Zeppelin's influence is a complex float through the mystical and the magical. Updating the partitioning between Stones fans and Beatles fans in the 60's, the 70's saw you sign in blood as either a snobby Zep intellectual or a drooling Sabbath head (Deep Purple was vaguely tolerated by both camps.) Zeppelin were clearly the artists, Sabbath the unabashed bashers. On a purely mythical, mystical, poetic level, Zep's influence has been immense — the band, through all their effortless rock star poses, coming in second only to the Beatles as the prime catalyst for the next generations of rock stars. Zeppelin worship caused rafts of teenagers to hit the skins and strings with a determination to escape the burbs in a squeal of fat tires and bootlegged rum. Zeppelin was insanely famous, revered, good-looking, debauched, and all the while were tossing off great record after great record that defied categorization, much to the chagrin of the press who just wished they could write their brief dismissals and go back to studying Dylan.

But herein lies the band's slightly diminished contribution to a specific animal called heavy metal. Like Queen or even Thin Lizzy, Zeppelin disowned any sort of association with

copyright 1984 Phil Anderson / KA S2000 Magazine

the jean-jacketed armies who called them friend. But unlike Queen, who seemed to invade the idea of metal, blow it out with the last word on the subject until they felt like teaching you lot again, Zeppelin, seemed to just wander into the genre during the course of going about making monumental art. Hence you got *Communication Breakdown*, one of the first post-Kinks riff-rockers; *How Many More Times*; *Livin' Lovin' Maid* (maybe the second smart-ass riff); *Whole Lotta Love*; *Immigrant Song*; *Out On The Tiles* and *Black Dog*. But this was all spread over four albums, all before 1971 came to a close. But then again, Sabbath had stomped Zep's pretentious curly fuss-pot locks by then with BLACK SABBATH, PARANOID and, horror of horrors, MASTER OF REALITY, three records that would out-power the Hoover Dam if it abandoned its cement shackles and bought some tight red leather pants.

As time went on, the Zeppelin legend grew larger and louder, and the band's influence on metal composition was equally fleeting, but deadly important if you met the glance. *Stairway To Heaven*, *No Quarter*, *In My Time Of Dying*, *Kashmir* and *Achilles Last Stand* were almost progressive in their epic sweep, taking metal to new heights (and lengths) of drama and making conceptual leaps that carry into the power and prog of today. *Kashmir* is also cited as one of the first metal tunes to add middle eastern flavours, the product of the band's globetrotting to the subcontinent, as likely to sample the hemp, as buy up instruments. Also, throughout the band's tragically truncated catalogue, Jimmy made it acceptable to use acoustic guitars, offering stunning, peaceful, uncompromising passages of folk beauty betwixt the money-burning rock god postures. By extension, Zeppelin made it OK to break all the rules, demonstrating that you can be a heavy rock band simply by somewhat arriving there and grazing the salad bar. Write the songs as they may flop onto the grass, and maybe some of them will rock. If they don't, well, maybe next record.

copyright Rock Classics

And finally, Zeppelin made sure they surprised us just one more time on the record that was to be their swan song, IN THROUGH THE OUT DOOR being the last before the level-headed and well-advised retirement of the name caused by the vomit-choked death of Bonzo. Unwittingly perhaps (and reportedly simply because keyboardist and bassist Jonesy just got up earlier than everybody else), IN THROUGH THE OUT DOOR just might have caused the introduction of synthesizers into hard rock. A very specific thing came out of this record — the synthesizer as riff-taker, something which showed up on Rush's

SIGNALS, GRACE UNDER PRESSURE and on, plus starkly so on Van Halen's 1984 record, specifically *I'll Wait* and *Jump* and an overlooked one-record-back predecessor called (surprise?) *One Foot Out The Door*. Small point, maybe unwarranted, but it just goes to show that Led Zeppelin sprinkled their pixie dust in all sorts of unpredictable locales, infusing metal with a creativity it may never have seen had Zeppelin not been at least passively enamoured with the power chord.

copyright Rock Classics

Discography

- ○ LED ZEPPELIN (Atlantic, 1969)
- ○ II (Atlantic, 1969)
- ○ III (Atlantic, 1970)
- ○ IV (untitled) (Atlantic, 1971)
- ○ HOUSES OF THE HOLY (Atlantic, 1973)
- ○ PHYSICAL GRAFFITI (Swan Song, 1975)
- ○ PRESENCE (Swan Song, 1976)
- ○ THE SONG REMAINS THE SAME (Swan Song, 1976)
- ○ IN THROUGH THE OUT DOOR (Swan Song, 1979)
- ○ CODA (Swan Song, 1982)

⚡ 3 ⚡
Deep Purple

Deep Purple's influence on metal is tied like an albatross to their shambled, chaotic, often brilliant, often paralytic catalogue. Their first shiny badge is awarded for the fact that they just may have made the first metal album ever, IN ROCK, getting the band excused for past Austin Powers transgressions with a scintillating, scientific and nimble new form of guitar rock that resembles modern metal more than anything Sabbath had assembled through to the Dio years. And don't forget — the year is 1970, the same year that Sabbath beat them in temporal space with BLACK SABBATH but then lost the album-to-album war with PARANOID.

> Deep Purple speaks:
> *Ian Gillan on writing Deep Purple lyrics into the new millennium . . .*
> "Well, Roger and I do the lyrics. Interesting really that you mention that. Because a couple of years ago, Roger and I were, I think it was in Portugal, we were walking on the beach, talking about things as we do, philosophizing about this, that and the other, and putting to rights the problems of the world, like we'd been doing since 1965. The topic of the day was naivety, basically what makes young kids' music so powerful? Because we were looking at the lyrics for example of *Black Night* and the stuff we wrote in 69 and 70. And we were saying, we can't even figure out what it means, but it sounds great. So we thought you know, when you're at that age you're immortal, you don't think twice before you say anything, you just do it because it's cool. And as you get a little older, you start thinking about everything before you say it, so everything becomes a little more considered, not just in songs but in life itself. You get a little cautious, or not exactly cautious, but experience in life tells you to weigh things up a bit before you speak. And the consequence is that in a very slow process, you end up, your songcraft improves enormously, you think you're writing better songs, in fact you probably are. But what you're writing is probably becoming a little more boring. As you become more and more remote from activity, because you're trying to write about fast cars and loose women and all that. But of course that's not the reality in your real life anymore. You're doing things on a far more philosophical level. But naivety is lost and we figured that, and said we'd happily replace it with all these conclusions. If you're going to write something about love, just make sure it's not over-sentimental blah blah blah. And then we'd go into this process of analyzing everything. I remember sitting bolt upright in bed a few days later and saying this is ridiculous, just nonsense. Of course I'm naive. I'm just a naive fifty year old. I'm not a naive twenty year old. But I've never been fifty before in my life, so what are the things we should be writing about? Let's not try and play this sort of 'from memory' stuff anymore. Let's write about the things that really make us angry, just like we used to. But it's different things these days. So let's go for that. So the stories can of course be more anecdotal because we've experienced a lot more, and a lot more spiritual, your spirit develops, or a lot more philosophical. Plus also hopefully, there'll be humour in it. But, having said all that, the point is really not to care about it and really concentrate on making the words sound good, or to put the sound of the words before the meaning of the words. So anyway, after a long process we finally figured out (laughs) where we'd been going up the wrong path."

IN ROCK wins due to its highly evolved riffage, with classics like *Speed King, Blood Sucker, Hard Lovin' Man,* and *Flight Of The Rat* slashing and burning with the first metal bite — no garage rot lethargy here, nothing based on the blues — metal's second guitar hero (we'll give #1 to Pagey) based his riffs and runs and sense of Nietzschean

(Wagnerian?) superiority more on classical music than on Robert Johnson. And there lies the rub. Ritchie Blackmore, throughout the mere handful of his pre-1975 records more or less established metal's ground rules — ground rules used by more than half of the metal bands in Europe to this day, power metal or otherwise. I mean, basically all Euro metal, prog metal and power metal tracks trace back through Helloween and Yngwie through to Ritchie, and for that matter Jon Lord.

Future Purple accomplishments are mere concentric, unfocused restatements of the IN ROCK theme, save for one discernible moment fused with pure original passion and the wide commercial acceptance that re-fuels such passion. We are talking of course about MACHINE HEAD, with its penultimate wrench rock anthem *Smoke On The Water*, sister song to *N.I.B.* and *Iron Man* (think about it.) This record is a metal deity that far outweighs the band's own ranking. It alone rubs shoulders with ZEP IV as a heavy record that was both important to (and loved by) many cross-sections of music fans as well as to the begrudging critics. Enjoyable, artistic and regal, MACHINE HEAD could swing from the uplifted grooves of *Highway Star* and *Pictures Of Home*, to the prog metal of *Space Truckin'*, and finally to the eternal blues jam of *Lazy* with an aplomb driven as the white snow by the perennial light touch of Ian Paice.

Deep Purple speaks:

Ian Gillan on IN ROCK . . .

"We wanted to write our own songs. I think Jon, Ritchie and Ian, that's why they wanted to change the line-up of the band from the one that did *Hush, Kentucky Woman*, etc. They wanted to be writing their own stuff, so that's why they brought Roger and I in, because we were already a kind of songwriting team. And so it just happened really, pure luck. If you listen to Jethro Tull, and see that they're very obviously based in folk music, if you listen to Free, you see they're very obviously based in soul music, and if you listen to Zeppelin, it's blues as you said. With Purple it's kind of weird, because Jon grew up in The Royal College Of Music, so his background's in orchestral music and jazz. Ian Paice grew up in the Buddy Rich school of music, so big band, swing, stuff like that was the major influence in his life. Roger Glover was into Lonnie Dunnegan and every form of ethnic music you could imagine, folk music basically. And of course when Dylan came along, that was Roger's idol. And Ritchie and I were pretty much pop, rock, sort of country, and then delving into blues and jazz. So we had a fairly diverse set of influences. So when the band came together, just an expression, it was enthusiastic and loud (laughs.) I don't know, I've always just been lucky I think, standing in the middle of these guys. They're just great musicians, that's what it is. I've never, ever imagined . . . we never even had any ambitions to even have our photographs taken. There was never any ambition to be stars or anything like that. We just wanted to play music, you know. IN ROCK really is the start of something. It is, you're right. With the benefit of hindsight, it looks to be a pretty significant record. And I think there are things like that that exist, these seminal records. Because, for example, I've listened to almost everything that came out of Seattle, and I can trace it, almost directly to Tony Iommi, in my opinion."

But like I say, even as the influence persists through the 70's, 80's and 90's, it felt like kiosk samples between five mile walks. MADE IN JAPAN is both Yngwie Malmsteen's and Roger Glover's favourite live album. FIREBALL had *Strange Kind Of Woman* and the sonic speed metal gauntlet of the title track. WHO DO WE THINK WE ARE! had *Smooth Dancer* and little else that charged. Once Ian Gillan left, the Coverdale years brought us the *Fireball* sequel *Burn* and the new metal experiment *Stormbringer* (we need only talk about the songs of those hallowed names, not the doggy bag albums.) And once Gillan and Ritchie patched it up in their usual fragile, smoothed-over and ultimately doomed manner, we got a reunion with Second Coming buzz, PERFECT STRANGERS and to a lesser extent HOUSE

Deep Purple

OF BLUE LIGHT giving added roots-connecting fuel to the already adequate supply of metal press in the mid-80's. Later still, Deep Purple made two of their very best records ever with the versatile Steve Morse in the guitar slot — a disputed claim, but like, just go listen.

> Deep Purple speaks:
> *Roger Glover on* IN ROCK . . .
> "Yes, IN ROCK. I remember back, because of our orchestra album and the subsequent misrepresentation in the press of us as this artsy, pseudo-classical band, there was this resentment. So we had a determination to put, once and for all, our stamp on what we were, which was a rock band. And it became hard rock, because heavy metal wasn't even a term that was around at the time. And I think that's the reason that the album is the way it is. I remember Ritchie saying at one time, 'if it's not dramatic or exciting, then it doesn't have a place on this album.' And those were pretty good words to live by."

But summarizing on influence, Deep Purple excels primarily for two reasons; one being the early albums, the metal acumen of IN ROCK and the purple prescience of MACHINE HEAD (with a spicy splash of early speed metal through FIREBALL's title track); and two being the castle gray tones of Ritchie Blackmore, who coupled with his disciple Yngwie Malmsteen, is largely responsible for all the classical power metal making waves in Europe today, as well as a general but wobbly elevation of metal's reputation to that of classical music (OK, stop laughing.)

Discography
  o SHADES OF DEEP PURPLE (Parlophone, 1968)
  o THE BOOK OF TALIESYN (Harvest, 1969)
  o DEEP PURPLE (Harvest, 1969)
  o CONCERTO FOR GROUP AND ORCHESTRA (Harvest, 1970)
  o IN ROCK (Harvest, 1970)
  o FIREBALL (Harvest, 1971)
  o MACHINE HEAD (Harvest, 1971)
  o MADE IN JAPAN (Purple, 1972)
  o WHO DO WE THINK WE ARE! (Purple, 1973)
  o BURN (Purple, 1974)
  o STORMBRINGER (Purple, 1974)
  o 24 KARAT PURPLE (Purple, 1975)
  o COME TASTE THE BAND (Purple, 1975)
  o MADE IN EUROPE (Purple, 1976)
  o POWERHOUSE (Purple, 1978)
  o DEEPEST PURPLE (EMI, 1980)
  o PERFECT STRANGERS (Polydor, 1984)
  o HOUSE OF BLUE LIGHT (Polydor, 1987)
  o NOBODY'S PERFECT (Polydor, 1988)
  o SLAVES AND MASTERS (RCA, 1990)
  o THE BATTLE RAGES ON (BMG, 1993)
  o COME HELL OR HIGH WATER (BMG, 1994)

- PURPENDICULAR (RCA, 1996)
- ABANDON (EMI, 1998)
- TOTAL ABANDON (Deep Purple, 1999)
- IN CONCERT WITH THE LONDON SYMPHONY ORCHESTRA (Eagle, 1999)

Judas Priest

When you mention the name Judas Priest, people seem to immediately think, "yeah, great band, big influence, BRITISH STEEL, SCREAMING FOR VENGEANCE, etc." But even though these were the cash cow days for the band, Priest's earlier, more subtle contributions place the band first in line after the trinity of old-timers topping our list. In essence, Priest comprised the first, practically un-noticed new wave of British heavy metal.

And the reason is simple. After one timid false start of a debut, Judas Priest no less than re-engineered metal in their name through three futuristic and God-fearing works of high metal science: SAD WINGS OF DESTINY (1976), SIN AFTER SIN (1977) and STAINED CLASS (1978.)

These works were the first real advancements in metal since its bloated inception in 1970; the first shiny new articulated, reticulated, calculated riffs; the best early example of twin-guitar leads this side of Lizzy; lyrics that were all razor-edged evangelical fire and brimstone, surrounded by tales of anguished criminal and potentially criminal outcasts, metal machines, monsters, everything a punter wanted to hear; themes that were hazily remembered from somewhere way back in their Sabbath collections. And Halford was the first high-end belter who didn't seem to get there by falsetto, accident, or a crazy night of chemicals, a vocal technician who would become perhaps the most respected singer in metal, the standard to which all power and prog metal front men are measured.

Tipton and Downing, well, like I say, the riffs they came up with were from another world. Their detailed construction resembled nothing from the previous caveman chording that plagued most of metal, save for the handful of Ritchie diddlers that slightly vaulted Purple a leg up over Priest — *Blood Sucker, Speed King, Highway Star, Supertrooper*, and most important to the Priest way of doing things, *Hard Lovin' Man, Fireball, Burn* and *Stormbringer*. Songs that the dual dueling Priests came up with that were improvements on said classics include *Tyrant, Genocide, Sinner, Starbreaker* and most pertinent to the next level that no one else even dreamed about, *Call For The Priest* and *Exciter*, which ushered in a new drag strip era of speed metal, one that Priest would own alone until Metallica. And while the riffs were something else, the two wove thoughtful, pre-fabricated solos that marked a subtle metalizing of Lizzy en route to Maiden, while showing flashes of rapid fire that wouldn't be lost on an impressionable young Yngwie.

In between, the band wrestled with geometrical progressive power metal (*Victim Of Changes, Dissident Aggressor* and *Savage*), plus more convoluted light touch stuff that highlighted the magic of studio whiz extraordinaire Simon Philips, and after that, Les Binks, who would batter a new heaviness into the band's best synthesis of power and might HELL BENT FOR LEATHER (KILLING MACHINE in the UK, a title deemed too direct for American tastes.)

> **Judas Priest speaks:**
> *Ian Hill on the band's influences . . .*
> "Ken and Glenn did the lion's share of the music, but I don't think there were very many outside influences. I try not to have that happen, because it will show in my bass lines. And I'm sure it's the same for K.K. and Glenn as well. But we all liked Cream, Ken was a Hendrix freak, you always keep those. But it was almost a conscious effort not to sound like anybody else, and it used to baffle people because they couldn't put a tag on us and say, 'yeah they sound just like Sabbath or Zeppelin.'"

But if Judas Priest should rightly be praised for this new and insane creativity shot deep into the arm of a ridiculed genre, it's the following four records that made the biggest commercial impact on the scene. BRITISH STEEL with its pop hits *Living After Midnight* and *You Don't Have To Be Old To Be Wise* (both uncharacteristic of the band or album) helped drive the graying contingent of the NWOBHM, along with a re-energized Sabbath, a re-energized Ozzy and semi-established newcomers like Maiden and Saxon. POINT OF ENTRY was even poppier, while SCREAMING FOR VENGEANCE broke the bank, as did to a lesser extent the heavier but over-processed DEFENDERS OF THE FAITH. These records, as much as the originals, prompted droves of punters to quit spectating and start participating, also no doubt, driven by the leather, lights and bikes stage show that the band had choreographed down to a sweet circus science.

> **Judas Priest speaks:**
> *K.K. Downing on the band's influences . . .*
> "When people set the precedent, like I have to agree with you, Deep Purple — IN ROCK is one of the greatest albums of all time. But growing up in England, there had to have been another 150, 200 bands who were equally as influential, from John Mayall's Bluesbreakers to bands like Cream, Hendrix, The Who, Rory Gallagher, Free, Bloodwyn Pig, you've got Jethro Tull, Chicken Shack, a lot of blues bands, Savoy Brown, Foghat, Fleetwood Mac, great bands like Budgie who are pretty much unknown now but whatever. They did some great stuff. They were all great influences, so if you were going to compete with the likes of Sabbath or whatever, you damn well better come up with something pretty good and unique. Otherwise you're not going to go anywhere. And even if you were good, it was hard to make any headway. So we decided to come up with stuff we thought was top quality, exert quality control over what we put out, and that's stayed with us to this day."

Years later, the Priest is still grinding, fronted by a more than capable young hotshot called Tim "Ripper" Owens, an obsessed mid-west Priest fan turned surprised member. Whereas Ripper's debut JUGULATOR, and pretty much all of the post-DEFENDERS output lapses in and out of Priest-puerile parody, the band kick it live, digging into their astonishing catalogue of anthems that range from the complex and pioneering to Twisted thumping Sisters that have one pining for lost brain cells misplaced in pimply youth.

copyright 1980 Phil Anderson / KAOS2000 Magazine

Judas Priest

Judas Priest speaks:

Rob Halford on the band's influences . . .

"Well, I think coming up with our signature sound was all self-invention really. I don't think any of us were kind of driven or inspired by what was around us, because it was all so new and unique and creative. I think it was just one of those special cases of musical talent comes together and being able to do something special. There really isn't one particular thing that I could say was responsible for inspiration or anything like that. It was just the makeup of the writing team that was able to create that kind of material."

Discography

- ROCKA ROLLA (Gull, 1974)
- SAD WINGS OF DESTINY (Gull, 1976)
- SIN AFTER SIN (CBS, 1977)
- STAINED CLASS (CBS, 1978)
- BEST OF JUDAS PRIEST (Gull, 1978)
- KILLING MACHINE (CBS, 1978)
- UNLEASHED IN THE EAST (CBS, 1979)
- BRITISH STEEL (CBS, 1980)
- HERO, HERO (Gull, 1980)
- POINT OF ENTRY (CBS, 1981)
- SCREAMING FOR VENGEANCE (CBS, 1982)
- DEFENDERS OF THE FAITH (CBS, 1984)
- TURBO (CBS, 1986)
- PRIEST LIVE (CBS, 1987)
- RAM IT DOWN (CBS, 1988)

Judas Priest

○ PAINKILLER (CBS, 1990)
○ METAL WORKS (CBS, 1993)
○ JUGULATOR (CMC, 1997)
○ '98 LIVE MELTDOWN (CMC, 1998)

5
Kiss

If there's one band you had to grudgingly push up the pedestal with Zeppelin and the Beatles with respect to this catalytic effect of causing bands to grow like weeds, it's Kiss. This perhaps is the band's most substantive contribution. Kiss (literally) lit a fire in the eyes of those who would become metal's prime practitioners in metal's prime years. For, mathematically, if you were a hormonally charged 15-year-old when KISS ALIVE! hit the

ground runnin' in a crash of thunder, you were 25 in 1985, ready to strike those Ace Frehley poses for the next generation of adoring metal fans: peak age stuck in the middle of metal's peak rage age.

Yes indeed, Kiss could not be ignored by teenagers, their parents, their fellow parishioners, or even their dead and buried grandparents. In a flash of black leather, smoke, strobes, sirens, blood, pyro and face paint, Kiss assaulted the senses with a post-glam nightmare that squashed Alice Cooper's middling Mott upratchet but good. As I've said before (I can quote myself, can't I?), Kiss were the Oakland Raiders on acid, the bad boy champions of flaming youth, the very best perhaps ever to practice shock rock, likely in the light of history, to beat out Alice or Marilyn or Zombie or Slipknot, while its 80's comparatives like WASP or Crüe wallow somewhere down the list.

> Kiss speaks:
> *Gene Simmons on life at the top . . .*
> "Life does not suck. I've never had anything to complain about. My worst day would be any band's best day. If scaling Mount Olympus is a measure of success, then I've got a year-round condo there waiting for me, whenever I want it. Christ notwithstanding, it's good to be a God walking the earth. Now I know what the other Jewish guy felt like. It's great to be worshipped, but I don't want to be crucified . . . certainly not for being Jewish."

So the band's main influence in this respect was to raise the bar in terms of the spectacle fans might expect from now on. Oddly, it didn't really happen that way in a direct sense. Sure, the giants like Floyd or the Stones exploded in girth and worth, but it wasn't until the 80's that the aforementioned WASP and Crüe led a minor glam / shock movement that spilled over into Poison, David Lee Roth (heck, even Van Halen and the 80's version of Kiss), Warrant and to some extent Maiden and Ozzy. Kiss' groundwork on the circus that is rock can be thusly felt, but it wasn't like every band immediately after the Kiss ALIVE II album had modular hydraulic stages.

> Kiss speaks:
> *Bruce Kulick on his guitar style . . .*
> "Well, the last few records with Kiss, I was really able to spread my wings, mostly meaning REVENGE, although I'm very proud of UNPLUGGED, of course and ALIVE III. But on REVENGE, I got to experiment with a lot of the styles that really define me. But even more-so on CARNIVAL OF SOULS. The track *The Jungle*, which I co-wrote is right now, really exploding on radio in the states, and I hope it spreads to Toronto too. I'm really excited about that. But, as a whole, it's a record where I got to play with a lot of my vintage pedals. There are companies now that are making guitar pedals also that are inspired by vintage pedals and are of course brand new. But my influences are all these British invasion guys like Jimmy Page and Jeff Beck and certainly Eric Clapton in Cream, plus of course Tony Iommi. But all those British influences are on this Kiss record. But to be honest with you, when it comes to what I play in a solo, I think I have a definable sound, but I'm flexible. To me the guitar solo and the guitar parts should just bring the song to the next height. The song's gotta live on its own, even if it's played on two acoustics. Everything else is just icing on the cake. So if I hear, 'oh this should be a Hendrixy thing or a Beatles thing,' I don't really think about it, or where I got that vocabulary from. But that's what guitar playing is, when you're learning and you're learning. So I always learned from the people who gave me chills. I always have those people inside me. It's like an encyclopedia of riffs. So all those styles are there."

copyright 1982 Phil Anderson / KAOS2000 Magazine

Musically, what the band came up with was perfect for the stage show, which they pretty much always admitted was more important anyway. The Kiss sound was a curious mix of early, brand new metal (let's give the band credit: they rocked hard and early), teen

Kiss speaks:

Gene Simmons on flying through the air, spitting blood . . .

"Oh yeah, 55 feet into the air. I'm scared of heights, scared to death. But, you know, you gotta do it. It's amazing. It's the same God Of Thunder throwing up on everybody's head from up above and nobody scatters. They just sort of gather under it, like when you throw bait to fish, they just go right for it. I guess it's because people want to go out and say 'you see that blood on my head? Gene threw up on me.' It's a badge of courage. So everybody can say 'wow, that came from inside his throat.'"

> Kiss speaks:
>
> *Peter Criss on the Kiss reunion being the ultimate revenge . . .*
>
> "Oh sure. It's the second and third coming, my lucky number. I'm grateful. I have a lot of enemies that were very happy to see me suffering. Now I'm grinning all the way to the bank. I'm glad those people hate me, because now, I'm having a great time. I have a lot of great friends who are also very happy for me, and are glad to see that I've deserved and worked hard for this. Last night, my wife and I were showing the guys in the band pictures of our new house. Gene was saying 'wow, I'm really happy for you. It's a beautiful house.' We really pat each other on the back a lot about our success."

dreem pop, early 70's east coast party rock, British glam (most specifically Slade), and an odd southern-ish boogie rock, ironically best portrayed by Canadians Bachman Turner Overdrive. This had its own sparked influence, as mop-headed, bell-bottomed 70's teens discovered that they could learn these retardo rock anthems easily and early, egging them on to the next academic plateau until they found themselves playing their high school and, for once in their lives, pulling the chicks.

So in conjunction with pointing out the possibility of regular rockers becoming larger (and taller) than life, Kiss also pointed to the possibility of a kind of loony cartoony superhero status in a new, supercharged live environment. It all looked pretty cool to a kid. One last area of influence: Kiss really took rock merchandising to another level of exploitation. Anything Gene could slap a Kiss logo on, he did — something that quite irritatingly continues to this day with the whole PSYCHO CIRCUS reunion junket and farewell tour subplots. And not surprisingly, the stuff ain't cheap.

> Kiss speaks:
>
> *Peter Criss on the "time warp" . . .*
>
> "I look at it like we've almost made time stand still. It's amazing when we do put the make-up on. We're twenty years old again, and everybody is treating us like we're twenty. The vibe is like that when we're on stage, until we leave and we're all limping and complaining about muscle aches and looking for a bottle of Geritol or Advil. We've found the answer to keep time and it's amazing. Ace calls it a 'time warp' for him. He's found a passage to get back to being a kid. I have to agree with him, because it's really true."

Discography
- KISS (Casablanca, 1973)
- HOTTER THAN HELL (Casablanca, 1974)
- DRESSED TO KILL (Casablanca, 1975)
- ALIVE! (Casablanca, 1975)
- DESTROYER (Casablanca, 1976)
- ROCK AND ROLL OVER (Casablanca, 1976)
- LOVE GUN (Casablanca, 1977)
- ALIVE II (Casablanca, 1977)
- DOUBLE PLATINUM (Casablanca, 1978)
- DYNASTY (Casablanca, 1979)
- UNMASKED (Casablanca, 1980)
- MUSIC FROM THE ELDER (Casablanca, 1981)

copyright 1982 Phil Anderson / KAOS2000 Magazine

- CREATURES OF THE NIGHT (Casablanca, 1982)
- LICK IT UP (Mercury, 1983)
- ANIMALIZE (Mercury, 1984)
- ASYLUM (Mercury, 1985)
- CRAZY NIGHTS (Mercury, 1987)
- SMASHES, THRASHES & HITS (Mercury, 1987)
- HOT IN THE SHADE (Mercury, 1989)
- REVENGE (Mercury, 1992)
- ALIVE III (Mercury, 1993)
- MTV UNPLUGGED (Mercury, 1996)
- YOU WANTED THE BEST, YOU GOT THE BEST! (Mercury, 1996)
- CARNIVAL OF SOULS (Mercury, 1997)
- PSYCHO CIRCUS (Mercury, 1998)

⚡ 6 ⚡
Alice Cooper

I'll never forget that Time magazine article — the ripped tights, the black top hat, the jagged make-up, and most of all that whopper of a snake! Regular folk were sure it was the face-melting atomic death of rock and roll when, of course, it turned out to be nothing more than a jiggling Little Elvis Jerry Lee Richard re-birth.

Once Alice Cooper (the band) had stumbled out from behind their absurdist Zappa-esque culture jam, this confused vestige of what an art collective in the 60's was supposed to be, things went morbid real fast. Shock rock was born. Alice often remarked how their band drove a stake through the heart of the love generation. And how indeed. Big boas (feather and reptile), big stories (just who is Alice?), and big boys in big girls clothes had Alice building a tasty triple-decker sandwich that was full of American junk for punks. This is undoubtedly Alice's major contribution to metal: the big rock show, the fact that theatrics were now to be shoveled at the crowd no-holds-barred, chickens, teddy bears, mannequins, ritual beheadings, glitter and glam, you name it, the more confusing the better.

Alice Cooper speaks . . .

Alice Cooper on Alice's style in today's metal world . . .

"When I say I don't like the hi-tech stuff, and I'm missing a lot of the heart in that stuff, I do like what Rob Zombie is doing. Because he injects himself into it. And suddenly then, it has a sense of humor. It has a sense of humanity. And he wraps himself inside the package, inside of that sound, and it works. Because I hear all kinds of stuff that comes right from his personality. What I hate is when I hear an album that literally sounds like it could just be a computer writing an album, and the person doesn't even really need to be there. But I do like what Rob Zombie has done. I'm never going to get away from the fact that an album, to me, if you notice, almost all of my songs pay off in the chorus. It pays off with a melody line all the way through. I am never going to avoid melody lines. Because I think, to write a song, if you take every one of these songs, and took all of the heaviness out and all the crap out, and just played them on piano? They're good songs. And I think that is what we strive to do. We said let's get to the energy of Rage Against The Machine, but let's pay it off with a great song. So it is a combination of, sure, tapping into that sound, but never losing Alice's melodic sense or his sense of humor. Even while this new album, BRUTAL PLANET, is so pessimistic, it's got a great sense of humor to it. And all of my albums I can listen to, and I would say 80 percent of them have a lot of humour to them."

And the cool part is that this was happening on a large scale as early as 1971. The Cooper show pre-dated Kiss, who stole Alice's macabre make-up and general malevolence, blowing the faux-art bolts off the beast, becoming the visually loudest example of shock rock in history, although never to be deemed the first. Alice also pre-dated the New York Dolls who sampled the cross-dressing, something which cropped up in a form even closer to Alice in another New York band called Twisted Sister, who actually embodied the Lizzy Borden element of the Alice concept as an additional rip-off. Then there was Ozzy, who actually mimicked the Alice shtick most closely, while rarely

Alice Cooper

getting called on it, this whole house of horror thing, even using Alice's hanging idea, his thrones, even a shade of make-up when the glam gods briefly required it. Flash to the 90's and the modern version of this, straight-up, is White Zombie / Rob Zombie, while a disturbing, more artistic, but surprisingly similar post-information / post-marketing / post-internet take on Alice can be found within the man's equally scrawny monster children Marilyn Manson and Coal Chamber.

Alice Cooper speaks:

Alice Cooper on his staying power . . .

"I honestly think it's because I do a good show. I think it's because I make really good records, and I'm not fat and bald (laughs.) I've maintained my artistic energy and my physical energy for all these years. I mean, I can still go on stage and blow any young band off the stage. That is my objective. I've never gone up there with the attitude of like 'well, here we are, a bunch of old guys, just want to do our hits.' I've always gone up there with the attitude that these songs are still viable, and not only that, but here are a bunch of new things to digest. I like to give them the old stuff, but then I like to hit them with new stuff, say, 'guys, let's not live in the past, we also have this.'"

While all this was going on, the band made music too. Starting out as untalented Arizona street punks eager to mangle any in-vogue musical trend (only always late, well after it had died), the band eventually stumbled onto their unique Doors-y style of metal, finding it a sufficient soundtrack to the band's much more interesting visual mayhem. But then these songs were crafty in their own bumbled way, not really all that heavy, more mass-market upon first inspection, and not without disarming eye-winked humour. The golden era (say, 1971's KILLER to 75's WELCOME TO MY NIGHTMARE) consequently brought us *Under My Wheels, Be My Lover, School's Out, Hello Hurray, Elected, Billion Dollar Babies, No More Mr. Nice Guy, Muscle Of Love, Only Women Bleed, Cold Ethyl* and *Black Widow*, a strange amalgam of the anthemic, the melodic, the glam and the mock-horrific — just enough going on to let us know there had to be some patronizing patter between golf swings and Bud swigs.

Alice Cooper speaks:

Alice Cooper on the idea of concept albums . . .

"I think that is one of the important things about Alice is that I write mini-novels. Any one of my albums can be written into a movie or a story. I almost write my albums as soundtracks for the story. You could write a comic book on almost every single album I've ever done because they definitely all lean towards story lines. So I tend to try to write some sort of cohesive work every single time. I really don't like writing twelve songs that don't connect. I like them all to connect. In fact, I like them to connect to other albums, sort of like a Vonnegut thing where certain characters keep coming back."

So Alice was the master of ceremonies, the creator of serious rock theater, as well as a band that could choke up a generation with *I'm Eighteen*. Both had the effect of lighting sparks in the hearts of future rockers, and many in interviews have said so. But a bunch of other stuff can be traced to Alice. Before Kiss would get a hold of the idea (but granted, after the Beatles), Alice did his own movie WELCOME TO MY NIGHTMARE, which could be seen as one of the cornerstones of the video craze as it exploded in 1983. An attendant phenom is this idea of concept records, Alice coming up with a few along the way (such as FROM THE INSIDE and THE LAST TEMPTATION), while also having an epic effect on the world of packaging, offering within his records at various times, calendars, panties, billion dollar bills, punch out postcards, cardboard box sleeves, innovative die-cuts, embossing, and comic books.

But alas, it's not the greatest story for Alice (and whoever the vampire had in his band that week) throughout much of the 80's and 90's. It just seemed like the man oscillated between trend-chasing and caricatures of his former glory like a panicked dog sucking the tail-pipe of the rock biz. Rest assured though, Alice Cooper's place in metal history is secure, having seared his image to the foreheads of those who made metal through the 80's. Now into the 90's, Alice being lauded as the grandfather of the shows garnering attention across the country, most notably the Rob Zombie and Marilyn Manson phenomena, not to mention those of younger shock pups like Coal Chamber and Slipknot.

Discography
- PRETTIES FOR YOU (Straight, 1969)
- EASY ACTION (Straight, 1970)
- LOVE IT TO DEATH (Straight, 1971)
- KILLER (Warner, 1971)
- SCHOOL'S OUT (Warner, 1972)
- BILLION DOLLAR BABIES (Warner, 1973)
- MUSCLE OF LOVE (Warner, 1973)
- ALICE COOPER'S GREATEST HITS (Warner, 1974)
- WELCOME TO MY NIGHTMARE (Atlantic, 1975)
- ALICE COOPER GOES TO HELL (Warner, 1976)
- LACE AND WHISKEY (Warner, 1977)
- THE ALICE COOPER SHOW (Warner, 1977)
- FROM THE INSIDE (Warner, 1978)
- FLUSH THE FASHION (Warner, 1980)
- SPECIAL FORCES (Warner, 1981)
- ZIPPER CATCHES SKIN (Warner, 1982)
- DADA (Warner, 1983)
- CONSTRICTOR (MCA, 1986)
- RAISE YOUR FIST AND YELL (MCA, 1987)
- TRASH (Epic, 1989)
- HEY STOOPID (Epic, 1991)
- THE LAST TEMPTATION (Epic, 1994)
- A FISTFUL OF ALICE (Guardian / EMI, 1997)
- THE LIFE AND CRIMES OF ALICE COOPER (Warner Archives, 1999)
- BRUTAL PLANET (Spitfire, 2000)

Queen

I really had to get the crowbar out and bend the definition of influence to get Queen in here, for Queen live in that no man's land between scant direct or material influence and sheer euphoric godly status, something which rains down an influence which is immeasurable, filmy, refreshed and refreshing.

Queen spent their whole career confounding the rock world, flirting and flouncing their feather boas into hard rock, coyly spurning its advances, but occasionally bashing the door down with carnal attacks that briefly flashed horrific innovations and then were gone in a puff of dry ice. Specifically, one would have to look to *Modern Times Rock 'n' Roll, Ogre Battle, Now I'm Here, Stone Cold Crazy, Sheer Heart Attack* and *Let Me Entertain You.* Wade through the violence, and you'll find considerable metal brawn, sparked like fireflies with ideas that betray the band's alternately well-checked and garishly-paraded intellect.

Some of the band's novel musical accomplishments were so small and specific that, if you blinked, you missed them. Others were so all-encompassing and abstract that you had to view them from the Concorde to get the picture. Specifically, Queen brought an elevated

Queen

level of studio trickery to rock, established on the band's legendary Roy Thomas Baker-produced debut, a record crafted with the benefit of unlimited studio use, spawning all sorts of experimentation with guitar sounds, drum sounds, multi-tracking, backward-tracking and operatic vocal harmonies. Brian May emerged as the biggest material influence in the band, inspiring guitarists to experiment with electricity and effects. Few actually copped the man's bizarre licks (many of which died outside of context), but an army of players became glassy-eyed in the presence of this odd new type of guitar hero,

copyright 1980 Phil Anderson / KAOS2000 Magazine

a man within whose shrinking violet presence, lurked one of the most vicious, though sparingly exploited, guitar sounds on the planet.

Through their baroque pastiche of sounds, Queen also came to be seen as a sort of fey cousin to Rush and, in a dodgier respect, to Purple and Heep, within this new progressive rock world, for lack of a better name. The conceptual QUEEN II and the explosively conceptual *Bohemian Rhapsody* (the track's promo video is now considered the world's first) invented heavy metal opera, or at least heavy metal theater, something inherent in many prog metal albums today (most prolifically within the works of Savatage and Blind Guardian), and odd detritus like Therion, romantic goth metal and fruity black metal solo and supergroup side distractions.

As time went on, Queen experimented with synthesizers, disco, techno, rockabilly, folk, balladry of many types, party metal, all in creation of a catalogue that is, in its Zeppified breadth and width, an inspiration to those whose muse is unbridled, unchecked and gleefully, fanatically undefined. Stylistic absurdities which, at the time, were considered creative blasphemies eventually began to leach into metal and hard rock. And prophetically, most of the band's wayward vagaries have been excused and embraced on various ironic and kitschy levels. Queen's fanbase is now somewhat thankful for this nutty variety of work that could simply be no other way.

But the untenable and the unquantifiable influences from this band are much more important than their ultimately microscopic imprint on any of today's metal subgenres. The chemistry between May, Mercury, Taylor and Deacon was practically a pantheoned ambassador for the idea of chemistry, imploring bands to look for this vital bit of abstract magic found amongst the superstars. This chemistry manifested itself most accessibly in the band's graceful, regal live spectacles. Indeed Kurt Cobain in his suicide note singled out Freddie Mercury as the blinding rock-powered antithesis to his brooding self. Freddie was a star who waded through each day as a work of art. This concept in itself is a sort of potentially perverse, potentially purifying influence.

So consider Queen's influence as the instructive effect of four lifetimes focused on the pursuit of great art. The fact that the band liked a good hard rock wank is merely a pleasurable sidebar to the main story coursing through the history of rock. Issues wrapped up in the fickle attention of the muse are much more vital to what happens within a band than we all might surmise. The inspiration of a songwriting standard to which one might aspire, with all the attendant cross-genre risks that might entail, is a crucial catalyst when those brain-crushing mental blocks threaten an artist's very existence. Queen sits in that hallowed zone waiting to shoot the sparks that just might move the art forward to its fruition, representing an influence that might be hazy and abstract, but one that permeates all of metal and elevates it in untold ways.

Discography
- QUEEN (EMI, 1973)
- QUEEN II (EMI, 1974)
- SHEER HEART ATTACK (EMI, 1974)
- A NIGHT AT THE OPERA (EMI, 1975)

○ A DAY AT THE RACES (EMI, 1976)
○ NEWS OF THE WORLD (EMI, 1977)
○ JAZZ (EMI, 1978)
○ LIVE KILLERS (EMI, 1979)
○ THE GAME (EMI, 1980)
○ FLASH GORDON (EMI, 1980)
○ GREATEST HITS (EMI, 1981)
○ HOT SPACE (EMI, 1982)
○ THE WORKS (EMI, 1984)
○ A KIND OF MAGIC (EMI, 1986)
○ LIVE MAGIC (EMI, 1986)
○ THE MIRACLE (EMI, 1989)
○ INNUENDO (EMI, 1991)
○ GREATEST HITS II (EMI, 1991)
○ LIVE AT WEMBLEY (EMI, 1992)
○ MADE IN HEAVEN (EMI, 1995)
○ QUEEN ROCKS (EMI, 1997)
○ GREATEST HITS III (EMI, 1999)

8
Rush

Rush's scope of influence on the world of metal is both simple and loomingly large. Basically, Geddy Lee, Alex Lifeson and Neil Peart are the godfathers of progressive metal, toiling away within a format they alone created (studied locals Spirit Of Christmas notwithstanding.) What is amazing, however, is that no one dared participate in the genre until Rush had nine studio records under their Canucklehead belts, 1983 and 84 seeing the first struggling steps of something similar within the early work of Queensryche and Fates Warning.

Rush began their recording career without their literary drummer Neil Peart, crafting a raw and raucous debut that was an adequate muscling up on hard Zeppelin, something the world desperately needed. But all that changed with the arrival of Peart. Instantly, the band started experimenting with odd time signatures, concept songs, concept sides, and concept albums, wild bass and guitar work, and tuned tom-tom fills which went beyond the call of duty, thereby flipping the band into their own time and space.

By the time 2112 was released in 1976, the band had broken the states, mostly through relentless money-losing touring. Their obsessed but compact fanbase now viewed them as intellectual virtuosos who rocked with might, while the critics reveled in jocular ridicule at Geddy's Donald Duck voice wailing away over tasteless displays of showy pomp and circus pants.

Rush speaks:

Geddy Lee on the band's influences . . .

"There are two terms that are often confused for each other. One is hard rock and one is heavy metal. I've always thought of us as progressive hard rock, owing more to bands like The Who and Zeppelin than bands like Black Sabbath. To me Black Sabbath was metal, The Who were rock. Zeppelin were metal-ish rock, and kind of began a whole style of rock. They really invented metal as far as I was concerned. But you can go back farther than them to Blue Cheer, and say that they invented metal, because they were really doing that kind of thing before anybody was, even though they could barely play. So I would say that we are kind of a mixture of those influences. I think we tried to stay more on the rock side of metal through our career. But we have moments where we indulge in metal because it can be a glorious, raw medium. But I don't think we were ever very gothic about our metal (laughs), whereas a lot of metal bands are very gothic. We were also influenced by bands like Yes, Genesis, Van Der Graaf Generator, Gentle Giant and ELP. They were progressive bands in every sense of the word, and as musicians we were influenced by that kind of playing and structure. So the fact that we were born out of a love for rock and metal, whatever you want to call it, I mean that's how we started, admiring bands like Cream and The Who. And when the progressive movement came along, we were so impressed with the musicality and the complexity, we became kind of complex freaks. We wanted to write things that were heavy but complex."

But Rush had the last laugh, building and evolving through seven more studio and two more live albums before the 90's were through, eventually receiving The Order Of Canada in the late 90's. All of this output, which saw the band move into Police-ed new wave guitar and synth textures, odd bits of electronic detailing, and eventually to a fairly stable blend of new technologies and traditional power trio tooling, has reinforced and assured the band's status as the greatest progressive metal band that ever was. Which speaks volumes given the fertile prog metal scene we're currently, experiencing both in Europe and the US, bands from all corners of power, speed and prog proudly wearing their Rush influences on their sleeves, rockers the world over remembering fondly the wood shedding sessions they would have with each Rush release as it arrived on LP, cassette or wobbled 8-track.

Rush speaks:

Alex Lifeson on the cult of Rush . . .

"Rush is a whole different thing. We're still a cult band after so many years. Talk about alternative, I think we've always been the alternative band. I used to think it was luck. Now I feel that opportunities came our way at a certain point and we just worked really hard. We've been lucky because we do what we do and if you like it great, and if you don't like it, too bad. Fortunately for us, there are a lot of people who really love our music and have grown with us and respect that in us. Every Rush fan will tell you what their favourite song is and what their least favourite song is and that's part of the magic of the relationship. They seem to accept that we are always moving forward and doing something different with every record that we make. Rush has never been a band that's gotten a lot of airplay. We certainly don't get much in the way of video airtime although MuchMusic has been great over the years. Certainly MTV couldn't give a shit about Rush. That used to bug me, but not so much anymore because I understand it's another commercial network and they are selling things. That was never important to the band. I think there's always been more of a mystique and that may make Rush into a cult band. People who were into the band were really into the band and the people who weren't, weren't. There was no sort of middle ground and that seems to exist to this day."

copyright 1981 Phil Anderson / KAOS2000 Magazine

Rush speaks:

Geddy Lee on the different eras of the band . . .

"Oh geez (laughs.) You could probably figure that out better than me. I guess I see ourselves as one band, really. But we've gone through an evolution. I see Rush as a continuing experiment, to be honest. But it's not like it's so inaccessible like fusion jazz or something. There's still a basic rock / metal thing, so we're still accessible. But I'd say the first period up to 2112, we were a band desperate to find our own voice. And I think 2112 marked the creation of our own sound for the first time really. And I think the next period up until and beyond MOVING PICTURES, we were still exploring our new sound, but I think our confidence grew, and the complexities became more overt in what we were doing. And then we went through a very textural period, a synthesizer-influenced period with POWER WINDOWS and HOLD YOUR FIRE, which began with SIGNALS. That was where the band kind of went from a three-piece hard rock progressive band into acting more like a four-piece band. That was a fairly profound change in attitude for us. And I would say that the last two or three albums have been an effort to kind of take what we learned through that four-piece period and try to reestablish a three-piece architecture. It's kind of like a weaning off of the elements that we learned. By going through that keyboard period we learned of lot about songwriting. So I think we are trying to apply those things we learned but within a more direct structure."

Rush speaks:
Alex Lifeson on Rush's experimentation with keyboards . . .
"During the SIGNALS era, I felt frustrated, but it was my fault. I should have stood up for what I felt. In all fairness, we were trying different things. We were experimenting more with keyboards, which were relatively new. That whole technology was new and how you applied it was new. I certainly didn't want to feel close-minded about it. In retrospect, SIGNALS was one of my least favourite records for a lot of reasons. Not just because the guitars were weak. The period with POWER WINDOWS and HOLD YOUR FIRE was very elaborate. I changed my guitar sound around that time, going for an thinner, spikier sound. Part of that was because I couldn't fit into the same range the keyboards were in. We made the mistake of doing the keyboards before doing the guitars, only because of convenience. We were doing beds in England and I was left with this very dense material that I had to fit the guitar into. And I thought I was one of the key people here. I was used to going into the studio with 30 percent prepared and doing everything on the day and that was part of the fun of recording. That kind of density to the music did not allow that approach any more, so I had to prepare myself much better. The last few records we've done, I'm much more prepared when I go in. I have all the parts worked out and I have a very clear idea of where things are going to go and if they're going to work. We can experimental a little bit on the day, but I have a much clearer picture before hand."

This is an element of the story that cannot be overstated. Through the invention of prog metal, each member of the band had unwittingly thrown down the gauntlet in each of their areas of expertise. Geddy offered bass patterns which more than occasionally

copyright 1980 Phil Anderson / KAOS2000 Magazine

Rush

strode to the fore as melody lines or brief but acrobatic fills, and later in the game the man added keyboard explorer to his resume. Alex, always restless and easily bored, became a sort of texture player, chiming, screeching and feedbacking well to the perimeter of the obvious (see also one Edward Van Halen.) Neil Peart offered lyrical depth around various moral subject matters, delving into his literary heroes such as Ayn Rand for inspiration. Meanwhile, he was busy building one of the most formidable drum kits of the day, adding numerous tom-toms, chimes, gongs, triangles, and later electronic drums to his repertoire. His work was always memorable and the stuff of air drumming legend (think *Tom Sawyer*, *Limelight* or *New World Man*.) The man is constantly being chatted up for drum magazine features and Peart is always eager to demystify his justifiably mystical band. All of this collective and individual creativity became a root system upon which, after serious study, countless metallers improved their game and the genre as we know it. Rush drove the next generation of players to take the high road into whatever corner of music they were attracted to.

Rush speaks:

Geddy on Alex's approach to the guitar . . .

"Well, Alex is a guy who gets bored very quickly. And he's never been a purist about playing guitar. He doesn't really like a simple guitar sound, and he doesn't like to play parts that are in anyway conventional. So he spends a lot of his time thinking of different ways of grappling with distortion. And he utilizes a lot of effects to try to give himself a unique character. Sometimes that's very difficult to record. But most of Alex's sound comes from his fingers. It comes from the different kinds of chords and patterns that he invents, which to me are very unique. I think Alex is a great soloist, but what I think he really excels at as a guitarist is someone who invents really great arpeggios. That aspect of his guitar playing, I think he's very underrated. I think when people realize that they are listening to one part of a song that sounds like three guitars, and it's really one part, I think it's really easy to take that for granted, because you just think it's an overdubbed thing. He invents some amazing patterns."

Discography

- RUSH (Moon, 1974)
- FLY BY NIGHT (Anthem, 1975)
- CARESS OF STEEL (Anthem, 1975)
- 2112 (Anthem, 1976)
- ALL THE WORLD'S A STAGE (Anthem, 1976)
- A FAREWELL TO KINGS (Anthem, 1977)
- ARCHIVES (Anthem, 1978)
- HEMISPHERES (Anthem, 1978)
- PERMANENT WAVES (Anthem, 1980)
- MOVING PICTURES (Anthem, 1981)
- EXIT . . . STAGE LEFT (Anthem, 1981)
- SIGNALS (Anthem, 1982)
- GRACE UNDER PRESSURE (Anthem, 1984)
- POWER WINDOWS (Anthem, 1985)
- HOLD YOUR FIRE (Anthem, 1987)
- A SHOW OF HANDS (Anthem, 1989)
- PRESTO (Anthem, 1989)

- CHRONICLES (Anthem, 1990)
- ROLL THE BONES (Anthem, 1991)
- COUNTERPARTS (Anthem, 1993)
- TEST FOR ECHO (Anthem, 1996)
- DIFFERENT STAGES (Anthem, 1998)

9
Aerosmith

Aerosmith have been called America's Greatest Rock and Roll Band. And it's kind of nice that heavy metal can claim them as their own. So where greatness and hard rock bisect, one can't help but notice influence.

As we've seen, America's metal history is scant, accidental, dated and steeped in garage-hoovered drugs. It wasn't until Aerosmith's and Kiss' ascendance in the mid-70's that the States could claim their own locked-down metal institutions that weren't embarrassing trundle spoo like Iron Butterfly, Steppenwolf, Mountain or Grand Funk.

Aerosmith

Aerosmith was the band that actually made good music, fusing the blues via the Stones with the knock-'em-down city boy riffs flowing from one Joe Perry, the band coming up with quintessential show tunes like *Same Old Song And Dance*, *S.O.S. (Too Bad)*, *Sweet Emotion*, their blistered cover of *Train Kept A Rollin'* (take that Foghat!), and the fledgling speed riffery of *Toys In The Attic*, all before 1975 came to a close. Additionally, *Dream On* is often bandied about as the first metal power ballad, while *Walk This Way* is viewed as the first rap metal, something re-emphasized when Run DMC covered the tune with the band, thereby unwittingly reviving a career on the needle mark skids. Finally, in the time-honoured tradition of the Stones, Aerosmith carried on a quiet but vigilant education towards the blues, continually covering obscure old music, even if much of this happened because the band was too groggy from chemicals to write their own material.

But in terms of influence, Aerosmith touched many, becoming media-drenched rock and roll bad boy role models for armies of jean-jacket soldiers, many of whom would pick up their first guitars stunned by the power chord shangrilas promised within the sexy, high volume grooves of ROCKS, the band's definitive 1976 barnstormer. Basically, the Americans had their first hard rock heroes, a band who could finally compete intricacy, hook and subtlety with the British aristocracy, a band that even the critics had to accept as musically worthy despite their adoption of chemical cocktails that would make their unfortunate down-coast (and later hometown) doppelgangers the New York Dolls wilt in shame.

It was this impregnation of a prolific body of work (five solid albums from 1973 through 77) into the golden age of stadium rock that was the band's lasting achievement. This forever rose-coloured look back at a hard rock heyday caused Aerosmith to become the distinctly craft-conscious US forebearers of all the pop metal hoopla that that nation would turn out, from Ratt in 1983 to Nirvana's metal death knell in 1991. Bands like Mötley Crüe, Tesla, Poison, the Black Crowes, Great White, Winger, Slaughter and finally most graphically Guns N' Roses would pick up bits 'n' bones from Aerosmith's amalgam of glam and blues, and finally overthrow Britain as the reigning snob kings of all that rocked in the world. And Aerosmith didn't die with grunge, their influence reigned simply by joining Metallica, AC/DC, Megadeth and Ozzy in selling scads of metal records (granted with highly corporate albums) when the genre was supposed to be dead. Once more, the brute influence of sales rears its green-with-dollars-and-envy head, driving many a disenfranchised mophead to create a life above and beyond the Joneses next door, and Tyler, as a Keith Richards icon, and his largely soft and sparingly spoken band, rise as mythical sage-like survivors at the eye of a Phoenix-risen tornado.

Aerosmith

Discography

- AEROSMITH (Columbia, 1973)
- GET YOUR WINGS (Columbia, 1974)
- TOYS IN THE ATTIC (Columbia, 1975)
- ROCKS (Columbia, 1976)
- DRAW THE LINE (Columbia, 1977)
- LIVE BOOTLEG (Columbia, 1978)
- NIGHT IN THE RUTS (Columbia, 1979)
- GREATEST HITS (Columbia, 1980)
- ROCK IN A HARD PLACE (Columbia, 1982)
- DONE WITH MIRRORS (Geffen, 1985)
- CLASSICS LIVE (Columbia, 1986)
- CLASSICS LIVE 2 (Columbia, 1987)
- PERMANENT VACATION (Geffen, 1987)
- PUMP (Geffen, 1989)
- GEMS (Columbia, 1989)
- PANDORA'S BOX (Columbia, 1991)
- GET A GRIP (Geffen, 1993)
- BIG ONES (Geffen, 1994)
- NINE LIVES (Sony, 1997)
- A LITTLE SOUTH OF SANITY (Geffen, 1998)

⚡ 10 ⚡
Iggy And The Stooges

They never sold that many pancakes, but somehow these Detroit disasters poisoned rock and roll irreparably, with Iggy's influence covering no less than time, sound, sight and emotion.

First of all, in terms of timing, The Stooges' debut was arguably the second American metal album after MC5's flame-thrown live record KICK OUT THE JAMS. However, while the UK was busy getting it right, Iggy, Dave, Scott and Ron, were getting it fantastically wrong. Barely able to stand, let alone play, the Stooges, through the guiding hand of a major label way out of their comfort zone, actually managed to put together a fairly disciplined affair, starkly so in contrast to its feral and ferrous follow-up FUNHOUSE or semi-official tragedy METALLIC K.O.. The Stooges revolved around fairly perky anthems like *No Fun*, *1969*, and *I Wanna Be Your Dog*, all early tracks to focus on riff, especially the latter which, although three-chord simple, was close to something Sabbatherian despite those silly hippy sounds tinkering about. The rest was also heavy enough to sound like the band meant it. Their second fuzzbeast, FUNHOUSE, put the "D" back in danger, rocking with visceral grime, wayward volume and sinister riffage that was previously absent on records stateside.

But it wasn't until RAW POWER, the band's third and last official record together, that Iggy's ghouls compacted then imploded — bad mix courtesy of David Bowie, sick, Munster riffing courtesy of James Williamson. RAW POWER's classics are many, the biggest being the tooth-puller *Search And Destroy*, second biggest being the chooglin' title track, both oft-covered. But best of all there's a consistency of high volume depravity — RAW POWER offers six rockers and two dirges during what is still, in 1973, temporal infancy for American metal.

Iggy And The Stooges

The influence of this hapless gathering can be felt anywhere that chemical swillage, spontaneous combustion, or immediate peril can be claimed to exist in rock and roll. Both the records and the live experience struck fear into the hearts of spectators, with heckled and harangued folks quickly realizing that they may be asked to participate with their own spilled blood and bruised baby fat.

So squalid metallers of every ilk can claim Iggy as their rusted root (misfits like the New York Dolls, Hanoi Rocks and Guns N' Roses come to mind.) But it's through the Stooges once removed where metal gets an almost thin but sooty film that permeates tattoo-like with the passing years.

First off, the Stooges influenced punk, notching up covers by the Pistols, the Damned, the Dictators and the Dead Boys, while Iggy himself became a punk off and on, although his late 70's were spent in naughty Berlin with Bowie as some sort of disenfranchised icon making real art records closer to avant garde New York punk than the textbook version of the form. Then later on, punk influenced metal, giving us hardcore and thrash. Later still we got grunge — an eclectic mix of metal, late 70's punk already derived from Iggy's garage noise, and Stooges rock itself in its most pronounced form since 1973, most pertinently through revisionists like Mudhoney. Finally, at the end of the 90's, we got a concerted stoner rock movement which, once more like grunge, grabbed a little of James Osterberg along with absolutely anything else bong-blue and righteous.

So like black exhaust on your fresh paint job, the Stooges just seem to coagulate on rock's dented psyche with nary much notice, always there in spirit when the world becomes safe and predictable, looming up like a foggy-headed poltergeist when rock and roll's demon heart is subjugated for planning, patronizing and pleasantries.

Discography
- THE STOOGES (Elektra, 1969)
- FUNHOUSE (Elektra, 1970)
- RAW POWER (Columbia, 1973)
- METALLIC K.O. (Skydog, 1976)

Rainbow

Leaving Ritchie to his tyrannical devices proved to be prodigious bounty for the metal world. Maybe some of you think Deep Purple served as a great balance between volatile creative personalities, and it was. It worked often. But allowing one piece of that Purple puzzle to become unquestioned leader, to allow him to assemble various fiefdoms to serve his will, well, that worked nicely too, thank you very much.

After screeching out of town in one last impetuous rage, Ritchie absorbed a little-known New York band called Elf and began Ritchie Blackmore's Rainbow. Elf's vocalist, Ronnie James Dio proved to be a synergistic catalyst for Ritchie's axe-driven flights of fancy, Ronnie providing the medieval verbiage, Ritchie matching him note-for-syllable with classical-derived tones that were mostly his own and his alone, with a little bit of epic Pagey thrown in for middle eastern measure.

Rainbow speaks:

Jimmy Bain on tour and ON STAGE . . .

"Pretty well everything that was in the live show went on it. It's quite a long record. It was just a lot of fun to do. That came out after I was out of the band, so that was kind of a bonus for me. You know, I liked doing a live stuff obviously, and it came out after I had been let go. I can't recall anything funny that was done recording-wise. I mean, it was all funny at the time, because Ritchie was pretty neurotic to say the least at the best of times. There was all kinds of stuff that went on, but not on stage. You'd come back and your room would be completely gone. You'd come back to the hotel and there would be nothing there, just a light bulb, no dresser or anything and it was all in the bathroom. They would spend hours and hours and hours trying to keep you away from your room so they could do all this stuff to you. And there were a couple of instances where we got kicked out of hotels in the middle of the night because of something one or the other of the guys had done. Cozy, at one time I remember, scaled up the side of this hotel in Germany. I think he was on some kind of medication at the time (laughs) and he had a fire extinguisher and he let it go. But unfortunately he had climbed up the side and had gotten the floors mixed up. He was supposed to be letting it off in Ian Broad's room, Ritchie's roadie at the time, but he misjudged the floors and he let it off in some German salesman's room. Then we were woken up at three o'clock in the morning and we were all ejected from the hotel. It was a lot of crazy stuff. You'd wake up to somebody axing your door down. It was crazy, but it never really affected your performance or the records. It was always done on the side."

It was this configuration that would form the band's golden era — three studio albums and one live record that were the springboard for a stunning, essential Dio career, and a large wedge comprising the birth of power metal.

Through the debut's *Man On A Silver Mountain* and *Sixteenth Century Greensleeves*, all of RISING and all of LONG LIVE ROCK 'N' ROLL, Rainbow sets a new standard in dragons and wizards music, dramatic, often foreboding fantasy themes buttressed by the Egypto-creep of Ritchie's refreshingly un-bluesy guitar modernism. In essence, Ritchie got to pursue one aspect of his persona, which he honed into cohesive records devoid of light diversion, save for the odd track on the debut still wrestling with Elf. It is this well from which today's large and commercially fertile power metal community samples, slurps and gains strength. And in one particularly crucial link through the 80's to the late 90's, Ritchie is unarguably the biggest influence on another first class metal mover and shaker, Yngwie Malmsteen. Yngwie took the torch from Ritchie when he was fiddling with Joe Lynn Turner and keyboards, and forged a new, more fanatical, hysterical and castle-maniacal classical metal that's also a key chromosome in the make-up of today's power, speed and prog.

As conductor and landowner, Ritchie has also made sure to surround himself with great players, resulting in another level of influence. Rainbow was always Ritchie's vehicle, but one could always find sub-personas from which to derive inspiration. We've talked about

Ronnie, but let's not forget Rainbow at various times also included Cozy Powell (R.I.P.: drove too fast), Jimmy Bain (a great songsmith in his own right, now back with Dio) and Tony Carey (all gathered for the classic 1976 album RISING), plus Bob Daisley, Graham Bonnet, Roger Glover, Don Airey, Bobby Rondinelli, Joe Lynn Turner, David Rosenthal and Chuck Burgi.

> Rainbow speaks:
>
> *Jimmy Bain on the chemistry between Ritchie and Ronnie . . .*
>
> "During RISING, Ritchie and Ronnie were pretty happy with each other. Ritchie was definitely happy with Ronnie's vocals, having done the first album. He was happy with Ronnie, who had a really down-to-earth personality. And Ronnie could handle doing a bunch of interviews, which Ritchie didn't really like doing. He had this image of not talking to the press, and he worked on that really hard. So Ronnie could sort of answer questions and was very personable. In essence Ronnie's lyrics is probably what he loved as much as anything about Ronnie. Because that was really where Ritchie was at. He was into the medieval period and Ronnie was into it too."

Cozy Powell gave perhaps the best performance of his life on RISING, and the Joe Lynn Turner years marked an interesting chemistry between Turner's Bad Co. / Foreigner pop stylings and a new keyboard-ready Ritchie (which is surprising given Ritchie's usual insistence on dominance), but the flavour of the day took its cue from Zeppelin, Rush and Van Halen.

So through the 70's and the early 80's Rainbow brought us perhaps three distinct eras — the Dio years; the Turner years; and one flash of brilliance, my favourite record by the band, 1979's DOWN TO EARTH, which is perhaps the greatest Graham Bonnet album ever recorded amongst many triumphs. As time insistently marched through new metals, Ritchie oscillated back into Deep Purple twice, eventually making a weak caricature of a Rainbow record in 1995's STRANGER IN US ALL. Now he's shunted the baggage and directly confronted his medieval interests, no longer transforming (through electricity and rock and roll) those castle tones, but playing them straight. The result has been Blackmore's Night, an acoustic project with his wife Candice Night as vocalist.

Add it up and you've got a mountain of memorable guitar work, an equal mountain of timeless classic rock compositions and almost as importantly, the first heavy metal work from an influence as big a big shot as Ritchie himself, Ronnie James Dio.

Discography
- RITCHIE BLACKMORE'S RAINBOW (Polydor, 1975)
- RISING (Polydor, 1976)
- ON STAGE (Polydor, 1977)
- LONG LIVE ROCK 'N' ROLL (Polydor, 1978)
- DOWN TO EARTH (Polydor, 1979)
- DIFFICULT TO CURE (Polydor, 1981)
- BEST OF RAINBOW (Polydor, 1981)
- STRAIGHT BETWEEN THE EYES (Polydor, 1982)
- BENT OUT OF SHAPE (Polydor, 1983)

º FINYL VINYL (Polydor, 1986)
º STRANGER IN US ALL (RCA, 1995)

Scorpions

The metal hopes of a whole nation have ridden on these boys for a long time, with only Accept and perhaps Helloween even coming as close to homeland identification as the mighty Scorpions.

Having no clue for maybe two records (all of LONESOME CROW and half each of FLY TO THE RAINBOW and IN TRANCE), Scorpions quietly began assembling a flotilla of new

Scorpions

metal anthems that would eventually cause the world to take notice. The band's influence runs deep; first off, through their early metal innovations sprinkled throughout their second, third and fourth albums. *Speedy's Coming, Dark Lady, Top Of The Bill, Robot Man, Catch Your Train* and *Virgin Killer* all swagger with a new rock groove, laced with ripping leads and a steady eye toward the stadiums across the ocean.

> Scorpions speak:
> *Rudolph Schenker on the band's sound . . .*
> "We always had in mind that we had to do something very different from what the others were doing. We respected other bands like Deep Purple, Led Zeppelin, but we said no, no we want to do it different. We were a different generation. I would go into the studio and write something and then Uli would write something and we'd come out with stuff like *Steamrock Fever*, which was maybe influenced a little bit by the punk generation in England, because we had seen a lot of that on tour that year. I think punk was similar to the Seattle thing, you know? We wanted to make something interesting, but very guitar-oriented, that people would go and say 'wow, what's that!?' It was a mixture, because Uli was very much Hendrix-oriented, and Klaus and me already had a type of Scorpions thinking, and to mix that Uli Roth sound with our feel, it was very interesting. It was like having Jimi Hendrix playing modern rock."

What pushed the band to the forefront of 70's metal was the canny guitar chemistry between flash rockin' Rudolph Schenker and Hendrix disciple Uli Jon Roth. Together they formed a twin-lead attack that was all business except for their astonishing nods to the production wizardry of Queen and Sweet. Uli left after TAKEN BY FORCE, finding the rest of the band's rapid Americanization at odds with his old escapist rock purism. After his subsequent arcane solo records, Roth now lives in a castle in England, toiling away at classical albums.

So, even before the band broke big in the states (the first step up being the commercial hard rock uniformity of ANIMAL MAGNETISM, and the second resounding whomp being BLACKOUT), the Scorps had an hour's worth of novel heavy metal proposals. *Sails Of Charon* and *Steamrock Fever* offered middle eastern-toned power chords previously heard only within Zep, Purple or Rainbow. *He's A Woman She's A Man* just rocked, as did *Another Piece Of Meat* and *Can't Get Enough*. Essentially, Scorpions was one of a half dozen acts laying a blueprint for the elevated possibilities of riff rock, despite Klaus Meine's treacherous, lecherous English as a second language lyrics.

> Scorpions speak:
> *Klaus Meine on individuality . . .*
> "In order to record an authentic Scorpions record, we had to find the strengths in the band. In order to do this, we decided to record it at home. Since we write our music at home and we've got the studios that we usually do pre-production in, it made sense. But the most important thing was that we had to find Scorpions music inside ourselves. That's the only way to get out there and be successful. It would be stupid for us to try and catch up to what's going on in America. All we had to make a really great album was to bring out Scorpions: pure instinct, pure magic, pure Scorpions. It's called personality. To find personality in songwriting is what it's all about. We haven't mastered songwriting quite yet, but hopefully we are heading in the right direction. But that's all that matters — it's not the pose you strike on stage."

Into the 80's now, and Scorpions are causing an influence that I kind of wish had never happened, one that pre-cheesed and exterminated metal in the low 80's with just as

copyright 1982 Phil Anderson / KAOS2000 Magazine

much force as Nirvana did in 1991 — the dreaded power ballad. Despite BLACKOUT's stuffed handful of searing metal mavens (*Dynamite*, *China White* and the title track), it was *No One Like You, You Give Me All I Need* and *When The Smoke Is Going Down* that pointed to the puerile future of the band. Next came smash-selling limp noodle *Love AT FIRST STING*, *Still Loving You*, *Wind Of Change* and *Under The Same Sun* and it was all over. Power ballads were everywhere, uniting the world in lighter-flicked get-a-life sentimentality. Vomit on vinyl.

Actually that 'uniting the world' bit is also a pretty important part of the Scorpions mystique. Klaus and crew are probably metal's biggest nation-hoppers, only perhaps

copyright 1982 Phil Anderson / KAOS2000 Magazine

Maiden and Purple being as cosmopolitan. In this role, Scorpions can be seen as metal ambassadors of the world, taking the genre to far-flung spots on the globe, educating the masses on the form (although I would argue that once educated, they would move on pretty quick from the Scorps' ill-conceived, off-expiry metal second-guesses as they existed throughout much of the 80's and 90's.)

Scorpions speak:

Rudolph Schenker on ANIMAL MAGNETISM . . .

"This album, it's a very interesting album. It's also one of the albums which is not finished. We came back from the LOVEDRIVE tour which was over a year long. Then we went directly into the studio and we had a very short time, and then we went on an English tour. In the short time, I think we did a good job. I think a very important song off the album is *The Zoo*, which I like very much, it's a classic, no question about it. *Lady Starlight* I like very much. And *Make It Real*, maybe for the European market. *Animal Magnetism* is even a great song. It's a very heavy kind of album, but it is somehow an album in between, an album in between LOVEDRIVE and BLACKOUT. I know many people like the album very much, probably because it is rare. It's rare like uncooked meat. We didn't take the time to make something really really precise. I think that's what some people like about it."

Discography
- LONESOME CROW (Metronome, 1972)
- FLY TO THE RAINBOW (RCA, 1974)

Scorpions speak:
Rudolph Schenker on his least satisfying album . . .
"I think SAVAGE AMUSEMENT, because the production wasn't as good as it could have been. Somehow that was one album too much for Dieter Dierks. Because we were very much a team in the early days, and somehow Dieter had different ideas for SAVAGE AMUSEMENT. And for us it was always important to work as a team, but on that record it was more like a dictatorship. But he sees the situation in the same way, because we met up a few days ago at a concert in Cologne, and he sees it the same way now that we have some distance. In this world you can't do everything 100% right. There are always things going wrong and all you can do is repair them."

- IN TRANCE (RCA, 1975)
- VIRGIN KILLER (RCA, 1976)
- TAKEN BY FORCE (RCA, 1978)
- TOKYO TAPES (RCA, 1978)
- LOVEDRIVE (Harvest, 1979)
- ANIMAL MAGNETISM (Harvest, 1980)
- THE BEST OF SCORPIONS (RCA, 1981)
- BLACKOUT (Harvest, 1982)
- LOVE AT FIRST STING (Harvest, 1984)
- WORLD WIDE LIVE (Harvest, 1984)
- SAVAGE AMUSEMENT (Harvest, 1988)
- BEST OF VOL. 2 (RCA, 1990)
- CRAZY WORLD (Phonogram, 1990)
- FACE THE HEAT (Phonogram, 1993)
- LIVE BITES (Phonogram, 1995)
- PURE INSTINCT (Warner, 1996)
- EYE II EYE (Warner, 1999)

⚡ 13 ⚡
The New York Dolls

No one much cared for The New York Dolls as they nodded half-heartedly through their bent-ankled, high-heeled, playtime career. Then again, they didn't care much for nurturing any sort of fanbase, perennially showing up late and in no shape to show off their oven-mitt-rudimentary rocks skills.

But the band was a sparked catalyst for other music makers who, through deliberate strategy or casual osmosis, took to heart inspired fashion tips from the band's presentation. Early on, and almost simultaneously, the band's managers Leber Krebs were taking the bed-headed rock and roll look of the band along with their Rolling Stones

fixation, and seeing in the two, a reason to back a slightly more reliable, recently transplanted contingent from Boston called Aerosmith. There was an appealing formula there, and an actual serious rock band who could milk it. They just weren't housed in the same five bodies. That got fixed real Frankenstein-like and Aerosmith went on to be a much more significant contributor to metal, arguably the biggest American band to further the cause, while the New York Dolls found themselves marginalized and finally driven insane by their declining fortunes.

In parallel with lighting up Aerosmith, the Dolls had an effect on another hometown band called Kiss. Kiss took a lead from the Dolls' over-the-top glam stylings and took them to a new smoke 'n' black leather level. Luckily and erroneously, Kiss got to see the Dolls' magic way beyond proportion to the band's actual fame, for the only town (outside of London, England) that crazy over the band was New York City. Fortunately Kiss was inspired to thwart practicality and the rest is Kisstory.

The New York Dolls

On top of inspiring the two biggest American metal influences ever, the Dolls became unlikely spiritual heirs to punk rock, making a deep impression on Malcolm McClaren and his new charges The Sex Pistols, while back stateside, the band unwittingly started off the whole art punk scene with Andy Warhol, Max's Kansas City, the Talking Heads, Blondie, The Voidoids, Television and the Ramones (the latter having their own peripheral effect on metal's evolution through the 80's.)

Then there's the band's general and specific fashion effect, generally that of glam, specifically that of cross-dressing. Both would show up pretty in pink on another big New York band Twisted Sister, glam (with various bits of femalia) thenceby sprouting sparkle all throughout metal in the 80's as all the newcomers (as well as the rocking chair contingent: Ozzy, Kiss, Van Halen) would become hair bands. Sassiest of the bunch were Mötley Crüe, Poison, Warrant and Ratt, as well as lesser phreaks like Roxx Gang, Nitro, Finland's Hanoi Rocks and UK's Wrathchild, all owing considerable truck to the front covers of the only two records the New York Dolls ever made, covers which brought into play the power of good photography with respect to a band's lasting impression.

And finally, like the Stooges, the New York Dolls loom as heavy-lidded apparitions everywhere danger can be found in rock 'n' roll, from the volatile relationship of Axl and Slash (you can slot David Johansen and Johnny Thunders between Mick and Keith and the Toxic Twins of Aerosmith) through the dope-fueled dirt component in grunge. Rarely is there a band that has had an effect on the seemingly disparate camps of glam metal and that of punk and/or grunge. But the Dolls managed it despite being unable to keep any sort of schedule, biting the many hands that would feed, bleeding money like it was rash-causing Hudson River water and generally smashing-with-smirk through the carefully arranged pastry strata necessary to create life sandwiches for those under the squinty glare as well as those puppeteering the strings, be they jivers close at hand or suit-types stuffed into veal-fattening pens at offices far away and floors up.

Discography
- THE NEW YORK DOLLS (Mercury, 1973)
- TOO MUCH TOO SOON (Mercury, 1974)

14
Thin Lizzy

One of a few all or nothings on this thorny matter of influence, Thin Lizzy belong simply because they were one of the greatest hard rock bands of all time, spanning one entire decade while lurching short and shocked into a second, punctuated by the post-break-up death of leader Phil Lynott January 4th, 1986.

Looking at specific points of influence belittles Lizzy's huge contribution to the advancement of British hard rock through the 70's. But we must point out a few things.

First off, Lizzy reflected the rock star hopes of an entire wee nation, being Ireland's biggest flash since Van Morrison, only to be eclipsed by the mind-and-body juggernaut that is U2. To this day, there's an annual Lizzy pilgrimage to Dublin that finds reverent rock stars, past Lizzy members and Phil's mom convalescing over pint and song.

Thin Lizzy speaks:

Scott Gorham on Thin Lizzy's lasting power . . .

"To be quite honest, it never went away. I was fully expecting when the band broke up in early '84, that people were going to remember us for a few years and then boom, it was off into the sunset. But it just never happened. Everybody that was associated with the band was always asked to talk about Thin Lizzy. Nobody would ever really let Thin Lizzy go. I think it was the kind of thing where the audience saw the integrity of the band. We worked so hard at being in that band and being Thin Lizzy, it was kind of frightening. It was like nothing else in your life mattered except for Thin Lizzy. That went for Phil, me and Brian Downey specifically. A lot of other guys fell by the wayside over time. But for the three of us, it was this one track mind business of the whole thing. I think the audiences over time bought into that and stuck with us because of it. Another thing is that we toured relentlessly. We were never out of people's faces."

Second, Lizzy has been the repository of much memorable guitar work of many hues, beginning with Eric Bell, moving through Scott Gorham, Gary Moore, Brian Robertson, Snowy White and finally John Sykes. Each has brought his own unique flavour to the band (and their collective resume pre- and post- is in fact daunting), but the all-encompassing trademark that has enveloped them all has been Lizzy's legendary twin lead harmony work, Lizzy being third in line past The Allman Brothers and Wishbone Ash, but the first to bring the concept to heavy metal, soon to be usurped (with credit, mind you) by Maiden, along with over half the NWOBHM bands to ever spawn an indie single. This idea remains Lizzy's crowning achievement, something which is now a trademark of many a power metal act, filtered through the fast science of Priest and Helloween right to front-edge purveyors of the new millennium like Steel Prophet and Jacobs Dream.

Thin Lizzy speaks:

Scott Gorham on Thin Lizzy's trademark sound . . .

"I clicked big time with Brian. He and I were the ones that actually came up with the Thin Lizzy sound, that twin guitar and harmony thing. There was no premeditation going on there at all. It was all by accident. That whole thing came about when we were sitting in rehearsals with an eight track machine and one of us have a line, and someone suggested that we add a harmony line over it. We worked the notes out, put it down, recorded it, listened back and went 'that's pretty cool.' We just started playing those things more and more. The only time that we realized that we actually had a sound was when we read it in a review — 'that amazing, harmony, twin lead guitar sound of Thin Lizzy.' I remember looking at Brian and saying 'shit man, we got a sound!'"

But leaving the shackles of specifics, one would have to pay reverent homage to Thin Lizzy simply for being there, for inspiring their followers, their peers and indeed all those headliners Phil was bent on upstaging, to be better songwriters, to be more attuned to melody, and to show a little class and self-respect. The list of great anthems is stuffed full of magic hard rock moments; *The Rocker, Wild One, Freedom Song, Jailbreak, The Boys Are Back In Town, Emerald, Cowboy Song, Old Flame, Massacre, Bad Reputation, Got To Give It Up, Hollywood, Cold Sweat, This Is The One,* and finally, *Bad Habits* and *Heart*

Attack ... blessed experiences that three generations of metal fans and practitioners of metal grew up to, under the watchful winking eye of roving Phil.

> **Thin Lizzy speaks:**
> *Scott Gorham on the swan song that was* THUNDER & LIGHTNING . . .
> "That was another problem. We thought we were losing and beating our heads against the wall because there weren't enough people that were actually getting what we were doing. That floored Phil especially, because he absolutely was Thin Lizzy all the way. I think what should have happened was that we should have given it a rest for a year and then maybe thought about coming back. I was too far gone at that point to think in those terms, so it never got said. Phil kept getting worse and worse, deeper and deeper into the drug thing until finally his body couldn't take it any longer and he died."

But despite the band's vast and varied studio catalogue, Lizzy's legacy also has much to do with the stage. Perennially touring as both back-up and headliner, Lizzy sparked many a player to pick up the guitar (and in Phil's case, the bass), touched by the melodies, Phil's delivery that was both vacant and steely-eyed, soulful and glam-showy, the sinewy guitar work, and the graceful Ian Paice-like touch of drummer Brian Downey. The band's talent converged for two live albums and one live EP (along with posthumous releases like the BBC sessions), the best being the legendary LIVE AND DANGEROUS set, which is often cited as one of the most inspired and inspirational live albums in metal history.

> **Thin Lizzy speaks:**
> *Scott Gorham on the impact of Phil's death* . . .
> "I think a lot of people started looking in the mirror after that happen. The thing with Phil was that people looked at him as the Mike Tyson of rock 'n' roll. This guy could take more drugs, stay up late, play more gigs, do more interviews. Like Mike Tyson, Phil got knocked out. But people actually saw that and they thought 'if it can happen to this guy, it can easily happen to me.' There was a whole slew of people around at the time who took a double-take at their own life and eased off. In my case, that was one of the reasons why I wanted to quit because I had to get better. The last time I saw Phil was three weeks before he died and at that point I was actually clean for about a year. He was still hard at it. It's down to determination more than anything else. I wanted desperately out of that drug scene to save my ass."

Ultimately, it's a rarified, untenable influence that this band has had on metal. Universally loved but never rewarded with huge record sales, Lizzy likely never saw themselves as a metal band like all those other poncy blokes. Instead, they partook when the muse directed them, an occurrence which came quite early in metal's development (arriving somewhere's around 1973 with their third record's *Gonna Creep Up On You*, *The Rocker* and the curiously prog-ish title track) and quite often after that, Lizzy finding themselves able to compose and deliver anthems that connected with a populace yearning and hungry of heart.

Discography
- THIN LIZZY (Decca, 1971)
- SHADES OF A BLUE ORPHANAGE (Decca, 1972)
- VAGABONDS OF THE WESTERN WORLD (Decca, 1973)
- NIGHTLIFE (Vertigo, 1974)
- FIGHTING (Vertigo, 1975)

º JAILBREAK (Vertigo, 1976)
º JOHNNY THE FOX (Vertigo, 1976)
º BAD REPUTATION (Vertigo, 1977)
º LIVE AND DANGEROUS (Vertigo, 1978)
º BLACK ROSE A ROCK LEGEND (Vertigo, 1979)
º CHINATOWN (Vertigo, 1980)
º RENEGADE (Vertigo, 1980)
º ADVENTURES OF THIN LIZZY (Vertigo, 1981)
º THUNDER AND LIGHTNING (Vertigo, 1983)
º LIFE / LIVE (Vertigo, 1983)
º DEDICATION — THE VERY BEST OF THIN LIZZY (Vertigo, 1991)

UFO

Maybe for some it seems blasphemous to put UFO so far down the list of big metal influences. Maybe others are questioning why they're here at all. That's the problem. I'm swinging wildly both ways, having the same problem with Thin Lizzy and even to some extent Queen. I mean, I consider these bands among the best the genre has to offer, yet their influence is questionable, almost all of it in a positive sense, all three being bands too talented, too unique, and too damn difficult to copy.

Thin Lizzy

In any event, UFO has to be mentioned for a few reasons. In the most general sense, the band's catalogue is studded with great metal, much of it coming early, such as *Rock Bottom, Doctor, Doctor, Let It Roll, Mother Mary, Natural Thing, Can You Roll Her, Light's Out* and *Love To Love*. These were the anthems that the metal greats of the 80's cut their teeth on, especially in the UK, UFO being this mythic but ironic working class type of experience woven into the fabric of everyday hard rock life. In essence, they were England's answer to Aerosmith, led by a toxic, combative duo (a borderline insane Michael Schenker and his sonorous bluesy vocalist Phil Mogg) who spent as much time growling at each other as they did trying to match pints with their party monster bassist Pete Way.

UFO speaks:

Michael Schenker on his approach to guitar . . .

"I don't really focus on listening to music at all. If I do, I write, I invent. I especially don't listen to rock music, because I want to keep it all fresh and exciting for myself. If I listen to rock music all day long, when it's time to make an album, I'm all worn out. It's like eating too much chocolate, you want to make sure you keep it special."

Looking deeper into the music, UFO was one of these classic, classical traditional metal experiences that inspired writers from many corners of the genre. For example, UFO could be said to be an influence on power metal, AOR, even prog metal and speed metal. In the same hallowed headspace as Deep Purple, Uriah Heep, Priest, Rainbow, Scorpions and Thin Lizzy, UFO were a prolific and productive bunch of writers, working in a zone that was pure art. Unhindered by tag or trend, the band just wrote great songs, many of which just happened to be heavy metal (see Zeppelin.)

But the two main influences that fall out of a survey of the catalogue would have to be on the worlds of power metal and AOR. In terms of the former, that's all Schenker, Michael being the closest thing to a classical, medieval, Egyptian, Arabian, middle eastern (somebody's gotta come up with a good way of describing this!) sound, this side of Ritchie. But Michael seemed to sample this cliché with selective maturity. He was just this sort of pure music man, reaching into his tool kit for the appropriate wrench without fumbling, plucking the right one on first try ever time. Consequently, his solos and his riffs are legendary and memorable, the DNA for what good power metal songwriting is today.

UFO speaks:

Michael Schenker on his relationship with Phil Mogg . . .

"Well, I had been with UFO over the years because of music, not because I had such a great relationship with the people. It's a musical relationship basically, and with UFO, nothing can happen until they find management that is there with heart and soul, and not just opening their hand for cash. They have to be good in organizing and working out details, I look at the big picture. We thought we had a good manager, but it turned out a different way. There wasn't enough heart there for details. We would get ready for a tour and I wouldn't even know what plane I was supposed to take, or where the rehearsal studio was, or what hotel I would be in. And when I would finally get there, there would be nobody there to rehearse with. And I don't like to waste my time. And I think UFO in general deserves better. So if this person ever turns up, maybe there's a future for UFO."

copyright 1984 Phil A   erson   OS2000 Magazine

With respect to AOR, UFO was one of the metal acts brave enough to use, liberally, keyboards and piano (hail Paul Raymond and Neil Carter), reinforcing the sweetness with sympathetic melodies, crafting songs that were among the best early examples of pop metal. Ergo the syrupy heft of *Shoot Shoot, Highway Lady, Too Hot To Handle, Only You Can Rock Me, Cherry, Young Blood, Money Money, The Wild, The Willing And The Innocent* and *Let It Rain*. One instantly thinks of fellow Chrysalis homers The Babys; while also seeing parallels within other early AORists like Journey and Piper; then into the big wallets of the 80's, Billy Squier, Bon Jovi, even Toto.

And speaking of the 80's, it would be a disservice to mention that the band's influence waned almost immediately after Schenker left after 1979's monumental live album

STRANGERS IN THE NIGHT. It would be a greater disservice however, to deny the power and grace of the next few UFO albums, 1980's NO PLACE TO RUN and 81's THE WILD, WILLING AND THE INNOCENT being my personal faves from the catalogue, 82's MECHANIX and 83's MAKING CONTACT also proving to be underrated and overlooked in the UFO canon. Best not talk about the rest of the situation (until 1997's elegant and forceful WALK ON WATER comeback), much of the next ten years featuring a revolving door of guitarists writing weak commercial pop metal that was as tired as it was ignored.

UFO speaks:
Michael Schenker on the business of music . . .
"Yes, I think everything works out the way it's supposed to. And you just have to learn from it and make better decisions, and take responsibility for the choices you made. And as a consequence of that I decided to become more independent and make sure that I can play what I want to play, no matter how bad the music scene gets and carry on doing my own thing. That's why I opened my own record company and that's why I'm selling most of my stuff as an independent, and building a first class recording studio and carrying on doing the things I enjoy for the people that enjoy the same thing."

In any event, UFO's influence is simply one of presence. Their place as one of the pillars of UK hard rock through the 70's (not the most successful either critically or commercial), is just one of a mere half dozen essential pieces of that country's crucial contribution to the form.

Discography
o UFO (Beacon, 1971)
o 2 - FLYING (Beacon, 1971)
o LIVE (Nova, 1972)
o PHENOMENON (Chrysalis, 1974)
o FORCE IT (Chrysalis, 1975)
o NO HEAVY PETTING (Chrysalis, 1976)
o LIGHTS OUT (Chrysalis, 1977)
o OBSESSION (Chrysalis, 1978)
o STRANGERS IN THE NIGHT (Chrysalis, 1979)
o NO PLACE TO RUN (Chrysalis, 1980)
o THE WILD, WILLING AND THE INNOCENT (Chrysalis, 1981)
o MECHANIX (Chrysalis, 1982)
o MAKING CONTACT (Chrysalis, 1983)
o HEADSTONE — THE BEST OF UFO (Chrysalis, 1983)
o MISDEMEANOR (Chrysalis, 1985)
o AIN'T MISBEHAVIN' (FM Revolver, 1988)
o HIGH STAKES AND DANGEROUS MEN (Essential, 1992)
o LIGHTS OUT IN TOKYO LIVE (Essential, 1993)
o WALK ON WATER (Eagle, 1997)
o WEREWOLVES OF LONDON (Zoom Club, 1999)

The 80's

⚡ 1 ⚡
Iron Maiden

If Metallica was the first real paradigm shift in metal since Priest, Maiden at least was a symptom that the guard would be changing. Touted as the successors to Priest, Maiden were punk's equivalent within metal, placed just to the disciplined right of Motörhead as the foreground aspiring street rockers of the NWOBHM, a movement which was both a reaction to punk and a reaction to metal's old guard at the same time, although more-so a reaction to commercial soft rock from America.

Maiden made it cool to be heavy and dark again, just when their forefathers all seemed to be flirting with American-bred commercial metal hybrids. Instantly we had monsters, devils, phantoms, harlots, wrathchildren and prodigal sons, all competing under a Total Eclipse for the green-with-envy attention of Eddie. Maiden, by record III, the first with Bruce, was making its rapid rise.

Iron Maiden

So right, influence. Let's start with generalities. Maiden were basically the biggest of the NWOBHM warriors, excepting Def Leppard, who rightly should be excepted as they basically abandoned metal for puerile infinitely multi-tracked pop. So we were left with Maiden, the one entirely new band aside from Saxon proving by example that you could be British, heavy, not write love songs and still succeed: influence through inspiration, pure unapologetic metal masquerading as nothing but, arriving jean-clad and beer-fed in the parlors of rock royalty.

Iron Maiden speaks:
Steve Harris on the initial Maiden philosophy . . .
"All I knew is that I wanted to play hard, aggressive music with lots of melody, with lots of harmony guitars and lots of time changes. And that's pretty much what I did I think (laughs.) I was really influenced by heavy stuff like Sabbath and Deep Purple, Led Zeppelin. But I also really loved stuff like Free and Wishbone Ash, The Who and progressive bands like Jethro Tull, Yes, early Genesis. I wanted to incorporate all that stuff. Lizzy wasn't so much the influence on the guitars. I liked their stuff to a point but it was mainly Wishbone Ash. I know they weren't as well known over there. If you listen to an old album called ARGUS you can really hear it."

On a more specific level, Maiden brought a number of things to the game that we weren't used to, stemming from the band's appreciation for Jethro Tull, Wishbone Ash, King Crimson and Thin Lizzy. From Tull and Crimson came the prog metal window dressings. From Wishbone Ash and Lizzy came something more subtle and valuable. Maiden could be considered the third in line after said pioneers (one might add the Allman Brothers) to come up with a large quantity of memorable, high quality twin guitar harmony solos, which became the band's trademark sound. Although no single band or handful of bands has taken this torch and run off with it, it's a technique that permeates all of metal, indeed rifling its way exhaustively through a large chunk of the New Wave Of British Heavy Metal, many baby bands simultaneously emulating Lizzy and then Maiden as Eddie trooped his bad-ass self around the UK.

Iron Maiden speaks:
Bruce Dickinson on Seventh Son Of A Seventh Son . . .
"SEVENTH SON really revitalized my enthusiasm. The idea of doing a concept album, I loved. It was a great idea. I was probably responsible in a large part for the cover, with Derek. The idea was to do something surreal. We wanted a surrealist Eddie. And Derek came up with that, which I was really pleased with. I guess what I found strange is that we took the album to a certain point, and then it never got developed any further. And in the same year, while we were in the midst of mixing or something, I heard some advance tracks from Queensryche's OPERATION: MINDCRIME, and was blown away. And I remember thinking, I was driving down a street through a park in Germany, and heard these four tracks from MINDCRIME, and then stopped the car, and sat there with my head in my hands, and thought that they had made the album that we should have made. SEVENTH SON should be this. And could be this. If we'd only forced it, if we'd only thought it through, and sat down and planned it, and discussed it. You just don't make a concept album like that in five minutes. You don't just loosely glue a few things together and say 'okay, that's a concept album.' So that was my feeling. I was proud of it, but there was always this thought, Goddamn, artistically we were in second place. Review-wise we were as well. In terms of the way the world perceives everything, MINDCRIME was a ground-breaking album, and SEVENTH SON was not quite. For Maiden fans it was, but there was this feeling I had then, that there was this world of Maiden, and there was the rest of the world."

copyright 1982 Phil Anderson / KAOS2000 Magazine

A third, more abstract influence Maiden had is just this example of owning a multi-hued catalogue studded with classics, a catalogue that nicely spans the teen years of pretty much all the folk plying the trade today. Maiden virtually dominated metal in the 80's and as a result everybody's got their Maiden memories. You've got the DiAnno years, a big first record with Bruce, the critical favourites PIECE OF MIND and POWERSLAVE, and then ponderous progressive pickings throughout the rest of the 80's, records that bombed stateside but did surprisingly well in exotic lands thirsty for heavy-handed mythologies.

Last and most importantly, Maiden are the undisputed fathers of power metal. Dabblers in prog and dabblers in more traditional 70's styles, Maiden were nicely positioned

copyright 1982 Phil Anderson / KAOS2000 Magazine

between the two, which is where the latest champs like Hammerfall, Primal Fear, Nocturnal Rites, Iced Earth, Nevermore, Pink Cream 69, Iron Savior, Steel Prophet, Kamelot, and even Children Of Bodom, In Flames, God Dethroned, Deceased and Arch Enemy all lie, as well as the previous, still-pumping generation, consisting of Helloween, Gamma Ray, Angra, Queensryche and Virgin Steele. Hence the recent round of Maiden tributes, the Irons in fact being one of the first half dozen bands to get tributized repeatedly in the late 90's.

Iron Maiden speaks:

Steve Harris on the highs and lows of his Maiden experience . . .

"I suppose when we played in Rio in '85 was amazing. We weren't headlining, but we were special guests of Queen, and Whitesnake and a few other bands were on the bill. It was the first time we played a major festival, with like 300,000 people showing up. So that always sticks in my memory. Also the first time we headlined Donnington, or both times really. But the first time really, because we had over 100,000 people there, in our own country, headlining. In terms of low points, I suppose it was pretty depressing when Bruce left. Not the fact that he was leaving as such, but the time of it. It was like for awhile we were four people in the band instead of five. Before, any time when we had changes there always seemed to be someone there to step in. So it was never very long until we were a unit again. So that was a bit strange. But to be really honest with you, there haven't been too many low points really. I've really been very lucky in that respect. We've really had a lot of success, and it's always been success on our own terms. It's been very enjoyable. I think Bruce had just lost the passion for the band. He's always been into doing a lot of other things, writing books and screenplays, this, that and the other. And he went off and did a solo thing. I think he just, I don't know? Maybe he just thought he didn't have time to do everything. Something had to give I suppose."

So basically it all adds up to what has become icon status, despite the band's ruthless efficiency in almost destroying their reputation with the Blaze albums. Maiden was the first name (and one of only around four or five) to break out of the NWOBHM, and a whopping big band of the 80's all over the world; one with a long, deep, rich catalogue worthy of detailed study. Additionally, they were the modern masters of the twin lead, as well as the wellspring from which all power metal flows. Can't argue the influential status of a list like that.

Discography
- ο IRON MAIDEN (EMI, 1980)
- ο KILLERS (EMI, 1981)
- ο NUMBER OF THE BEAST (EMI, 1982)
- ο PIECE OF MIND (EMI, 1983)
- ο POWERSLAVE (EMI, 1984)
- ο LIVE AFTER DEATH (EMI, 1985)
- ο SOMEWHERE IN TIME (EMI, 1986)
- ο SEVENTH SON OF A SEVENTH SON (EMI, 1988)
- ο NO PRAYER FOR THE DYING (EMI, 1990)
- ο FEAR OF THE DARK (EMI, 1992)
- ο A REAL LIVE ONE (EMI, 1993)
- ο A REAL DEAD ONE (EMI, 1993)
- ο LIVE AT DONNINGTON 1992 (EMI, 1993)
- ο THE X FACTOR (EMI, 1995)
- ο VIRTUAL XI (EMI, 1998)
- ο BEST OF THE BEAST (EMI, 1996)
- ο ED HUNTER (EMI, 1999)
- ο BRAVE NEW WORLD (EMI, 2000)

Metallica

Metallica is another band whose influence is one of substance, sheer inspiration through their success, and a refreshing lack of visual style, until, that is, the cigar-chomping look on the band's latest Loads of whatever.

In terms of sonic accomplishment, one can consider RIDE THE LIGHTNING and perhaps KILL 'EM ALL as the power-paired third great metallic upratchet, first being the invention of metal with Purple and Sabbath, second being the trinity of Judas Priest albums from 1976 to 78 (with a little help from ten or so frightening Scorpions compositions.) If Judas Priest invented a new fast and furious speed metal, Metallica (along with Slayer) perfected it. And along with the velocities, Metallica added the froth of California punk plus the grime of Motörhead, and called it thrash, an unseemly, inadequate term for something as bolted down as *Fight Fire With Fire* or *Trapped Under Ice*.

copyright Rock Classics

Metallica

Metallica speaks:

James Hetfield on making LOAD . . .

"Listening to the Black Album compared to this one, it's like 'whoa!' It was so anal! It started to turn that way towards the end. It was like 'don't mess with it, dude. Let's leave it.' We started to put the thick glasses on, so we took them off. We just let things be and let our hands play. Going in and recording live, it's gotta be fun. We sit and play live when we do drum tracks. When we go in the studio we start fiddling with textures and all that little stuff, but without losing the grip, integrity and meat of it. It's not frosting — we wanted some meat under all that. Then we go and play live and we just wing it."

Basically Metallica brought new electrocuted power to metal, barked-out vocals that preceded the more extreme growls of black, death and grind, production sent to the crisp edges of technology's capabilities, and intelligent playing at inhuman speeds. It all marked a new extreme, Metallica leading through sheer verve and magnetism a rough batch of bands like Exodus, Death, Testament and Megadeth in the invention of Bay Area thrash, and by extension, thrash in general, a genre that moved rapidly through the Midwest down to its current home in Florida, transformed into faster flavours of death.

Metallica speaks:

Jason Newsted on Metallica's development . . .

"A few years ago, just after we put out the METALLICA album, we were the fad in rock 'n' roll. I'm glad we've made it through that period. A lot of bands start to go in a heavier direction and the labels were starting to sign bands that played heavier rock. I hate the fad concept. To me it's just to make a quick dollar, to join the crowd. That's something we'll never do, and never did. If you listen to the last studio album, or even the recent live stuff, you can hear that we've progressed as a band. I don't think we've really changed that much as people. We're all basically the same as we were a few years ago, but we're a little more mature. A band has to go through a period of maturity when you start evaluating what you've done and what you still want to do. Lars in particular is biting at the bit to get back to work. It was really his idea to do this tour. He eats, sleeps and breathes Metallica! I don't think he enjoys his time away from the band. I've actually enjoyed our break, but I'm also looking forward to seeing what this band will come up with next. We opened so many doors with the last album. Working with Bob Rock really made us reach our full potential. I don't really have any idea when the next album will be ready to go, but I can promise it will be very interesting."

Metallica speaks:

James Hetfield on surviving the 80's . . .

"I don't think we were content being down there. There are some bands who are fine with it. They love what they do and they don't like change; they're afraid of it. They just want what they are doing. That's fine. We got some bug up our asses that makes us want to go: 'we've done that, let's do something else, I'm bored, let's go somewhere.' We've had that hunger since day one. That mixed with a total, pure, from the heart honesty. This is what we're doing. We aren't candy-coating nothing. We're not putting a cloud in front of you. We're not trying to fool anyone. We're playing music for ourselves and if you like it, then that's good. If you can't please yourself, it's near impossible to please other people. There are bands that do that. They get so trapped. They get so worried about what they think. We were never like that. When it comes down to it, it's the music. Looks or whatever just get in the way. People seem to hear the honesty and how pure it is to us and our 'not give a shit' attitude. That's kept true over all the years and that's the main goal for us."

Later on, the record …AND JUSTICE FOR ALL helped to invent the progressive thrash practiced by Watchtower, Atheist, Anacrusis, Cynic, At The Gates and Death, a format that thrives to this day, with that record becoming seen only now as a type of a watershed for experimentation in metal. As a wee side note, JUSTICE's innovative cold steel production values can be seen as a predecessor to the Pantera sound generated on COWBOYS FROM HELL and practiced to this day.

Metallica speaks:

Lars Ulrich looks back on the old days . . .

"I think we fit in as one of the less trendy main contenders. We're less extreme in the way we're sitting in the musical landscape than we were in 1983. We are, obviously, a lot more embraced by the mainstream than we were. We are a lot more recognized than we were. But millions of records later, the same things still fuel us. I'm more into the creative process than I used to be, and less into the endless mindlessness of touring than I used to be. Those are probably the main differences between now and back then. I don't think that anybody who was there in 1983 would get the same vibe as they do from LOAD. But that doesn't mean that we have to deliver anything else than what we want. Part of that vibe that you're talking about, which is a vibe that I've had myself a lot with bands that I was into, was that you are the only kid on the block who was into that type of thing. I certainly got that vibe with a Diamond Head or whatever, but I never got that vibe with an Iron Maiden because Iron Maiden was just so big and there was a guy next to me who knew who Iron Maiden was. So I think that what certainly has happened was we are one of those rare bands that, as we grow older, we don't let age not interfere with what we do. I mean that the way I said it. We don't let age not interfere with what we do. We don't pretend that doesn't happen, where as I think a lot of other hard rock bands do that. I think they try and suppress that. I think that one of the things I'm very psyched about, generally, is the fact that that happens. You draw different influences and inspirations than you did five years ago, ten years ago."

Now, through the oscillated, vacillated, supposed and/or real sell-outs of the "Black Album", LOAD, RE-LOAD, and the amorphous and annoying classical blob known as S&M, the band can claim a new type of influence reserved only for One, that of the biggest metal band in the world. Naysayers might frown that this happened through embracing the mainstream, by slowing down, by actually singing, by using acoustic guitars, AC/DC beats, Marianne Faithful, an orchestra, or through Bob Seger covers. But this is an integrity that runs beyond. Hetfield can quite rightly claim that Metallica's mold was cast through relentless touring, through almost evangelical identification with their fans, and by a steadfast belief in substance beyond style, and not a deliberate cash-grab through marketing ploys (although seeing the way the band's singles are released these days, I may have to take that back.) It's likely that the band's current sound simply reflects their current tastes, and that their merely creating records that they want to hear. After all, when you're #1, who gives a damn what anybody thinks?

Discography
- KILL 'EM ALL (Megaforce, 1983)
- RIDE THE LIGHTNING (Megaforce, 1984)
- MASTER OF PUPPETS (Elektra, 1986)
- THE $5.98 EP GARAGE DAYS RE-REVISITED (Elektra, 1987)
- …AND JUSTICE FOR ALL (Elektra, 1988)
- METALLICA (Elektra, 1991)
- LIVE SHIT: BINGE & PURGE (Elektra, 1993)

○ LOAD (Elektra, 1996)
○ RELOAD (Elektra, 1997)
○ GARAGE INC. (Elektra, 1998)
○ S&M (Elektra, 1999)

3
Slayer

Whether Slayer places first, second, or third in terms of metal influence in the 80's, depends on where you place the importance of today's black, thrash and death scenes among the less brutal contributions of Maiden and Metallica. Maiden is a looming presence through all of prog, speed and power metal, also contributing to the idea of epic concept albums and multi-coloured live shows to match. Metallica helped invent thrash and speed, pushing the genres to new heights of skill. In the 90's, their influence is that special inspiration that comes from being kings of the entire heap, that glow that comes from an abstract called fame.

But certainly Slayer can also claim much of the above and then some. After all, Slayer and Metallica are the two biggest names in speed metal (the pronounced and verified 80's version), and by less accurate extension, its unwound, unshaven cousin thrash, which careens uncontrollably into Venom, Exciter, Razor, Sacrifice, Coroner, Sodom, early Voivod, Destruction, and even Tank and Warfare.

Slayer speaks:

Jeff Hanneman on Slayer's legacy . . .

"I think we were best at combining punk with metal, adding all that speed, and that violence of punk with big, heavy metal riffs. That's it. I've been asked that question before, and that's basically what it is. When I started writing for this new record I was telling Rubin and our manager, 'send me stuff, I want something to beat. I want something that will make me go wow!, something that's really heavy.' But there's not a hell of a lot out there. But in terms of influences, Tom, he likes, I think, every song that's ever been written by anybody! (laughs), like old 60's classics. He actually likes happy music (laughs.) I can't stand happy music. I like death and sadness and stuff like that. He likes The Beatles for one. He likes a lot of 60's music 'cos that's when he grew up, He's like a couple years older than the rest of us. He's definitely the one who has the weirdest tastes out of the band. I'm the punker! When, we first started the band, I introduces punk into the band, and that's what got Dave all hyped up about punk, and Kerry just recently got into it a couple of years ago. Yeah, I shaved my head and everything. In the early 80's, I was just getting out of Priest, Iron Maiden, Led Zeppelin, Aerosmith, that kind of stuff and Kerry I guess, was just getting INTO that kind of music. That's when I was getting into punk. So that's kinda how Slayer formed. My punk influence, you know like 'we should play fast, we should play fast', and Kerry's influence on riffs and stuff like that, and we kinda combined the two."

And Slayer pan-seared the finish line while Metallica was still kicking away the vodka bottles in search of the gas pedal. Compare the velocities on SHOW NO MERCY, HELL

AWAITS and REIGN IN BLOOD to the mean average of those on KILL 'EM ALL, RIDE THE LIGHTNING and MASTER OF PUPPETS, and Slayer is out of their leathers and into their Raiders before Metallica even wake up.

Slayer speaks:
Jeff Hanneman on getting back to work after such long breaks . . .
"Well, we had a lot of things to do. We had to get rid of Lombardo, you know try out new drummers, plus we had that festival in Europe to do, then after that, you know, we do like our leisure time. We like to hang out, like going to hockey games. Once we got started, it pretty much fell into place. We pretty well practiced the whole time off, working out new songs. I, especially, didn't know what I wanted to write about. I was kinda thinking about different things, so I came up with a few songs, a few riffs here and there, then Kerry pretty much finished it. He kinda just kicked in and finished the songs. We all have our little hobbies, like Paul likes cars, Tom and I like hockey. But Kerry's into his dogs and his snakes. We all have our other interests, but once we all get focused it all falls into place. We do a lot of work at home, and then usually Kerry or I will come in with a riff or a song, or a whole total song, and then we'll play it and make it better, so we usually do our writing at home. But the record was a pretty long, drawn-out process, because we had lyrics to finish, and Paul, as opposed to Dave, is a perfectionist. So Paul, we'd like do the song, and go 'that sounds good, Paul', and he'd go 'no, no, no, I can do it better, I can do it better', and when it came to mixing, he was the same way, he'd want to listen! Like we'd all say the song sounds fine, perfect, and he'd say 'I just want to check out the drums', and we'd all leave the room, and Paul would sit there by himself and tweak the drums a little bit. It took a little longer than usual, but it was worth it."

Slayer is also the first and second word in the as-yet-undefined crooked branch of the genre called black metal, second because Venom emphatically arrived first, and first because Venom couldn't play, or at least chose not to. Slayer conversely were fast, riff-mad, scientific and mathematical, able to lock it down at ridiculous speeds, which although short of today's blastbeats, were at the time bordering on the absurd, many finding them incomprehensible and unmusical. Slayer also adopted a whole Satanic look, lyric and image, although this was more of an artificial prop (or propeller.) In essence, the music was amphetamized Priest and everything else about the band was Americanized Venom. Now well into the black metal revolution, Slayer is without a doubt the highest musical influence on the form, while sharing visuals and lyricals with Venom, Celtic Frost and Bathory. Heck, early in the game, they even slapped on a little eyeliner.

And let's not forget that as Slayer's lyrical material evolved away from superficial devilware to man-made death and gore, they became a big influence on what was initially an American phenomenon, death metal. Deicide, Morbid Angel, Obituary, Cannibal Corpse, Malevolent Creation, Sinister, Suffocation and Immolation are all sick offspring of Slayer's legendary (stomach) turning point REIGN IN BLOOD.

Time marches on, and Slayer hilariously shuns the limelight, over the years becoming icons who are sort of there then not... a new record, lots of interviews and touring, and then back to watching sports on TV. Over the years they've stayed the faith (at one point, through their covers album UNDISPUTED ATTITUDE, reminding us about the hardcore heritage in metal), but generally screeching by in a blur of complex mayhem. It's no longer an innovation; there are faster, more extreme bands, bloodier bands, probably better players, but Slayer remains an influence just by being there, staying with us, and importantly, demonstrating that extreme musicians can sell a pile of records.

Discography

- SHOW NO MERCY (Metal Blade, 1984)
- HAUNTING THE CHAPEL EP (Metal Blade, 1984)
- HELL AWAITS (Metal Blade, 1985)
- LIVE UNDEAD (Metal Blade, 1985)
- REIGN IN BLOOD (Def Jam, 1987)
- SOUTH OF HEAVEN (Def Jam, 1988)
- SEASONS IN THE ABYSS (Def American, 1990)
- DECADE OF AGGRESSION (Def American, 1991)
- DIVINE INTERVENTION (American, 1994)
- UNDISPUTED ATTITUDE (American, 1996)
- DIABOLUS IN MUSICA (American, 1998)

Van Halen

It was time for new blood. And if it wasn't time, Van Halen was going to personally change all the clocks in America. Oblivious to all the snob-faced critical fawning over gob-spittle punk rock and the supposedly well-deserved death of musicianship, Van Halen re-lit the fire first forged by Aerosmith and by a little album the Halen-ites all loved called MONTROSE.

copyright 1982 Phil Anderson / KAOS2000 Magazine

Intent on eating headlines for breakfast, Diamond David Lee Roth, Michael Anthony, and virtuoso brothers Alex and Eddie broke out of California with a Ted Templeman-scorched

Van Halen speaks:
Sammy Hagar on his first two records with the band . . .
"The happiest times for me were OU812. 5150 I would say was the happiest time, but it went so fast, and it was so hectic, and we were doing so much press, and there was so much pressure, that I can't say it was the happiest. It was the most exciting, but the happiest was after the success of 5150, when it sold 7,000,000 records or something worldwide, and we went into the studio to start OU812. It was like, 'Wow, we can do this, we can do anything we want. We did it.' There were so many people betting against Sammy Hagar replacing David Lee Roth. I mean, the fans were into it, but there were a lot of press and radio and record company people, a lot of the old fans saying no way, it's not going to happen. Even some old Sammy Hagar fans weren't happy about me joining Van Halen. But when we did it, and boy we did it, we had our first number one album that band ever had, for 5150. And I remember sitting in Atlanta in a hotel room, and Ed Lefko said 'come on boys, we need to have a meeting.' I was like 'oh oh, what's going on now?', because there were always a lot of complicated legalities about me joining the band. And it was early after I joined, like three weeks into the tour, because it went to number one the third week and stayed there for three weeks. Anyways, he walks in and gave us the news, had a bottle of champagne on the table, we were so happy man, we flipped out. But we couldn't feel it. It was so weird. You don't really feel it. You do and you don't. Because none of us ever had a number one record before, so it was a big deal. But OU812 was a blast. That's when the band found itself and started having fun together. The first one, we had fun, but we were getting to know each other. It was uncomfortable fun. But OU812, we'd jump in our airplane after the show and just start cracking up."

copyright Rock Classics

debut record that delivered America its first guitar hero for the 80's, the first of a new breed that could do this new thing called shredding. Identified, bundled and forever immortalized with a titled guitar solo called *Eruption*, Eddie is perhaps the band's greatest contribution to metal through his sheer inspiration to other young guitarists. Eddie provided that catalytic Beatles effect, planting stars in the eyes of those perhaps on the verge of neglecting or abandoning their axes for regular mortgage-paying work, providing the motivation and knuckle-cracked challenge to succeed and exceed. Eddie single-handedly caused the shred craze of the 80's, a phenomenon that raised the bar for bassists, then drummers, keyboardists and vocalists, by extension raising the musical quality of metal until grunge made it uncool to respect yourself, like people and know things.

Van Halen speaks:

Sammy Hagar on the slow breakdown in relations . . .

"I came straight out of one of my solo albums, and did a month's press tour, a world tour, all the way around the world, and then straight into OU812. We were burnt. After that album and that tour, I had been on tour for five years straight, basically. I said, I need a break, the band needed a break too. Eddie was trying to quit drinking, because Al had quit drinking and Eddie was trying to go into rehab and he did that four or five times and it never worked with him. He was like a bull-headed guy, come straight out and hit the sauce (laughs.) So I built Cabo Wabo, and did all that stuff during that time, and then my wife, who I'm now divorced from, had a nervous breakdown, in the middle of that break, and I couldn't go back in the studio yet. And FOR UNLAWFUL CARNAL KNOWLEDGE was a difficult time. For me. Not for the band. The guys were really cool. Ed Leffler was still alive. He kept them cool. He said Sammy needs some time off. Sammy's wife's in the hospital. It was really difficult. So, the guys were so cool during that period, I can't tell you how cool. They were there for me, and we finished FOR UNLAWFUL CARNAL KNOWLEDGE and it was a great record. It's really one of my favourite Van Halen records. I think that's when we were becoming a little more artsy and we did *Right Now* and *The Dream Is Over*, what a wonderful tune. And *Poundcake*, what a rock track. But we spent a year making that record, because I'd come into the studio for awhile then I couldn't. But then after that, we decided to do the live album. That wasn't a pleasurable experience because the guys wanted to go in and change everything and fix everything and make all the mistakes perfect. And I'm going 'oh no, please don't take the goose bumps off our live album!' Van Halen, one of the greatest live bands in the world, didn't really have to fix things, but they did. And they drove me crazy with that. Like, 'oh no, now you have to re-sing it because I was out of tune, so now that the guitar's in tune and I fixed my part, now you're out of key!' And I'm going, 'you asshole, now I gotta go back in and fix something!' (laughs.) And I didn't want to. So that wasn't cool. It wasn't great, but it wasn't bad. Anyways, so that tour was hugely successful. That was Van Halen's most successful tour. Everything sold out so fast from that live album. And that live album wasn't a huge record. It was a big live album, but it wasn't as big as the other Van Halen records. So then after that Ed Leffler dies, shortly after the last show. I went to Cabo. I just tried to get away, and the band hired Ray Danniels, and it just was never the same. We had a little trouble making BALANCE. There's great songs on there. It's more of a Sammy Hagar record than any of the Van Halen records. This is what's odd about that. The one we had the most trouble making, the one where they gave me the most trouble, where they made me change things, they didn't like certain melodies, certain lyrics, you gotta re-sing that, do this, do that. Bruce Fairbairn gave me more trouble on that record than I'd ever had in Van Halen. Normally I'd go in and just sing it, boom. And they'd go, 'wow man, you can really sing!' And it was done. But that record was painful, pulling teeth a little bit. Not arguing, but Bruce would go, well, maybe we should just do it again, because Eddie says he thinks you can sing it better. And I'd be going, 'this is really weird.' But just on a couple of songs. But oddly enough, it's such a Sammy Hagar record, with *Can't Stop Loving You, Not Enough*, those are like my kind of songs, that's like my input strong. *Don't Tell Me What Love Can Do*. That's kind of a Sammy grungy type of thing. Anyway, that was a tough record to make. Basically after that tour, the band was over. I'm telling you right now. The rest is history. You see what happened after that. I knew it then that I did everything I could and tried to cooperate and try and be a team player but these guys didn't want to play ball with me. I can tell you right now, they had another agenda. They were looking forward to it, they had a big plan."

Van Halen also had that over-riding, convertible cruising through Hollywood effect, greedily snatching the torch from the 70's arena rockers (Aerosmith, Kiss, Journey, Styx, BOC and Ted Nugent) establishing themselves as the festive sun-drenched festival kings of the 80's. And leading the circus was the ultimate chrome-and-fins rock star David Lee Roth (cultural descendant of Black Oak Arkansas' Jim Dandy and Elvis before him) who

copyright Rock Classics

in his own right, inspired folks to join the carousel. Dave branding US rock as fun again, worthy of your blessed and all too rare night off from responsibility.

But it's kind of cool that Van Halen's influence remained on a level of intangible, emotional inspiration. Van Halen would remain a "don't try this at home" experience, few ever actually attempting the Van Halen sound, which was an odd amalgam of eccentric drumming, non-obvious, often unmusical guitar blurts, squeals and screeches, topped with vocals that often sounded casual, talk-showed and in search of the next rock-filled tumbler of Jack. It was all a volatile package, fierce acrobatics made easy, hard playing masking hard work, perhaps the perfect metaphor for the American metal experience and by extension the American dream.

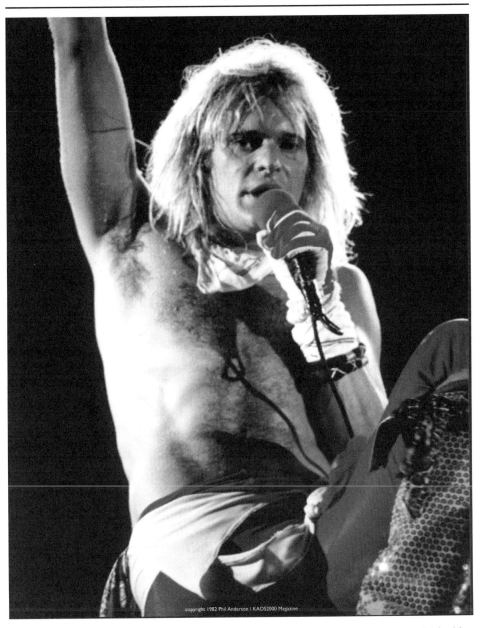

copyright 1982 Phil Anderson / KAOS2000 Magazine

As time wore on and, horror of horrors, Dave left the band, we were left with the Van Halen effect being split between a dimmer version of the band with Sam and the version of the band with precocious stand-ins that was Diamond Dave solo. The run for Dave was brief, but inspiring while it lasted. The Bissonettes, Sheehans and Vais of the world caused their own little Eddie quakes, showing up in all the technical mags discussing their post-Ed shred, endorsing the heck out of all sorts of gear, and all the while dressing like a Twisted Sister nearly out the door of a paint factory explosion. The new and diminished Van Halen soldiered on, influencing nobody anymore but selling a bucket of ducats at every stop for pretty much the next ten years.

Van Halen

As it stands now, Van Halen has entered the lexicon of classic rock, none of their latest product with Sam or the even newer textured noise with the in-out Gary Cherone making much difference in the world. Basically Eddie and Alex are somewhat frozen in time, reputations intact, hall of fame status assured through a bunch of brief, shockingly spontaneous and purely creative records, most of which feature God's gift to balding carnival barkers.

Discography
- VAN HALEN (Warner, 1978)
- II (Warner, 1979)
- WOMEN AND CHILDREN FIRST (Warner, 1980)
- FAIR WARNING (Warner, 1981)
- DIVER DOWN (Warner, 1982)
- 1984 (Warner, 1983)
- 5150 (Warner, 1986)
- OU812 (Warner, 1988)
- FOR UNLAWFUL CARNAL KNOWLEDGE (Warner, 1991)
- LIVE: RIGHT HERE, RIGHT NOW (Warner, 1993)
- BALANCE (Warner, 1995)
- BEST OF VOLUME I (Warner, 1996)
- 3 (Warner, 1998)

Venom

Venom would reply with a hearty chortle and a spray of warm draft at the thought of their humble three-piece as an instrumental cornerstone of metal evolution. But it would be more from the surreal, comical, inverted fact that they could not deny it; that in there bumbling, pokey, take-the-piss way, they corrupted an astonishing array of disciples.

Lant, Dunn and Bray unwittingly (and this can also be argued) snapped their arrow-headed tails in a number of directions. First off, they seemed to take extreme pain to record as badly and counter-productively as possible, something that would have critics scratching their heads for years. Through WELCOME TO HELL (1981), BLACK METAL (1982), AT WAR WITH SATAN (1984) and finally POSSESSED (1985), the world had larfed and barfed along until reality set in, with fans eventually realizing that they liked good music, and becoming fed-up with the band's muddy guitars, trash can drums, dropped-out bass, and bad hangover vocal mewlings.

Second, Venom were the first rock band since novelty acts like Coven and Aphrodite's Child to actively embrace Satanism and the occult (even if it was all a big joke) culminating in the band's second prophetically entitled album BLACK METAL. Third, Venom beat all Americans, Metallica included, in creating a din called thrash, or at least providing the unhinged, unclean, unsure component to thrash's make-up. And importantly, given Venom's temporality as having three records by 1983, Venom could be said to have provided something of a basic blueprint over which Anthrax, Overkill and their Bay Area counterparts injected virtuosity and production acumen.

> **Venom speaks:**
> *Abaddon on getting along . . .*
> "You don't have to get along with somebody particularly to get along with them. It's like a bad marriage. People have nuances and ideals and just because one of them doesn't necessarily mesh with yours, it still exists, so you have to give and take a little bit. I am sure other bands have done that. It's just that we're such bull-headed assholes that it was easier to run into each other than sit down and listen. We don't particularly like each other, but I think we can tolerate each other a lot better now."

Lastly, Venom provided England with their own naff version of Kiss. So the UK, years after the original thing had continually snubbed the place, got their own cheap date for an otherwise mundane Friday night, their own black leather, smoke 'n' pyro symphony, a visit to which the music became an afterthought tolerated but best left unscrutinized.

But the world this all converged upon is that of black metal, that frosty pro-Satan scourge from the right-north that took the metal world by storm in the mid to late 90's. Venom, along with Bathory, Hellhammer / Celtic Frost and Slayer, are black metal's spiritual heirs. Venom provided no less than the following: bad recording, spontaneous punk-ified thrash, overt Satanic content, an early extreme vocal sound, and an actual record after which the genre became named.

Let's take a look at that vocal. Cronos' annoying, cloying style is intrinsically his own, a product of his throat alone and not of trend. But it's woeful spew can be heard around the world, originating in the immediate thrashers Venom influenced (Sodom, Destruction, Voivod), through the death of Death and Obituary, and right 'round into the distinct crow-like scratch of black metallers today, most pertinently, Dani of Cradle Of Filth and Ihsahn of Emperor, both slight men with daggers for vocal chords. Venom is everywhere. Everywhere indeed, including one of the larger libraries of tribute albums and individual covers. Venom tributes arrived early and on par with those for Kiss and Black Sabbath, two bookends between which Venom sits perplexed and defiant.

> **Venom speaks:**
> *Abaddon on Venom's abstract qualities . . .*
> "I've looked at a million bands like Slayer and Metallica. They kind of have this thing about them, where it's almost like a commodity. Venom's never been like that. Venom's always been kind of, if we did something shit, you can turn around and say it. It wouldn't matter. If you went to Lars Ulrich and said that the production on the last album was shite, he'd massively offended. I think that's the difference with Venom. We kind of come across untouchable, but we can be touched. We're not made of glass. People can say what they feel, more or less, around the band and expect one reaction or another."

So there you have it. Beginning at the fringes, Venom became an evil spark for the origins of thrash, addressing in their hapless manner, elements of speed, noise and vocal terrorism. Venom also put on a metal show, reviving the glory days of Kiss, in tandem perhaps with bands like Mötley Crüe and Iron Maiden. But most pertinently, Venom's hooked claws scratch a methodical grid of blood-red gashes through all surfaces of black metal's serious make-up. The band established themselves as the first fast, furious, funny, noisy, loose, badly rendered trash-faced contraption, misunderstood in their early 80's heyday, destined to be revived only a full decade later with Mayhem, Enslaved, Immortal, Emperor, Burzum and other roars from the north.

Venom speaks:

Abaddon on the band's early popularity . . .

"It was incredible because we weren't just living a rock 'n' roll dream, we were creating a new feeling, a new sound, everything. Everything we did was original. We just went out to be the heaviest, the fastest, the loudest, the dirtiest, the most colourful, the most over-the-top. I guess every heavy metal band does that, but we were kind of getting it right. We weren't good musicians, but everything we did, it was the first time it had ever been done. The early 80's were just absolutely incredible — we couldn't do a thing wrong. We didn't need a press agent because the phone never stopped ringing. People were offering gigs like there was no tomorrow. The band never made any money because every cent went back into the band. At the beginning we were very serious about all that Satan stuff, which is why it worked really. After that we kind of went cold on the whole thing, exploring other lyrical ideas — more mystery rather than degradation. Lyrically it lightened up a lot after the first three albums. It got back to it with PRIME EVIL. That's personally my favourite record we've ever done. It's so f***in' heavy, so nasty and virulent."

Discography
o WELCOME TO HELL (Neat, 1981)
o BLACK METAL (Neat, 1982)
o AT WAR WITH SATAN (Neat, 1984)
o POSSESSED (Neat, 1985)
o EINE KLEINE NATCHMUSIK (Neat, 1986)
o CALM BEFORE THE STORM (Filmtrax, 1987)
o LIVE OFFICIAL BOOTLEG (Thunderbolt, 1986)
o THE SINGLES 80-86 (Raw Power, 1986)
o PRIME EVIL (Under One Flag, 1990)
o TEMPLES OF ICE (Under One Flag, 1991)
o THE WASTE LANDS (Under One Flag, 1992)
o CAST IN STONE (CBH / Steamhammer, 1997)
o RESURRECTION (Steamhammer, 2000)

Def Leppard

To anybody snapping up those first few New Wave Of British Heavy Metal records, it quickly became apparent which bands were going to break from the pack. Maiden had this instant buzz, the moderate shock rock stage shows, jovial beer-goggled horror metal songs and a red-eyed, green-faced mascot named Eddie. And don't forget the logo. As with the corporate American hard rock bands of the 70's, NWOBHMers had to have a spiffy logo.

Worlds away philosophically was a slick bunch of Sheffield boys named Def Leppard who wrote like they were Van Halen. None of this natty witch metal for these NWOBHMers. ON THROUGH THE NIGHT was basically "Hello America" all the way, big commercial riffs, solid mid-metal rock anthems, songs about rockin', competent production values — basically UFO crossed with Riot, spawning something akin to Priest without the serious overtones. And the Leps didn't forget either, that it's the logo that makes the band.

> Def Leppard speaks:
> *Phil Collen on the band's place in rock history . . .*
> "It really comes back to just the guitars. That's the main thing. We never really considered ourselves a heavy metal band. We've always considered ourselves a rock band in the tradition of like the Stones or Queen or The Who; or Van Halen, they were a rock band. That's what we wanted to be really. So I think the guitars are important and the attitude. Like I say, you can be a pop group that plays a rock song, but that's not us at all. We're really a rock band that crosses over into the pop thing. I really do think there's a difference. Especially in the 80's, you had a lot of a pop groups that would put on a fuzz box and go, now we're a rock band. And it's like, no it's not real. We were, and are, a real, sweaty rock band that crossed over into the other side of it."

Record #2, HIGH 'N' DRY, pumped up the party quotient with a detectable nod to AC/DC, but it wasn't until 83's classic smash album PYROMANIA that the band ascended to a throne so high (we're talking around 10 million pancakes sold) that a new party metal revolution was born. Oddly though, it was an American revolution, led by a bunch of Brits, the only ones in fact to participate in this new arena that fifteen years hence, would be deemed "hair metal".

Yea and verily, it was the Leps who became the first modern practitioners of the form, their predecessors such as Aerosmith, Van Halen, Boston, Journey and Loverboy giving way to the cheeky young pups who had been thrust unwittingly and luckily into the MTV age. PYROMANIA was the perfect vehicle, comprising solid pop metal hybrids crafted to perfection through the meticulous studio wizardry of Robert "Mutt" Lange, who brought us processing heretofore unheard of, strange new synthetic drum sounds, multi-multi-ed vocal harmonies, equally clinical layers of guitars, and all the while arriving at a deceptive simplicity that made it translate effortlessly on a portfolio of technologies, from crappy AM car radio to the best Trekkie geek, high paying union job stereo systems.

copyright 1984 Phil Anderson / KAOS2000 Magazine

Def Leppard's connection to this new animal called MTV cannot be overstated. PYROMANIA hit just as this strange new music video craze was taking hold. It was Billy Idol, Ratt, Quiet Riot, ZZ Top, Mötley Crüe, Twisted Sister and the Leps, swirling in heavy rotation, crammed down your throat like magic pop rocks.

Def Leppard speaks:

Phil Collen on the band's distinct sound . . .

"I think our main ingredient is the production, not just like, gratuitous production, but the fact that we spend time making a song right. What we did on the SLANG album and what most bands do, is they write a song and they record it. That's it. What we'd always done in the past, when Mutt was involved, on HYSTERIA, PYROMANIA and ADRENALIZE, is we would write the songs and we'd go, 'OK how do we make it better?' We've gotten a lot of flak for that, because sometimes it's taken us forever. You go back in the studio and you re-write, and you have people knocking on the door, 'Guys, what's going on?! Are you guys finished?' 'No, no, we're making it better!' And that's the main thing really. It's not the time or the production, it's making the song right. And that goes for everything, the backing vocals, everything. Playing everything separately, because we don't play as a live band. Again we did on SLANG and RETROACTIVE, and pretty much all the stuff through the 90's, but on those old albums, everything was done completely separately. There wasn't a microphone involved. It was all direct guitars, multi-tracked vocals. And again, that has to have the right attitude, because anyone can sing like two hundred voices, but you have to inject the right attitude or you end up sounding like a choir. You need a bit of a rock 'n' roll element to it. It really is a process of elimination. It's either right or it's wrong. A lot of it is experimental but you really don't know. You might have an idea. But you don't really know until you try it. It's a bit laborious, but the end result is really quite exciting."

Def Leppard

Def Leppard

And it was ever onward and upward after that. Drummer Rick Allen was to lose an arm in a New Year's Eve 1984 car crash, which surprisingly did not end his career. Instead, it seemed like a good reason to continue the trajectory of record-doctoring, Mutt Lange getting trickier and more deceptive with his drum sounds, more layers, more fakery, more sugar, less spice. HYSTERIA sold even more than PYROMANIA and the Leps were leading this genre they caused, once again, after a four year absence from the scene. Subsequent albums sounded exactly the same (save for the experimental and under-rated SLANG from 1996), further driving home the point that whatever Def Leppard did, for better or worse, was painstakingly intentional.

So the main area of influence has undoubtedly got to be this idea of good-time stadium rock and roll, a genre that begun with PYROMANIA, quickly adding Bon Jovi (indeed the two ruled quite evenly through the 80's), as well as the entire hair band army, a sampling of which would include the aforementioned Ratt, Quiet Riot, Twisted Sister, and Mötley Crüe, followed by the newly glammed-out Kiss, Poison, L.A. Guns, Great White, Warrant, Slaughter, Tesla, and finally this dirtier thing called Guns N' Roses.

The technological influence is also of some import. Mutt Lange changed the way records were going to be made. No more bashing it out face-to-face in the studio over a couple of takes and a couple more pints and a few more lines because the football's about to start. Bands now employed big budgets, bigger timelines, uncredited session musicians, computer-enhanced drums, all sorts of vocal trickery, samples, mistake-masking layer upon layer, all in the name of making deluxe product. Raw was out, perfection was in.

Def Leppard speaks:

Phil Collen on the making of EUPHORIA . . .

"It took about the same amount of time as PYROMANIA, which is about eleven months. Which is also about two years, three years shorter than HYSTERIA. I think part of it is that we really knew what we wanted. We absolutely knew the direction. And to be quite honest, some of the problems we had with HYSTERIA, the direction was a little hazy. Mutt had an idea, but for us it was all experimentation. For this album we kind of knew what it should be like and then it was just a matter of getting the songs to work. We had two studios which really made a big difference. We had done it over at Joe Elliott's house in Dublin, and we lived there, worked six days a week, Saturdays off, and took over one of the other spare bedrooms. It was actually quite funny, we'd go, 'you know that room you're not using Joe? Do you think we can put Studio Two in there?' We literally had done all the vocals upstairs in the other room. It really made a big difference."

And finally, you can't diminish the positive effect on metal the Leps caused simply by selling all those records. Def Leppard was a bustling third world economy unto itself, causing a trickle down of signings throughout the industry while metal commanded the spotlight from 1983 until its crash in 91 (oddly enough 92's ADRENALIZE was the record left to turn out the lights and toss the keys to Nirvana.)

Discography
o ON THROUGH THE NIGHT (Vertigo, 1980)
o HIGH 'N' DRY (Vertigo, 1981)
o PYROMANIA (Vertigo, 1983)

- HYSTERIA (Vertigo, 1987)
- ADRENALIZE (Vertigo, 1992)
- RETRO ACTIVE (Vertigo, 1993)
- VAULT (Vertigo, 1995)
- SLANG (Vertigo, 1996)
- EUPHORIA (Vertigo, 1999)

7

Ozzy Osbourne

Witness metal's greatest survivor, our very own Keith Richards, a man who is metal's biggest icon, rivaled only by Metallica or perhaps Aerosmith as the genre's biggest selling act today.

Ozzy's influence runs deep in many directions. First of all he brings to his solo career, a past as lead singer, hand-clapper and peace-signer of the band that is the first word in metal, Black Sabbath. And it's remarkable that he's able to make the grade twice, once with the Sabs, and a second time as ringleader of one of the biggest acts of the 80's, and one of only a handful to survive and thrive in the 90's, despite only two studio albums.

Ozzy's influence is indelibly linked to the teams he has created. Specifically, the Ozzy Osbourne band has been a vehicle for some of metal's guitar greats, beginning with the electrifying Randy Rhoads who was killed two records into his stint with Ozzy on tour in a fly-by prank. Ozzy then briefly had used Night Ranger's Brad Gillis, after which he found Jake E. Lee, who would later go on to make two stirring, soulful blues metal albums with Ray Gillen and Badlands. Other guitarists along the way included Joe Holmes and Steve Vai, with the most significant player from the later years being Zakk Wylde, who has made three hard, southern rock-tinged records of his own, as well as an acoustic album. Also attendant have been some of metal's legendary drummers (Lee Kerslake, Tommy Aldridge, Randy Castillo) as well as its senior bassists (Rudy Sarzo, Geezer Butler and Bob Daisley, who wrote more than you think!), making Ozzy's band a constant state-of-the-art construct worth watching and studying.

Ozzy Osbourne speaks:
Ozzy on getting it right . . .
"Every album I've ever done, I'd be walking up the road or I'd be in my studio at home, or in my room, or in the car, and I'd go F*** MAN! Why didn't I put that there or that here? I'm . . . that's why I always have to let go. I'm really not a pleasant guy . . . I'll say to you, 'well what do you think about this?', and you'll go 'well, I don't like it.' And I'll go 'WHY don't you like it?!' I want your opinion, but when you give me the opinion I don't want to hear, then I get pissed off. I'm like a living nightmare. My wife goes, 'I'm f***ing going away for a long time when you make these f***ing records.'"

copyright 1981 Phil Anderson / KAOS2000 Magazine

Ozzy Osbourne speaks:

Ozzy on how an Ozzy Osbourne album gets made . . .

"It's all a collaboration really. It's not all me at all. I mean if anything, all I do is have the luxury of sticking vocal lines over some amazing guitar work. Or vice versa, if I get a vocal line first. One of the more memorable albums I've worked on recently is NO MORE TEARS. Randy Castillo, Zakk Wylde and the rest of us sat down and we said, I mean, I never sat down and wrote airplay records. I just wrote albums, and if they got played on the radio, fine. But we all sat down and said, OK, without going cornball, we got to write each song with a treatment that it will at least have the possibility of being played on the radio. It won't be too whacked out. I'm fed up with singing about *Bloodbath* In f***in' *Paradise* and Satanic shit. I still wanted something dark, but in a different area, you know? So that's the way it came about. It was a lot of work, but it was a lot of fun, and it's the first time I'd ever done professional demos which is a good thing and a bad thing, because I ended up bouncing a lot of the stuff off of the demos and onto the masters. For instance, the harmony section on the end of *Mama I'm Coming Home*, I bounced it."

But Ozzy himself has been an inspiration and influence simply by standing there on two shaky legs and doing Ozzy year after year. He's a vital link to the past, a link to the excesses of the 80's and a walking, mumbling reminder that pure, unapologetic heavy metal at the humble hands of a past petty criminal can still beat the dim projections of naysayers back at label headquarters deep into the 90's. And the whole Crazy Train, right from the drink-sodden BLIZZARD OF OZZ debut through to THE OZZMAN COMETH have given us a wealth of anthems which deserve their own wing in the metal museum, songs like *I Don't Know, Suicide Solution, Mr. Crowley, Flying High Again, Over The Mountain, Rock 'n' Roll Rebel, Bark At The Moon, Miracle Man, No More Tears, I Just Want You* and *See You On The Other Side* exhibiting an astonishing range of rock styles that have defined at least a couple of generations of metal fan, with Ozzy oddly able to pull off the ballads as convincingly as the rockers.

One final area of influence, something that was totally unexpected, and likely more Sharon's doing (Ozzy's powerful manager / wife) than Ozzy's is the Ozzfest festival concept. Essentially a metal version of Lollapalooza, Ozzfest has been a consistent concert draw, as well as an excellent showcase for the cutting edge of today's metal, having aided the careers of Sepultura, Coal Chamber, Limp Bizkit, Fear Factory, Soulfly, Kittie and many other hot smaller acts who all seem to grow because of the experience.

Ozzy Osbourne speaks:

Ozzy on the difficulties of working on Ozzmosis with Michael Beinhorn . . .
"Oh absolutely. Working with producers, and Michael Beinhorn in particular, was not a pleasant experience for me. I don't know, he's a nice guy and all that, he's got a lovely wife and he's got lovely children, but f***, these guys turn into something else when they get into the studio. It's like being in the f***ing army and I'm not used to being treated like a f***ing idiot. I mean, when it comes to the stage where I have to question my f***ing sanity, where I know I sung a song one way, and I hear the mix and it sounds different. I mean this guy would have me singing all f***ing day, and I'd go, 'what is this guy looking for? what does he want?' And if you sing the same line time and time and time again, you forget what you're singing, you forget what the song is about and you can't put any emotion on it. I don't know about you, but I like to have the human factor there. I don't want a perfectly recorded record. I don't want it crystal clear, because that's not the way the music will sound on stage. And he would vari-speed my voice and slow the tape down so I could reach those notes. There was no f***ing way I could reproduce it on stage. Even if I dropped it down four octaves."

So that's Ozzy for ya, once a mere quarter of the genre's most important band, now, through seven consistently well-crafted and lyrically under-rated solo records, Sabbath's unquestionable marquee star and by default, the king of all metal.

Discography
- BLIZZARD OF OZZ (Jet, 1980)
- DIARY OF A MADMAN (Jet, 1981)
- SPEAK OF THE DEVIL (Jet, 1982)
- BARK AT THE MOON (Epic, 1983)
- THE ULTIMATE SIN (Epic, 1986)
- TRIBUTE (Epic, 1987)
- NO REST FOR THE WICKED (Epic, 1988)
- JUST SAY OZZY (Epic, 1990)
- NO MORE TEARS ((Epic, 1991)
- LIVE AND LOUD (Epic, 1993)

o OZZMOSIS (Epic, 1995)
o THE OZZMAN COMETH (Epic, 1997)

8
Mercyful Fate

In much the same eerie fashion that Judas Priest's SAD WINGS OF DESTINY just seemed to parachute in like a black seed, along came MELISSA, a merciless (!) state-of-the-art banquet of dark art that shook the bolts out of Priest's advanced tooling and directed the machinations unto the altar of Satan.

Struggling out of bands like Black Rose and then Brats, Denmark's Mercyful Fate showed up half-baked but well on the way to the banquet with EP and compilation tracks before unleashing the death-chilled falsetto cries of MELISSA. Tracks like *Evil* and *Curse Of The Pharaohs* featured locked-in proficiency that became all the more scary due to King Diamond's blatantly evil lyrical matter, the two together pointing to some sort of Paganini 'n' Robert Johnson devil dance at the crossroads, for metal hadn't been crafted so perfectly since Priest's STAINED CLASS back in 1978. MELISSA, and its equally high-minded follow-up DON'T BREAK THE OATH became the grail standards which, interestingly enough, few dared follow either immediately or years later.

So wherein lies influence? Well, first off, Fate could be seen as a viable link in the progressive metal chain. *Satan's Fall* from the debut was eleven minutes long, but not as

Mercyful Fate

tricky as the shorter, more info-packed masterworks on DON'T BREAK THE OATH. But given the band's wily cross-pollination — their prog metal straddled power metal — Fate was seen as the calming, slowing counter to Maiden and Helloween, helping to cause the variety in the burgeoning prog / power field today. What was important was the quality of the musicianship, King Diamond's eccentric portfolio of unholy voices, Denner's and Sherman's devilish lead duels, Hansen's disciplined bass grooves and Kim Ruzz's groovy metal heft, even during difficult time signature maneuvers.

Mercyful Fate speaks:

King Diamond on the band's sound . . .

"I've always been against labels, because it's so hard to label bands. Would we be black metal? I mean I think of growly voices. Then there's speed and thrash. And that certainly doesn't cover us at all. I just know that we're a band that plays heavy, and that there's not a whole lot of other bands that sound like us. And that has a lot to do with the artistic freedom we've been given by the record labels. That's a very positive thing, that we've been able to carry on writing and performing. And I think that has to do with why we're still around. I mean, the fans are still definitely out there for heavy metal. And it's a mutual respect between the fans and us. They know that we aren't pretending to be something other than what we are. So it's total honesty. And we have a lot of respect for the fans. It's not like we show up to gigs stoned, drunk or can't perform. We do whatever we can to perform as best we can under whatever circumstances. Every night. Because we know that it is those people that make it possible for us to do what we love the most. So you owe them a lot of respect, to not just blow them off."

So if Mercyful Fate were the original darklords poking and prodding power and prog, they were also causing a relentless up-marketing of something called black metal. Previously much the hazy domain of Sabbath, and then the more lyrically and visually direct domain of a trash can called Venom, Mercyful Fate filtered an unadulterated, uncensored evil through musician's music, something which wouldn't catch on until the second wave of modern black metal through later Emperor, later Rotting Christ, later Old Man's Child,

Mercyful Fate

Dimmu Borgir, Borknagar, Sacramentum, Cradle Of Filth, Arcturus, and onward into Children Of Bodom and Sinergy.

It's interesting that in both musical kernellings, Mercyful Fate's presence wasn't to be appreciated until much after the break-up of the original configuration in 1985. It was like their updated dust-off of Priest, Rainbow, Scorpions and Sabbath was too rich to be attempted until power metal really flourished in 1998. Similarly, in a black metal world dominated by the ear-splitting caterwaul of Venom, Bathory, Celtic Frost and Death SS, Mercyful Fate for years remained this stand-alone icon of perfection. Consequently, the first bunch of black metallers were an even noisier bunch, not coming around to the high-gloss prog metal ethic that Fate knew until the raft of conceptual, mathematical mind-melting records from the aforementioned musos hit and elevated black metal around 1998.

One also can't ignore the effect of future work from the band and, as importantly, King Diamond's solo work. King Diamond, the band, continued through the 80's and 90's, to the point where it overlaps and dovetails nicely with the newly reformed and thriving Mercyful Fate. King Diamond's unique contribution once more is to power metal, his clinical, keyboard-laden classicism and the involved story lines, both ideas thriving in the pomp of today's power genre.

Mercyful Fate speaks:
King Diamond on his hopes for Mercyful Fate. . .
"What I really wish for is for us to get a little more exposure. To get that special support tour with Slayer, or play for a bigger audience. That's what we need because I think there's a lot more people out there that have not been exposed to us fully. When you look into the audience, you see a lot of different shirts. I've seen everything from death metal bands to Bon Jovi and that's quite a crossover for people to hear our music. I think we do have the potential of breaking big, if we get the proper exploitation and get the right chances. We just want to make other people aware that we are there and to try and make them take that chance. I don't hear other bands sounding like us and vice versa. We just write what we feel inside and whatever we felt at the time we wrote the songs, that's what you hear on the album. I think that has a lot to do with us still being around, so many years later. We've created our own little niche and it's not affected by time."

One last note of influence: King Diamond was obviously the guy to bring something Kiss and Alice invented, face make-up, to black metal. We didn't call it corpse paint in the King's day, but that's what they call it now. In many an interview, black metal bands do cite Mercyful Fate as an influence in this direction, quick to add that the music was a big influence as well.

Discography
o MELISSA (Roadrunner, 1983)
o DON'T BREAK THE OATH (Roadrunner, 1984)
o THE BEGINNING (Roadrunner, 1987)
o RETURN OF THE VAMPIRE (Roadrunner, 1992)
o IN THE SHADOWS (Metal Blade, 1993)
o TIME (Metal Blade, 1984)

o INTO THE UNKNOWN (Metal Blade, 1996)
o DEAD AGAIN (Metal Blade, 1998)
o 9 (Metal Blade, 1999)

9
Dio

Dio, Lemmy, Ozzy ... there are only a handful of folks so big, they only hadda name them once. Ronnie James Dio easily cruises to a post in our Hall Of Flame because he's been in so many important places at the right time. He's the face and voice of the classic Rainbow line-up. His records during his first run with Sabbath (1980's HEAVEN AND HELL and 81's MOB RULES) comprise, in actuality, one of the band's most critically and commercially acclaimed golden periods. And his band Dio has seen its own fair share of accolades and crowds, having created a string of smash records in the mid-80's, the most celebrated being the first two — 1983's HOLY DIVER and 84's THE LAST IN LINE.

But because this is about bands, and not spell-casting warlocks, we're going to talk about Dio, a band certainly worthy of a chapter here on their own merits. Dio's effect on the evolution of metal is ironically much like Ozzy's. Both men operated and thrived in the mid-80's with well-written, well-crafted traditional metal records; their unique personalities driving the vocal and lyrical matter, and their backing bands prophetically chosen corrals of future hotshot metal talent.

> Dio speaks:
> *Ronnie James Dio on his approach to lyrics . . .*
> "The things I write, as the lyricist, are very personal. But for some reason, I don't write this song and say, 'that's about you, you bitch.' I don't normally do that. Once I start, I try to put it in somebody else's perspective. I try to think of how the injured party would feel, not me as the injured party, but somebody else as the injured party so I can speak for them. Because that's my point. So again, I put myself totally in someone else's place, and I don't really find any of them to be a autobiographical, but of course they are, because song writing is a very good therapeutic tool. You can really release a lot of demons by saying what you need to say. I write songs for people, how people feel about being lonely, for being pecked at for, not being the greatest physical specimens on earth; things like that just happen. *Last In Line* for me describes people who persevere through all the stones and slings and arrows that are tossed at them. The last in line, that's usually where people like that are placed, the end of the line. But to me, just because you're at the end of the line, doesn't mean that you can't succeed. And I usually find that the people who are willing to stay there at the end of the line will succeed."

Dio however, stylistically, is closer to what power metal is today, making the man and band, along with Iron Maiden, Priest, and (appropriately so) Dio-era Rainbow, the four pillars of power metal. Through the man's demons and wizards imagery and his passionate parables for the downtrodden and outcast, Ronnie is now seen as a sort of

metal sage, champion of hope, poet of the punters, a classic and classical rock Merlin. Power metal today is discussed nearly as much in terms of its proximity to Dio as it is to Helloween, Priest or Accept.

Dio

Dio speaks:

Ronnie James Dio on his shift in lyrical focus over the years . . .

"Well, in the early days with Elf, we wrote a lot of things that were perhaps more juvenile, being younger men then. And the music itself was a little more honky tonk rock 'n' roll, which didn't really lend itself to a lot of deep things. And then when I was in Rainbow, of course the music and the lyrics kind of tailored themselves together. So I wrote more escapist, fantasy-based kinds of things. Which I carried on into Sabbath, which was a perfect vehicle to be even darker and more doomy, which is what I really wanted to be more involved in anyway. Then the world changed. It had become a place where, even if you tried to escape, you could never escape the reality of it, because when you came back, it had become a pretty rotten world, especially for a lot of young people, with the lack of employment, and disease and wars all around the world, just all the horrible things that are out there. And I just found it really hard to talk about having your dreams come true and really applying yourself, and things will work out fine at the end of the day. It's just not like that anymore. So from the album DEHUMANIZER, which was of course the reunion record with Sabbath, I started to write in a much more realistic, observational kind of way. So that's what's really happened up to this point. So over the last three albums, which include ANGRY MACHINES, STRANGE HIGHWAYS and DEHUMANIZER, I've been a lot more factual and observant about the realities of life today."

Dio's influence also spreads past Ronnie to his assembled warriors of the road. His first incarnation of Dio contained no less than Jimmy Bain, Vinny Appice, Claude Schnell, and future Def Leppard axeman Vivian Campbell. Later records featured House Of Lords' Craig Goldy, AC/DC's Simon Wright, World War III's Tracy G, Dokken's Jeff Pilson and Yngwie Malmsteen's and Silver Mountain's Jens Johansson.

Dio speaks:

Ronnie James Dio on making MAGICA . . .

"I would never actually make albums in a home studio. I might if I had a full studio here, but I would never put a permanent studio in my home. You'd never get out of the house if you do that! I'm not getting out of the house as it is now! I mean, I have to be dragged out of the house in order to get away from it. Because Craig comes over every day, and we work for about twelve hours every day. At the end of the night, like 1:30 in the morning, I remember what I have to do the next day, which is take my dog out for a walk. If he doesn't have a walk, he'll kill me. He's always awake at seven o'clock looking at me, going 'hey, time for that walk.' So we're off. And then once I'm up, I'm up, I can't go back to sleep again. And by that time, Craig is back over and we do it again. So I don't have much chance to get out of here, and I wouldn't have a studio at home. Plus the fact that I like to go other places to do things. Because you create a completely different atmosphere in another place. So that's why when you choose a recording studio you pick something that you look forward to going to. And that's not my home. So we'll do the record I'm sure where we did the last one, with the same engineer, a guy named Wyn Davis, at a place called Total Access, which is in Redondo Beach — A great engineer, a great musician, a great guy, a great studio, and like I say, the studio is in Redondo Beach, to give you a hint of how nice it is down there."

This hiring practice, this passion to play with and create the best, turned out to be of utmost influence, as many of these minor rock stars became studied mentors for the next raft of precision players, those making metal of high craft today. Standing out from the pack would be Vivian Campbell and Vinny Appice. Vivian has sadly found himself restrained and dumbed-down through his clinical posting within the Leps. But for a brief instance, we got to experience the flash and rhythm of a man with a great ear. And

Ritchie Blackmore (first Deep Purple. reunion tour)
Copyright 1980 Phil Anderson / KAOS2000 Magazine

Francis Buchholz, Rudolf Schenker, Matthias Jabs and Klaus Meine (Scorpions.) Copyright 1982 Phil Anderson / KAOS2000 Magazine

Eddie Van Halen. Copyright Rock Classics

Rick Savage, Steve Clark, Phil Collen and Joe Elliott (Def Leppard.) Copyright 1984 Phil Anderson / KAOS2000 Magazine

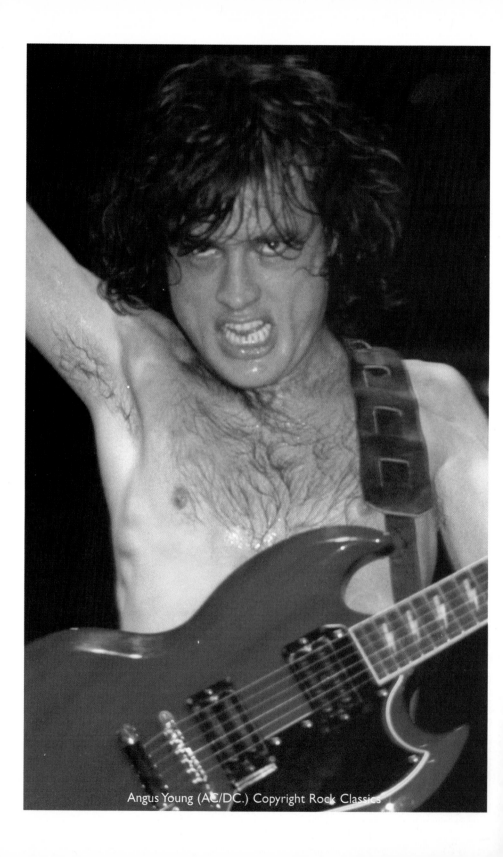

Angus Young (AC/DC.) Copyright Rock Classics

speaking of rhythm, Vinny is the man, the driving force behind MOB RULES, early classic Dio, plus later years output from STRANGE HIGHWAYS through the band's blistering, bottom heavy double live set. Vinny's stamp on the band was undeniable, the big man's groove king thump steamrolling Dio's memorable compositions along with the authority they deserve. Ironically, his booting from the band was a result of his percussive stamp over-reaching the bounds a drummer should arguably be afforded in a democratic band, or in this case, a benevolent dictatorship.

Ronnie's icon status was assured a long time ago. But by continuing to make meticulous, well-crafted records that somehow manage electric spontaneity, life-affirming messages, and riffs that riddle the top couple o' hundred of all time, Ronnie will have no problem entering the millennium as one of but a handful of icons worthy of hallowed and continued one-name status.

Discography
- HOLY DIVER (Warner, 1983)
- THE LAST IN LINE (Warner, 1984)
- SACRED HEART (Warner, 1985)
- INTERMISSION (Warner, 1986)
- DREAM EVIL (Warner, 1987)
- LOCK UP THE WOLVES (Warner, 1990)
- DIAMONDS — THE BEST OF DIO (Warner, 1992)
- STRANGE HIGHWAYS (Reprise, 1994)
- ANGRY MACHINES (Mayhem, 1996)
- INFERNO: LAST IN LIVE (Mayhem, 1998)
- MAGICA (Spitfire, 2000)

AC/DC

If you want to talk about steadfast belief in a chosen pathway, AC/DC are emphatically it, leading the charge ahead of Quo, the Ramones and Motörhead in bringing you one song served one hundred ways.

But the simplicity implicit within the early records by these Aussies was indeed refreshing, quickly resulting in a major launch stateside, leading with an altered HIGH VOLTAGE, followed by the electric upcharge of LET THERE BE ROCK. It was a stunning sound, built of an insistent single kick, single snare lock beat, riffs that mixed BTO boogie with ZZ southern, spiked with the unholy reptilian croak of one Bon Scott. After Bon's alcohol-related death (he froze in a car), we got the whisky screech of English Geordie bloke Brian Johnson and thankfully more of the same. Each singer could claim one of the band's two biggest testimonies to suburban hurling however, Bon taking us down the *Highway To Hell*, while Brian rang the *Hell's Bells* on BACK IN BLACK.

copyright Rock Classics

AC/DC's influence is like a deep river through all of metal's past twenty years. Masters of the mid-groove, their impression was felt almost immediately through the moderate success of Switzerland's Krokus, near clones in almost every department. Oddly enough, other mainland acts like Killers, Trust, Ocean, Warning, Ganafoul, Cinepalace and Defi (all from France!), Spain's Baron Rojo and even Accept (for one daft album) also took quite kindly to the band's scruffneck boogie.

And given the band's huge fame back home down under, the world was introduced to the dirty blues metal of Angel City, Rose Tattoo and Heaven (preceded by Buster Brown and Buffalo), all near clone-like at times, with only Angel City able to establish any sort of critical legitimacy on any level.

In a less direct sense, the band's simpleton, simpletoon joie de vivre coursed through the scrappers amongst the NWOBHM, followed by the US poverty party rockers of the low to mid-80's' mid-labels, and on into the sleaze bands of metal's hair heyday. There were the novelty rockers such as Rhino Bucket and Johnny Crash, but then there were those who selectively copped the band's blues, their swing or their riffs, so elements of AC/DC show up within Britny Fox, Great White, Poison, Cinderella, Slaughter, Quiet Riot, Tattoo Rodeo, Keel, Dangerous Toys, Sea Hags, Jackyl, Salty Dog, Guns N' Roses . . . you name it, they all flicked the switch.

AC/DC speaks:

Angus Young on AC/DC and the blues . . .

"Well we were always a band that started as a rock 'n' roll band but you know, blues runs right through good rock 'n' roll. Even in the early days on our first album we had songs like *The Jack* and that was all blues-based, and on DIRTY DEEDS we had *Ride On* and it was also blues and then on BALLBREAKER we did *The Boogie Man*. I think it's part of us. I mean myself as a guitarist when I pick up a guitar, the first thing I'm playing is a lick. But we've always been a harder-edged rock 'n' roll band. We do come on with the tough, rough sound. I think that's part of our style and our nature."

But in the grand scheme, this band was too daringly dull to copy forthright, too deconstructed, unplugged and barely composed. Only these particular shrimps were going to be able to pull it off and live to drink about it. Therefore, AC/DC sits as one of these top shelf, off to the side phenomena, commanding an entire corner of metal while inspiring others to blaze their own trail, bow to no trends, and in fact, not budge an inch to the vagaries of time.

And on another level, Angus and Co. inspired through sheer pleasure dealt — AC/DC is the brew you reach for when you don't want to think, when work is done, when you don't want to struggle to enjoy some music; it's an instructive tonic for all rockers who need reminding of that first rocker's buzz that they felt when jamming for buddies in their basements.

AC/DC speaks:

Angus Young on family . . .

"When Malcolm asked me to join when I was young, it was always the case that the music is what we were there for. We have the brothers thing, but between the two of us it's always the music that you look at and that's your end game. As kids we would scrap a lot I suppose, but as we joined together in playing and making music it was more professional. When we were working out our ideas for STIFF UPPER LIP, the thing that we wanted the most was to make a good rock 'n' roll record, something that was toe-tapping all the way through. We weren't thinking of anything like top 40 hits or anything; we were just aiming to make a good rock 'n' roll record. That's why we also brought in our other brother George because he made a lot of the early AC/DC, and it just seems so natural — the three of us. And if Malcolm's sitting between the two of us he makes a good referee too (laughs.) We all get on together. We are a family that grew up very bonded, very tight and we're all in agreement — we all love what's good in rock 'n' roll, especially George. He's a big fan of rock 'n' roll, especially the past; he knows a lot of the history of it. When he's got his two brothers there really belting it out, he loves it."

AC/DC speaks:
Angus Young on the early days . . .
"AC/DC was a live band. This is what we do well. We enjoy playing rock 'n' roll and we've made our reputation from that. In the early days in Australia, there was no way in the world that we were going to get any media coverage. The only media coverage we would get is if there was a riot here or brawl there. It wasn't like we were getting any airplay like some of the music coming from America or Europe. We were one of the first bands to break the mold and start selling records by word of mouth. People were coming to see us live and we started to outsell the pop music, which then was a shock. In the end they had to come to you and say, 'would you play our TV show?' We only laughed at things like that. In those days people wanted pop music sanitized and they were in for a shock the first time we were on television."

So take their lead and don't intellect the influence, just feel it. Soak it up through osmosis like raw pine takes in a dark walnut stain. Among practitioner and punter alike, AC/DC is an understood, a name which never fails to crack a smile, copied only sporadically and usually with untoward kitschy results, a band always there in spirit when the true and pure action of rocking out is about to take hold.

AC/DC speaks:
Angus Young on meeting Bon Scott . . .
"When Bon first came along and saw me and Malcolm, he sat behind the drums and started bashing away. We said 'we know a good rock 'n' roll drummer, what we want is a great rock 'n' roll singer.' Hence the song. This is what we wanted. For us it was great. He was a striking person. He did have the stuff legends are based on. I was in awe too, being the youngest. I laughed my head off and he laughed when he saw me! He said to Malcolm, 'do you want me to sing like someone?' Malcolm said, 'No, we're asking for you, not anybody else. We don't want a clone, we want you and what you are.' He loved that. He loved the fact that he could get on and be himself. He said to himself, 'I never got to be what I wanted to be.' Being in a pop band, the front guy would always have the image for the little girls. Bon used to call himself the background singer, the rhythm singer. He had the talent and nice guy looks. Some people wanted him to cover up his tattoos and all sorts of stupid things."

Discography
- HIGH VOLTAGE (Albert, 1975)
- T.N.T. (Albert, 1976)
- DIRTY DEEDS DONE DIRT CHEAP (Albert, 1976)
- LET THERE BE ROCK (Albert, 1977)
- POWERAGE (Albert, 1978)
- IF YOU WANT BLOOD (Albert, 1978)
- HIGHWAY TO HELL (Albert, 1979)
- BACK IN BLACK (Albert, 1980)
- FOR THOSE ABOUT TO ROCK (Albert, 1981)
- FLICK OF THE SWITCH (Albert, 1983)
- '74 JAILBREAK (Atlantic, 1984)
- FLY ON THE WALL (Albert, 1985)
- WHO MADE WHO (Albert, 1986)
- BLOW UP YOUR VIDEO (Albert, 1988)

o THE RAZOR'S EDGE (Albert, 1990)
o LIVE (Albert, 1992)
o BALLBREAKER (Atlantic, 1995)
o BONFIRE (Atlantic, 1997)
o STIFF UPPER LIP (Atlantic, 2000)

Motörhead

As remarked in the previous essay, AC/DC, the Ramones, Motörhead . . . there are only a handful of acts that have churned a sound so singular for so long that they've become a genre unto themselves. Motörhead is such an experience, having established this buzzing and brutal power trio blast way back in 1977 with their seminal self-titled debut. What was interesting about Lemmy's polluted proposal was that it almost pre-empted, sabotaged and hijacked punk rock. Arriving at this point after being ousted from notorious bong-headed space thrashers Hawkwind (yes, thrashers), Lemmy was encouraged by the dirt factor of this new music, coming up with an alloy that was equal parts garage rock, post-Pink Fairies (Larry Wallis was an early member) biker rock and an almost unintentional metal that was smashed together and slapped down in the alcoholic spirit of The Damned.

> Motörhead speaks:
> *Lemmy on his good qualities . . .*
> "Yes well, when I get drunk, I don't fight people. So that's one good thing. I can't stand those drunks, three drinks, and they're saying 'yes, I'll fight anybody in the place.' That's really boring. And another good point is that I persevere, and that I believe in the innate goodness of people. My bad point is that I'm terribly cynical, and I believe that we're all going to hell in a handcart (laughs.) I love rock 'n' roll, I really do, almost ever since I could remember I've been doing it. I mean, it's been good to me, and I been pretty good to it to. I don't think I have any reason to stop doing it. And I know this is the best version of the band we've ever had, because I'm playing in it and I know. This is certainly the best band I've ever had, but people are just stuck with it, you know? People won't come out of 1981. The old stuff is pretty ropey when you listen to it up against the new stuff, without the benefit of nostalgia painting it gold, you know?"

Then the NWOBHM broke, and Motörhead found themselves three records deep into their identity, suddenly seen as the instigators of the whole mess, logo, badge, pin, patch and death mask grandpappies of the new spirit of metal, the first of a generation who proposed to take the compositional complexity of metal and the anarchy of punk and make a new chaotic caterwaul all our own, from the street, for the street.

OVERKILL and BOMBER were the blueprints, spawning direct comparatives like Tank, Warfare, Jaguar, Avenger, early Tygers and Venom, while Maiden embraced a larger

proportion of 70's metal, fired in the crucible of Lemmy's unshaven new speed rock. Meanwhile overseas, fanzine and record store guy Brian Slagel and his buddy Lars Ulrich were sprinkling holy water from Lemmy's brow all over California (there's an image), with Brian finding and Lars creating bands who would become America's new trashy speedsters, fueled by the innovative double bass barrages of signature Motörhead blastbeat precursors *Overkill* and *Ace Of Spades*.

Motörhead speaks:

Lemmy on whether fans should have bands of their own generation exclusively . . .
"That's obviously part of it. That's the way it should be. But if the band is good, I think they should be heard. That's all. And I think we're good. I'm not complaining exactly, because I know people have their own age group. Of course they do, I have mine. But I don't really think we are in an age group as such. I don't think our music is older. It sounds young to me."

copyright 1982 Phil Anderson / KAOS2000 Magazine

So even as Motörhead were, through timing alone, the godfathers of the NWOBHM, and through intention, the first speed metallers, they could also be deemed the first true thrash band, purposefully recording loose and dirty, becoming the first intentional grime rockers, something which Lemmy's heroes the Ramones weren't even prepared to try. In fact, Venom was really the first band to raise a glass to Lemmy and say "bloody 'ell, we can be worse!", which did indeed happen, establishing a slippery slope which led finally to the extreme and anti-musically caustic experimental brutalities of early black metal circa 1995 to 97.

> Motörhead speaks:
> *Lemmy on the possible resurgence of metal . . .*
> "Well, it will be back. All we have to do is keep the faith. Rock and roll always returns, because they can't find anything to replace it. And rap is crap, you know? Rap is the worst f***ing thing in the world. People talking over a drum beat. Social distortion. That's what they think it is, social comment, but it's not, it's just people bitching. Metal seems to be coming back in the States here. It's never been away in Europe. We didn't have all this 'metal is dead' stuff in Europe."

It's also inspiring that Lemmy made only subtle shifts in his trademark sound as a staggering two decades passed. Motörhead continuously recorded with a number of line-up changes, and every record crackled with faulty electrical wiring, buzzing bass, Lemmy's distinct whiskey roar, firecracker drums and riffs dragged through the muck, mire and excrement like some sort of time-honoured biker colours ritual. Many believe that the ultimate distilled firewater shot from the band came with their shocking live album NO SLEEP 'TIL HAMMERSMITH, a blazing acid shower of volume that's now considered one of the best live albums in metal, along side the usual suspects, Judas Priest's UNLEASHED IN THE EAST, UFO's STRANGERS IN THE NIGHT, Thin Lizzy's LIVE AND DANGEROUS, Ozzy's

SPEAK OF THE DEVIL and Sabbath's LIVE EVIL (OK, I threw in those last two.) But the record captured the hard roadscrape of the Motörhead experience. Like AC/DC, Motörhead became a rock of confidence, an unswerving testimony to belief in one's art,

a fatherly example of gritty persistence tapped when the grinding inhumanity of the road wells up and threatens to crash the van.

The ultimate expression of Motörhead's hallowed place in metal history took place on Lemmy's 50th birthday, when Metallica donned wigs and jumped on stage as The Lemmys, tracking sacred mud through a half hour set of Motörhead classics. And to this day, the band continues to celebrate the underground essence of metal, soldiering on with regular touring and records that are, in my opinion, the best of the catalogue, with Lemmy finding in Mikkey Dee and Phil Campbell more than worthy compatriots on the road to live loud integrity.

Discography
- MOTÖRHEAD (Chiswick, 1977)
- OVERKILL (Bronze, 1979)
- BOMBER (Bronze, 1979)
- ON PAROLE (United Artists, 1979)
- ACE OF SPADES (Bronze, 1980)
- NO SLEEP 'TIL HAMMERSMITH (Bronze, 1981)
- IRON FIST (Bronze, 1982)
- ANOTHER PERFECT DAY (Bronze, 1983)
- NO REMORSE (Bronze, 1984)
- ORGASMATRON (GWR, 1986)

○ ROCK 'N' ROLL (GWR, 1987)
○ NO SLEEP AT ALL (GWR, 1988)
○ 1916 (Sony, 1991)
○ MARCH OR DIE (Sony, 1992)
○ BASTARDS (Zyx, 1993)
○ SACRIFICE (SPV, 1995)
○ OVERNIGHT SENSATION (SPV, 1996)
○ SNAKE BITE LOVE (SPV, 1998)
○ EVERYTHING LOUDER THAN EVERYONE ELSE — 1998 HAMBURG GERMANY (SPV, 1999)
○ PROTECT THE INNOCENT (Castle, 1999)
○ WE ARE MOTÖRHEAD (SPV, 2000)

\ 12 /

Yngwie Malmsteen

Yngwie (don't forget the J.) Malmsteen's contributions to metal are only now starting to bear fruit. Having left Sweden for ill-fated stints within Ron Keel's Steeler and Graham Bonnet's Alcatrazz (passing on a chance to join UFO), Yngwie instantly attracted accolades for his lightning quick baroque and classical runs, becoming the most buzzed-over hotshot axeman in California.

Moving on to an inevitable solo career, Yngwie's style blossomed, becoming a unique combination of lots of his signature solos and a gothic castle-gray metal that was like Ritchie Blackmore left to his own devices, or more accurately, the caricature of Ritchie's signature personality trait, sent megalomaniacal. This is Yngwie's first element of influence, the man becoming metal's next exciting guitar hero, the one with the most readily identifiable sound since Eddie Van Halen, with perhaps Randy Rhoads filling the shoes betwixt the two, both in impact and in style.

Yngwie Malmsteen speaks:
Yngwie on today's rock environment . . .
"I'd have to say that most of the time I've been really frustrated with how fashion rules everything. They don't allow room for innovative people. It has to follow a stern formula. And it's frustrating because I know that what I do is not fitting into anything really. But that's not why I'm doing it. I'm doing it because this is what's unique to me. This is what I do. And I think that it's inevitable that this sound will be coming around again."

Yngwie brought the serious, snobby, aristocratic and classical back to metal with a vengeance, taking that one medieval wedge from Ritchie (passing on Blackmore's very occassional *Lazy* blues), a smaller medieval piece from Michael Schenker, and an even tinier sliver of medieval from one Uli Jon Roth, and blowing the ball of renaissance

Yngwie Malmsteen

bombast sky-high, blathering on about Paganini and Bach, even covering classical music, just like Blackmore, eventually making a classical album, just like Purple.

The influence of a guitar hero is soon reflected in the influence of many a great band. First, Yngwie caused furtive challenged practice within the ranks of guitarists, causing academic discussion and practice within the form that raised it to higher levels. Second, many of these guitarists copied him, causing an imitative influence that finds a couple dozen clones among metal's power metal pack, folks who have become better, stronger, faster Yngwies, which I guess, is of some limited artistic value, if only as an expression of human ingenuity.

That brings us to Yngwie's larger spread of influence. The bands housing the Malmsteen clones are pretty much all practitioners of a type of speed metal, now somewhat inaccurately named power metal. People cite Maiden and Helloween as the evident wellspring of the genre, but its loftier, diddling, gothic persona comes from the Yngwie catalogue and its rougher road maps, those of Rainbow and Dio.

Simply because this one genre, power metal (not to mention its side-by-each brothers speed metal and progressive metal), thrives and multiplies at this moment, Yngwie's legacy is assured. Indeed, beyond the man's often-imitated axe mechanics, and the dripping ornate classical melodies driving his compositions, one could ascribe a tertiary influence to the man, one based on the players that he's harboured and nurtured. Primarily there are the vocalists which now read like a roll call of the 80's Euro-metal elite: Jeff Scott Soto, Marc Boals, Joe Lynn Turner, Goran Edman, Mike Vescara, Mats Leven, all before or because of Yngwie, entering the pantheon of power metal legend.

Yngwie Malmsteen speaks:

Yngwie Malmsteen on joining Alcatrazz . . .

Well, that's a funny story actually. I was gigging with Steeler around town, L.A., San Francisco, we did the club circuit. And I started creating a big buzz around L.A. Everyone was talking about me. 'Oh that kid's playing like no one else.' A lot of people were blown away. So I had a lot of people come and check me out, like Ronnie Dio came around a lot. We became good friends and still are, although I don't see him that often. And Phil Mogg from UFO was there, and a lot of other people I don't really know about. And Phil said 'I'm trying to reform UFO, are you interested?' and I'm like 'yeah, f*** yeah!' I love UFO, I thought they were great. And he says come over to my house tomorrow. And I said okay. And I lived with a friend of mine, because Steeler lived in a really bad place so I slept in this guy's house. I got a phone call in the morning, and it was from Graham Bonnet's manager, and he said come down and check this out. So I had to choose between Phil Mogg and Graham Bonnet the same day. So I went to play with Alcatrazz, although they weren't Alcatrazz then, they weren't anything. They didn't have a drummer, didn't have any songs or a band name, nothing done. Anyway, they liked me a lot and I liked them. But I went to see Phil Mogg, and he was at the time, really drugged out or something, I don't know the story. But he definitely seemed like someone I couldn't work with. So I said to Graham, 'OK, I'm in.' I already had a bunch of songs, and then I started writing more. So I basically wrote the whole album. I was not supposed to be anything more than the sideman. Graham Bonnet was supposed to be the star, but then I sort of took the show over (laughs.) Something happened there, I don't know, and then the friction started and they weren't all that happy at how I stole the show. I didn't mean to. I just did what I did. So that's when I decided to leave. I just wanted to do my own thing."

In other fretful, always fragile postings were John Leven (from Yngwie's pre-US version of Rising Force), brothers Anders and Jens Johansson (from Yngwie's old band Silver Mountain), Bob Daisley, Barry Dunaway, Mats Olausson, Bo Sundberg, Mike Terrana, Barry Sparks, Tommy Aldridge, Cozy Powell and David Rosenthal — once again a healthy chunk of well-regarded traditional metal production through the 70's and 80's.

copyright 1981 Phil Anderson / KAOS2000 Magazine

Yngwie Malmsteen

Yngwie Malmsteen speaks:

Yngwie on his catalogue . . .

"Well, my favourites would have to be RISING FORCE and TRILOGY. Actually I like MARCHING OUT as well. ODYSSEY for some reason, everybody else loves and I can't stand it. I thought ECLIPSE was a very good album, very song-oriented. FIRE AND ICE had a couple moments, but when SEVENTH SIGN came out I thought that was better. And then MAGNUM OPUS is complete shit. That was like my low. Very uninspired. Then INSPIRATION I think has a little bit of a happy feel to it. I had just finished my studio and I called up all my pals and said, 'hey, I just finished building my studio, come on down and let's record something.' And that's how it happened."

So all in all, Yngwie's influence is both overbearing and appreciatively subtle. The man, through his steadfast adherence to a sound that he built, record after record (save for radical diversions like his classic album and his covers album), became a guitar hero, a maker of careers, and a cornerstone of no less than three metal sub-genres thriving and striving as we speak.

Discography

- o YNGWIE MALMSTEEN'S RISING FORCE (Polydor, 1984)
- o MARCHING OUT (Polydor, 1985)
- o TRILOGY (Polydor, 1986)
- o ODYSSEY (Polydor, 1988)
- o TRIAL BY FIRE: LIVE IN LENINGRAD (Polydor, 1989)
- o ECLIPSE (Polydor, 1990)
- o FIRE AND ICE (Elektra, 1992)
- o THE SEVENTH SIGN (Music For Nations, 1994)
- o MAGNUM OPUS (Music For Nations, 1995)
- o INSPIRATION (Music For Nations, 1996)
- o FACING THE ANIMAL (Mercury, 1997)
- o CONCERTO SUITE FOR ELECTRIC GUITAR AND ORCHESTRA IN E FLAT MINOR OP.1 (Dream Catcher, 1998)
- o LIVE IN BRAZIL (Pony Canyon, 1999)
- o ALCHEMY (Pony Canyon, 1999)
- o BEST OF (Pony Canyon, 2000)

⚡ 13 ⚡
Queensryche

It was Queensryche and Metal Church that led the post-NWOBHM Northwest metal scene, with Culprit, TKO, Wild Dogs and Rail all showing promise but fizzling before they could get off the ground. Metal Church pursued an interesting Bay Area thrash / mainstream hybrid to moderate success, but it's Queensryche that rose above, first with their pioneering post-Maiden, pre-Helloween four-track EP, and then with the fussy, dressy, overblown epic metal churn of THE WARNING.

> Queensryche speaks:
> *Geoff Tate on individuality . . .*
> "I think all through our career we've had a lot of diversity, which I guess is what has kept us going all this time. We can still sell records, we can still play shows, because we have that kind of diversity. But then again it's also like a stone around your neck. Because the marketing people can't put a box around you and say, OK, this is what you are. Because you keep changing. Being called progressive is a label that gets attached to bands. I bet if you ask any of the progressive bands, none of them would put that little box around it. The honest truth is that we don't do this for anybody else. When we do live shows, that's for an audience. But when we make a record, I don't give a f**** what anybody else thinks of it. It's what I think about it. That's my personal expression. Don't ever write a song or record for anybody else other than yourself. It doesn't make any sense."

THE WARNING established the band as the first credible commercial face of progressive metal since Rush. The smell of self-seriousness was palpable, egos a flyin', everybody over-playing each over-written track, while a singer by the name of Geoff Tate combined glass-shattering highs with a dramatic thespian disposition that was soon to cause the band critical drubbing along side feverish fan worship last seen with Rush and Zeppelin, and concurrent to Queensryche, enjoyed by a band of English blokes called Marillion.

> Queensryche speaks:
> *Chris Degarmo on the band's methodology . . .*
> "I think we're a work in progress. I know we don't solicit requests from our fanbase (laughs) necessarily when we go in to design an album, because that really just gets you into a house of mirrors. Everyone has a unique perspective on what they like and what appeals to them and what they expect. What's worked really nicely for the band is just trusting our own chemistry and allowing ourselves to explore new songwriting approaches together and really just trying to reflect the moment. I could describe each of our projects, and there's been six full-length albums now and one EP. And each was kind of a snapshot of where we were at a given time, what we were thinking about or what was happening in the world, which is what gets reflected."

RAGE FOR ORDER solidified the band's standing as true prog metal risk-takers, adding futuristic electronic window-dressing to songs relentlessly lacking in rock and roll grooves, songs that sounded like the band's die-laughing new fashion makeovers. OPERATION: MINDCRIME followed, a hot and bothered Big Brother concept record that's now tossed about as one of the best metal concept records of all time, if not the very best — at minimum, it's the first that comes to mind. To this day, as the band's biggest contribution to metal, OPERATION: MINDCRIME could be considered the inspiration for much of the conceptual progressive metal written and released in droves throughout the late 90's, not to mention its effect on Bruce Dickinson, who saw his leaving Maiden inevitable after deciding how inferior SEVENTH SON was in comparison.

Further Queensryche spreads found the band retaining its hold on metal psyches prone to grandeur. EMPIRE sold surprisingly well, a vindication that progressive metal could be commercial if its excesses were held in check. *Best That I Can*, the title track, *Jet City Woman* and, most instructively, *Silent Lucidity* combined the morose melancholy of Roger Waters' Pink Floyd with the stadium rock of Def Leppard, resulting in an emotional alloy that was perfect for Queensryche's bi-polar mad scientist rock star riffing.

Queensryche speaks:
Geoff Tate on OPERATION: MINDCRIME . . .
"It was a funny time. Up until that time I think we had only sold 300,000 records or something like that, been on several tours around the world. We were sort of getting our feet wet in the industry, and I remember at that time, at the end of RAGE, we had separated from our first management company, which was kind of a traumatic time for us, since they had been there from the beginning. We had hooked up with Q Prime at that point, and I had taken off and gone to Montreal, and lived there for about six to nine months, and that's where I came up for the idea for MINDCRIME. And I came back to Seattle for Michael's wedding in March, I think, of 1987. I think we got together a couple of weeks later after his honeymoon and I launched this idea to the band, and none of them were really interested in doing it at the time. I remember I had to fight very, very hard to get them to accept the idea. It probably took about two months solid of hitting them over the head with it until they finally gave in and said 'all right, all right, we see what you're trying to do here, let's get working on it.' So we started getting on the same page, started rolling along and got a lot done on it. Then we hooked up with Peter Collins and James Barton; Paul Northfield worked on it pretty heavily with us, and all the recording sessions went great. It was just as very creative time, where everybody was throwing in ideas and pushing it along. And then I remember it came out for sale to the public and it just didn't sell anything. It was like a complete failure. And we were touring and touring and touring, and just not selling any records at all. I remember the guys saying to me once, 'Oh, really great idea Geoff' (laughs.) Then all of a sudden, *Eyes Of A Stranger* came out and boom, it started the ball rolling. That was a year after the release of the record."

PROMISED LAND, HEAR IN THE NOW FRONTIER and the sparse and ill-received Q2K mirrored evolutions taking place elsewhere in prog metal (Dream Theater's AWAKE and Marillion's BRAVE) and in mainstream hair metal (Def Leppard's SLANG and Dokken's SHADOWLIFE.) Bands were looking to make dark, artistic records outside of their albatrossed formats (don't call it grunge) and they were all crucified for it, Queensryche making somewhat of a critical return with HEAR IN THE NOW FRONTIER and its apocalyptic but hopeful hit single *Sign Of The Times*. This move towards succinct songwriting wasn't new. Yes, Rush and Kansas all went this route in the 80's, with perhaps the most extreme example being Genesis who went from the progger's prog of *Firth Of Fifth* and *Eleventh Earl Of Mar* to the minimalist electro claptrap of *Abacab*, *Mama* and *I Can't Dance*.

So Queensryche were, and are, upholding their progressive rock prominence by re-engineering their direction, record to record, and providing instructive creative inspiration to new generations of prog metallists who would do well to offer such variety and think outside of any parameters whatsoever. As it stands, Queensryche are second only to Rush (and ahead of Fate's Warning and Dream Theater) within the pantheon of prog metal, often criticized but even more often the object of intense debate and curiosity.

Discography
- ° QUEENSRYCHE (206, 1983)
- ° THE WARNING (EMI, 1984)
- ° RAGE FOR ORDER (EMI, 1986)
- ° OPERATION: MINDCRIME (EMI, 1988)
- ° EMPIRE (EMI, 1990)
- ° OPERATION: LIVECRIME (EMI, 1991)
- ° PROMISED LAND (EMI, 1994)
- ° HEAR IN THE NOW FRONTIER (EMI, 1997)
- ° Q2K (EMI, 1999)

14

Helloween

If Maiden was this lime-green commercial second generation expression of power metal, then Helloween would be the trim and disciplined third incarnation, importantly, the first that sounds dead identical to the common definition of the genre today.

Early Helloween deftly straddled thrash and traditional Maiden-style epic metal, in fact marrying two ideas that were still in their infancy and doing it well. With all the bluster and bravado of youth, the band seethed out of the gates like an agitated but basically happy bull, already not above a bit of self-deprecating humour with their pumpkin-headed mascot, already tuned to the ironies of playing self-important castle metal at these unsafe speeds.

The band's sound, save for a few critically carved experimental detours, hasn't changed much over the years. Helloween, through all the right motivations and commercial rewards thereof, become Germany's champions of Maiden metal mania, one step beyond, one step ahead, one step higher, always arriving quicker, and all without breaking a sweat.

And by the mid-90's, through their uncompromising hard work on their records, they all of a sudden found themselves the standard bearer for the new generation of retro-speedsters, or in the modern lexicon, those somewhat serious practitioners of power metal. The 70's had a bunch of bands, the 80's had Maiden, but it's Helloween that's the direct root of the current sound, a quick and progressive metal flurry built of rapid classical runs, slicing riffery and even sharper twin leads, high, operatic vocals, furious double bass, and these tales of moral triumph that instruct toward the good fight while attempting to rush you to the finish line.

Helloween speaks:
Andi Deris on the last few albums . . .
"Well, MASTER OF THE RINGS was definitely done with a few stomach aches. I really didn't have my confidence yet, I wasn't secure, but Michael helped me a lot. So I would say it was quite an experience for everybody. The band itself couldn't be a band in terms of having not been together for a number of years, playing together, being tight. So it was something that had to be put together with the help of various studio techniques. TIME OF THE OATH proved that we were actually a band. We already had a world tour under our belts, and suddenly the studio work went much easier, because we all knew each other. It was easier going in the studio, with less tracks to tie together. We could play more things as a band because we were tighter. When you are arranging a song, it's much easier to just play as a band, without having to look at each other and communicate verbally. It saves a lot of time. And then for BETTER THAN RAW I think we finally knew and understood each other as much as a band should, to be called a band. So after four years, we are now finally a band (laughs.) We've done several tours and now; there's no question we've arrived."

So Helloween first begat Gamma Ray (started by crucial 'Weenie Kai Hansen, and now power metal's second biggest band), then Brazil's Angra, Pink Cream 69 (current vocalist Andi Deris' old band), Blind Guardian, Hammerfall, Primal Fear (featuring ex-Tyran Pace, ex-Gamma Ray vocalist Ralf Scheepers), Iron Savior, everything coming out of Italy, and the transformation of Shrapnel Records from a guitar clinic zone into a home for musical chairs power guys. The scene is thriving and the records are always faultless, built of a work ethic that defies the listener to dismiss what he's hearing on any grounds other than personal taste.

Helloween

Helloween speaks:

Andi Deris on the title BETTER THAN RAW . . .

"That's a fun title, because we always have trouble finding titles for our records. We were sitting in our favorite club in Hamburg called The Backstage. We were having a chat and realized that nobody likes pumpkin. There's this sweet pumpkin that mainly Japanese fans give us after the show, and we all decided that raw pumpkin is the worst of all. Everybody hates raw pumpkin. And somebody said 'well, if we have to have pumpkin, anything's better than raw.' And that was it. And we're all Smurf fans, and instead of the evil sorcerer, we decided to use a sexy witch trying to cook the pumpkins instead of Smurfs, so that's the whole story."

Helloween speaks:

Michael Weikath on Rainbow's influence on the band . . .

"Rainbow it is the biggest influence on our particular approach to speed. I think they were way ahead with speed and the double bass approach. We're not influenced by those speed and thrash bands of the 80's. In fact, I think this is just a continuation of Rainbow, Deep Purple, UFO and even Led Zeppelin. Most of the other speed metal bands from the 80's lacked melody. They didn't create structures or even songs. Speed metal was always very primitive to me."

Continuing along this path of hard work causing influence, Helloween have added a number of layers to their reach. They've instructed the youngsters on metal's past through their many covers of obscure classics, and indeed a whole album thereof, called METAL JUKEBOX. They've given us elaborate concept albums and they've always printed their lyrics. They've spawned numerous offshoot bands and solo albums, both of a metal and non-metal nature, and they've continued to spread the metal word through relentless European touring, truly emerging from the shadow of Maiden as one of the traditional metal draws with their own rich back catalogue from which many a happy Hamburg Friday night's mosh was, and continues to be, born.

Helloween speaks:

Andi Deris on BETTER THAN RAW . . .

"It's definitely a record filled with self-confidence, definitely something we've allowed ourselves to go for, experiment sound-wise as well as the arrangement-wise. We went for new tunes, new rhythms, new things on the guitar, mainly because of the help of Uli, our drummer. He plays guitar pretty well, and he knows exactly how to combine riffs with the rhythms from his drums. And that's very interesting, hearing what's there between the songs. I really like it. The first time I was listening to *Push* or *Regulation* I was going like, 'Wow! What the hell is going on here!?' And basically everybody, I remember all of us sitting on the couch at the back of the studio, with these big smiles across everyone's faces. It's that smile you have when the power overwhelms you."

Discography
- o HELLOWEEN (Noise, 1985)
- o WALLS OF JERICHO (Noise, 1985)
- o KEEPER OF THE SEVEN KEYS — PART I (Noise, 1987)
- o KEEPER OF THE SEVEN KEYS — PART II (Noise, 1988)
- o I WANT OUT — LIVE (EMI, 1989)

Helloween speaks:
Andi Deris on the band's legacy . . .
"I would say our legacy is that we combine the artillery of speed metal with nice melodies. And we were the first band to come up with this, and we're still doing the job. We stopped doing the job for two albums (laughs), and it was this huge breakdown for the band. You can imagine. Suddenly the record sales all over the world fell to under 200,000. And actually now, the band, with its member changes, is quite sure where they have to go. And the band is thankful to have their own special originality, and we stick with it. We will definitely not go down that road again (laughs.)"

○ THE BEST THE REST THE RARE (Noise, 1991)
○ PINK BUBBLES GO APE (EMI, 1991)
○ CHAMELEON (EMI, 1993) ˋ
○ MASTER OF THE RINGS (Raw Power, 1994)
○ THE TIME OF THE OATH (Raw Power, 1996)
○ HIGH LIVE (Raw Power, 1996)
○ PUMPKIN BOX (Victor, 1998)
○ BETTER THAN RAW (Raw Power, 1998)
○ METAL JUKEBOX (Sanctuary, 1999)

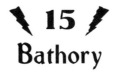

15
Bathory

You really can't credit Quorthon (son of Black Mark prez Borje Forsberg) and his one-man show Bathory with inventing black metal, given that Venom already had been in blasphemous operation for three years before Bathory's wall o' thrash debut. But the band can be credited with making the fledgling genre more than a one-band show. Bathory, along with Hellhammer, Celtic Frost, Slayer, perhaps Canada's Exciter and later California's Possessed, turned it into a scene with roots rather than a flash in the pan.

And after Venom, Bathory was the most prolific, uncompromising, mysterious and hellbent on a path straight down. The building blocks of damnation were the tried and tested, blistering speeds, awful almost industrial production values, a constant wall of simple riffs, and quite pertinently, a vocal style that is the predecessor of the sniveller style practiced by the early Norsemen. Quorthon was not above other innovations that are now the hallmark of the genre, such as long soundtrack-like horror effects and eerie smears of keyboards.

But it turns out that Quorthon was an intelligent, if not reclusive guy (he's never put together a touring unit), growing tired of the genre he helped create, and moving on to another field of influence, that of Viking metal, having as unlikely co-conspirators Manowar, a decidedly non-Viking bunch of New Yorkers who had themselves decided to adopt a Viking image, oscillating back to tales of Valhalla throughout their career. But Bathory and Vikings had true synergy. The roots in anti-Christian black metal had set the stage, as well as the fact that Quorthon was Swedish, and had grown up reading Viking legends in school.

Bathory speaks:
Quorthon on the band's influences . . .
"Well, the thing with Bathory was that those albums came in pairs. We changed every second album. And during the whole 80's I was listening to nothing else but classical music, trying to isolate myself, and not be influenced consciously or unconsciously by what else was going on. But the main influence when we started Bathory was the lyrics of Black Sabbath and the music of Motörhead, great bands, great influences. But I also had influence that none of the guys I was playing with knew about, bands like Mountain, and well, the great guitar god of all, Mr. Winter. I even listened to stuff like Johnny Cash, Chuck Berry and The Beatles, a completely different school. I mean the other guys even had to fill me in on like Iron Maiden and Whitesnake and shit bands like that."

So we got a trinity of records, BLOOD, FIRE, DEATH (1988), HAMMERHEART (1990) and TWILIGHT OF THE GODS (1991) (more-so the second and third) glorifying the cold black northern seas, the swirling nether worlds of Odin, Thor, blood brothers, fathers and sons, cold clashing steel, mountains, thunder and plunder. Attendant was a sound that marched to a trashy, crashy, often mid-paced vibe that once more was new to the Bathory sound and again would be a big part of black metal's anti-musical mystique. There were also female chants, acoustic guitar, wind, lapping waves and other elemental samplings, all used copiously in the Viking (or more dangerously, nationalist) side of the black metal duality.

Bathory

After this phase, Quorthon moved on again, entering a pure thrash era that saw his reputation diminish somewhat, with most fans becoming upset at the varied, seemingly tossed-off lyrical themes, the new slightly cleaner production and the more human element of Quorthon's vocals. Even less appreciated were his solo albums, one quite metal, one quite alternative. 1996 brought BLOOD ON ICE, the man's most complicated concept album yet, and one that took the band back to their Viking period with a theatrical vengeance.

Bathory speaks:

Quorthon on his phases and realms beyond . . .

"The Viking stuff was an emergency solution. We didn't want to write social stuff in the early 80's. So after the Satanic shit, the Viking shit was the most natural thing. We still wanted to be anti-Christian, or anti-social, or anti-establishment, whatever you want to call it. But really, Bathory should not be the ones people look to with respect to the Scandinavian spirit, because we have bands in Norway who say it all. They have all of it, being Satanic and into Odinism and national socialism. I mean, if you are a Satanist, you cannot be a national socialist and the other way around. And if you're the son of Odin or whatever, you cannot be a national socialist. So I think it's a truly weird situation we have here. As far as myself is concerned, when I came up with the conclusion that Satanism is really a product of Christianity, that is when I paused for awhile, and said to myself, 'what the hell am I doing here? I'm able to make a record once, maybe twice a year and all I'm doing is screaming Satan, Satan, Satan!' Sure we were doing it as a rebellion against the Christian church and the establishment. But it doesn't work once you come to the conclusion that it's all fake. I mean, certainly everyone wants to have this fantasy about what happens when we die. It's an abstract thing. We can't touch God. We can say whatever we want about religion and the afterlife, but my personal belief is that we're more or less like plants and trees. We die and we go back to earth. And then people go, 'well what about the soul?', and I talk about electro-magnetism, and things like pacemakers being more or less the physical, technical evidence of our bodies being run on electricity. Ultimately we just go back to earth. There's no such thing as a heaven or afterlife. That's why I had to go back to the time and place before Christianity was around, which was the Viking age. But the only guys doing that were Manowar, so I guess we were shut out somewhat from the black metal, death metal scene when we started to make that Viking epic shit. So after the solo record and celebrating ten years with the JUBILEUM records, the only natural thing to touch upon was everyday life, social shit. And I think that is something I want to develop a little bit more. But I'm very very confused at the moment. One third of our fans wants us to be Satanic, one third wants us to be Viking, so we've painted ourselves into a corner yet again."

So as we sit today, knee-deep in stacks of briskly-selling black metal, Bathory's legacy is assured, not to mention overtly acknowledged through my many interviews with black metal bands. Never really out of vogue, the two phases of the early Bathory material (pure black metal and his fur and fjord stuff) have served as the sound and subject matter of a good 80% of what encompasses the present genre, 40% going with the anti-Christian thing, 40% in various poetic ways addressing northern heritage, and another 20% blathering on about philosophy, fantasy, sci-fi, real life, or the blood-splattered rainbow of topics dealt with by death metallers.

Discography

o BATHORY (Black Mark, 1984)
o THE RETURN (Black Mark, 1985)
o UNDER THE SIGN OF THE BLACK MARK (Black Mark, 1986)

o BLOOD, FIRE, DEATH (Black Mark, 1988)
o HAMMERHEART (Black Mark, 1990)
o TWILIGHT OF THE GODS (Black Mark, 1991)
o JUBILEUM VOLUME I (Black Mark, 1992)
o JUBILEUM VOLUME II (Black Mark, 1993)
o REQUIEM (Black Mark, 1994)
o OCTAGON (Black Mark, 1995)
o BLOOD ON ICE (Black Mark, 1996)
o JUBILEUM VOLUME III (Black Mark, 1998)

⚡ 16 ⚡
Guns N' Roses

I'm sticking these guys in here pretty much against my will, because it's expected, highly expected. But (with a sigh) I must acknowledge that this fact alone bears significance, that GN'R must have had an enormous influence on something to do with metal, maybe not the genre's evolution per se, but maybe on the world's perception and enjoyment of it.

Why I perchance doubt the direct influence on metal is a dismissive amalgam of the following. GN'R were actually making their impetuous rock pig waves while metal was actually dying. To be sure, when APPETITE FOR DESTRUCTION came out in mid-87, metal still had three good years left. But the album didn't break big for on nigh a year. And then the band's next recordings (three records of strong material spread over two albums, mind you), didn't arrive until grunge was confidently howling out loud at anybody who would even think for a second about dressing like a gypsy. USE YOUR ILLUSION I and II were followed by a covers album and then a gradual disintegration of the band into a morass of safe, competent but forgettable solo albums. And the long and short of it was that, through it all, GN'R didn't inspire any new metal ideas. There was no new Axl Academy of Feline Caterwauls. There wasn't a sudden rash of top-hatted Slash clones.

Guns 'N Roses speaks:
Gilby Clarke on the band's guitar chemistry . . .
"When Izzy first came to L.A., I was one of the first guys who met him, because there was at first a very small clique of people who grew up on bands like Kiss and Led Zeppelin. But later we got into bands like David Bowie, New York Dolls, and more of the punk stuff like The Clash, Sex Pistols, so there was a small crowd of people who were into rock but then got into the punk rock stuff. And that's how me and Izzy clicked. So him and I were much more compatible with our music, Slash was more about metal. For myself, I would say in the earliest days my influences are people like Ace Frehley, Mick Ronson from David Bowie's band and then later I would say Keith Richards and Ron Wood. Those are my biggest influences in terms of style. And I love the Beatles! The Beatles — that's where you take lessons in songwriting (laughs.)"

Nobody copied the look, nobody copied the songwriting, nor the production values, nor the guitar technique. Sum total: Guns N' Roses emphatically had no innovations, nor did they spawn any innovators, a very different, diminished beast from our hallowed list of bands who caused no scenes in their wake, but were indeed innovators themselves.

But grudgingly, one can't deny this band's impact. Folks philosophize, with some kernel of truth, that GN'R brought sleaze and danger back into metal (although only the safe, California-commercial form of it) through their trashy look and spoiled-rotten behavior blustering a moderate glance back at The Stooges, the Dolls and their most pertinently toxic spiritual heirs Aerosmith.

Guns 'N Roses speaks:
Gilby Clarke on his time with the band . . .
"I was treated great. Look, I was paid well, I was in a rock band that I liked to be in. I never had any problems on the road. It's kind of hard to have problems or complain about the lifestyle in the band you are in when you are selling out stadiums every show you play, and people are buying the records, and people like the band. There's a lot of controversy that comes with it, but as far as I'm concerned, life could be a lot worse. But the guys were always great, we hung out every day together."

Furthermore there's that abstract fame thing. GN'R gave metal an early 90's hypodermic shot in the arm, propelling a sales bang to end its run, first through APPETITE and then when metal was supposed to be dead, through multiple ILLUSION hit singles like *Knockin' On Heaven's Door* (early launch), *November Rain*, *Civil War* (also early launch), *You Could Be Mine* (ditto), *Live And Let Die*, *Don't Cry* (ditto again!) and *The Garden*, which featured a cameo from Slash's hero Alice Cooper.

Guns N' Roses

And through these hit singles, which included many ballads and covers, GN'R triggered metal back into the mainstream spotlight. The band, like many great hard rock artists, especially Aerosmith (is that guitar?), blurred the line between what's heavy and what isn't. In one sense, they perpetuated the cynical "lead with the ballad" ruse that caused Extreme's PORNOGRAFFITTI's legendary store returns. In another sense, GN'R injected their grimy presence, and in turn that of hard rock, deep into the fabric of the mainstream. Compounding things was a band that loved punk and 70's glam, led by a guitarist who was more a Keith Richards-derived blues man than a poofy metal shredder. In terms of their unfashionable roots, the band flashed an endearing bit of fandom in pushing some of these unmetallic influences through their quite enjoyable covers album THE SPAGHETTI INCIDENT?, something Metallica had done before them, and something Slayer would do in 1996 through the pure punk snarl of UNDISPUTED ATTITUDE.

So add it all up, and GN'R, although not exactly a big influence on anything, at least contributed to the metal economy, causing the dollars to float around and trickle down for a few more years. And even if I'll never admit to the artistic levity others attach to APPETITE FOR DESTRUCTION (critics who merely dabble in metal liken it to the Pistols' NEVER MIND THE BOLLOCKS — give me a break!), I think the ILLUSION albums are a fine example of hard rock tooling being applied to a myriad of classic rock styles, impregnating metal into layers of fans who otherwise might have tuned out. Ergo, there's the financial contribution as well as a grudging acknowledgment of greatness, directly attributed to the band's universality.

Discography
- ○ LIVE ?!*@ LIKE A SUICIDE (Uzi, 1986)
- ○ APPETITE FOR DESTRUCTION (Geffen, 1987)
- ○ GN'R LIES (Geffen, 1988)
- ○ USE YOUR ILLUSION I (Geffen, 1991)
- ○ USE YOUR ILLUSION II (Geffen, 1991)
- ○ THE SPAGHETTI INCIDENT? (Geffen, 1993)
- ○ LIVE ERA 87-93 (Geffen, 1999)

⚡ 17 ⚡
Savatage

It's of questionable legitimacy including Savatage in the Top 50. I mean, despite their utter iconoclastic class and their importance as a vital link in the chain, their influence has been peripheral, for all the reasons one would want to be seen as such. The general point is that few have tried, and fewer succeeded, in accurately capturing their sound.

Part of the problem is that, like Riot, they've actually had two distinct lives. The early work of both was shoot 'em up traditional metal of the highest, defiant caliber, while each band's output in the 90's is a different spoke of the progressive metal wheel — Riot leaning toward the conceptual and speedy, Savatage to the conceptual and uh, conceptual (no other word for it.) Savatage's music feeds their involved story lines like soundtrack support.

Savatage speaks:

Chris Caffery on working with Al Pitrelli . . .

"It's gotten a lot better. Our relationship has been a slow moving one, but it is definitely one that through time is getting very strong. At first he hadn't worked with another guitar player since Alice Cooper, and I never worked with anybody in Savatage except for Criss. And I'm not even sure he had even heard a Savatage song before he went into the studio to do work on DEAD WINTER DEAD. So you had me, that had played 300 shows on stage with Criss Oliva, and Al who had never really played with other guitar players before in his life, and we went out and toured and I was playing all of Criss' stuff live, and there was just a little bit of confusion at first because he wasn't familiar with the band's past and I really wasn't ready to let the band's past go."

Savatage's crushing metal beginnings are spoken about in the language of enigma. SIRENS, POWER OF THE NIGHT, HALL OF THE MOUNTAIN KING . . . these are great records, universally loved by traditional metal fans of two decades and two generations, as well as participating purveyors creating the new power metal right now all over Europe. Yet only now are we seeing the first Savatage tribute album, and never have we found a band to embrace or denounce for being a Savatage clone. There were simply too many unreproduceable variables within the chemistry of the band, especially between vocalist Jon Oliva and his deceased brother Criss. There were elements of Sabbath, Priest and Dio, but there was something else — and not even anything new — just this timeless heavy outlook that absurdly could only come from a band, as Jon professes, who doesn't even listen to much hard rock. Nevertheless, enough were listening to reward the band with a major label deal, and history has borne out the significance of their first four years of work as top-flight songwriting within a classic, uncompromising heavy metal tradition, something which many a power metaller has admitted as having made a deep impression.

Savatage

Then came STREETS A ROCK OPERA, and Savatage entered a new, equally enigmatic and individual phase, one also interestingly not glaringly new, trendy or innovative, save for the sum of the parts. STREETS, followed by a string of concept albums heavy of plot and message, established Savatage as one of the most exciting, and one of the few, progressive metal bands operating in the early 90's. The band's records were not standard digits-flyin' prog though, more like Broadway production storyscapes, rockers linked by luxurious keyboard and piano-laden ballads, soundtrack effects, comprising a prog closer to Queen II than IMAGES AND WORDS. All the while, Savatage was operating during an unfashionable time for concept records, building a following mostly appreciated in Europe and Japan, while also flying the flag, along with Queensryche and Dream Theater, as the only major label bands allowed to get this deep into the narrative muck.

Savatage speaks:

Johnny Lee Middleton on the Savatage chemistry . . .

"Paul O'Neill is the producer and he's basically the sixth member of the band. We're like the Lynyrd Skynyrd of rock: we've got two guitars, keys, vocals, drums, bass. If it gets any more crowded, I'll have to build bigger stages. But that's what it takes to pull off our music live. Now we're in a situation that we can do everything that we want to. Anything. We have the talent on stage and enough people to play. We're just growing, which is the problem with a lot of bands. The weird thing about a Savatage fan is that they won't have just one Savatage CD, they'll have all of them. It's like smoking crack — one CD and you're hooked. It's really weird. I've got people that write me that are 50 years old. I've got people the write me that are 12 years old. We appeal to a broad spectrum and we're going to continue to grow and to do what we're doing. We don't want to get stuck with a record sounding the same."

Now, after five such records, plus the band's highly innovative two Trans-Siberian Orchestra Christmas epics and the Beethoven's Last Night opus of 2000 (also from TSO), Savatage have taken their place as one of the few big prog metal forerunners to inspire — through their hard work, their positive societal and political messages, their ambitious arrangements and their swirling keyboard and guitar work — subsequent generations of artists who might ply their trade in prog, among those who might veer towards more straight-forward metal, straight prog or indeed entirely different disciplines like dance, writing, or the theater.

Discography

- SIRENS (Par, 1983)
- THE DUNGEONS ARE CALLING (Metal Blade, 1985)
- POWER OF THE NIGHT (Atlantic, 1985)
- FIGHT FOR THE ROCK (Atlantic, 1986)
- HALL OF THE MOUNTAIN KING (Atlantic, 1987)
- GUTTER BALLET (Atlantic, 1989)
- STREETS A ROCK OPERA (Atlantic, 1991)
- EDGE OF THORNS (Atlantic, 1993)
- HANDFUL OF RAIN (Atlantic, 1994)
- DEAD WINTER DEAD (Atlantic, 1995)
- GHOST IN THE RUINS (SPV, 1996)
- FROM THE GUTTER TO THE STAGE (Koch, 1997)
- THE WAKE OF MAGELLAN (Atlantic, 1998)

\ 18 /
Celtic Frost

Celtic Frost's influence necessarily goes hand in hand with that of Tom G. Warrior's previous band, the notorious Hellhammer, long heralded as the worst band to ever exist. Listening to it now, after the brutal white noise bliss of extreme black metal, it seems almost comical, trivial, but not overly off-putting. But at the time, the band's six track APOCALYPTIC RAIDS EP had everybody throwing up their arms at the horrible production, the muddy bloshcore and the general past-Venom-ness of it all. Nevertheless, Hellhammer gets a posting along with Venom, Bathory, and its cleaned up incarnation as Celtic Frost as black thrash innovators daring to devil the dirt.

And so Satanic Slaughter changes his name to Tom G. Warrior and fashions a new band that's a mite less ragged, undisciplined and eclectic, leaving the odd Manowar-meets-Death SS tones of *Massacra, Triumph Of Death* and *Horus* for a curious new sound that's already worthy of the term old school.

I mean, fact is, MORBID TALES is like a stodgier version of Venom — slightly better production values, slower riffs, closer to a type of punked out poverty metal than pure thrash. But the cool thing was the mystique, the graphics, the whole image, Celtic Frost quickly lining up with Venom and Bathory to become the trinity of European thrash. And truth be told, the records got more artful quickly, TO MEGA THERION becoming an early classic, trashier of sound, less sociable, with odd symphonic touches that would find Celtic Frost doing the best early job of that hazy quality black metallists call "atmosphere." Through TO MEGA THERION and its equally revered follow-up INTO THE PANDEMONIUM (Warrior's favourite, with VANITY / NEMESIS a close second), the band built themselves this harsh, almost industrial climate in which to thrash away, creating a sound that was just this side of garbagey and garagey, just enough to clue you in that it was all part of the plan, part of the atmosphere.

Celtic Frost speaks:
Tom G. Warrior on the band's metal legacy . . .
"We were one of the few, at that time, in terms of heavy metal bands that weren't afraid to branch out. What we did, I don't think was very unconventional, but it was to the rest of the scene. We were essentially not just metalheads, we were music lovers. We came from violently varied musical fields. Reed was a trained jazz and classical drummer, Martin was a new wave addict, my influences were David Bowie and Roxy Music. What connected us was that we all really loved heavy metal. But because we had so much variety in our background, we didn't see anything wrong with combining these backgrounds with our heavy metal. So what to us was normal, to the rest of the scene, it was perceived as unbelievably unusual. Because at that time a word like jazz or new wave was almost like a curse word in metal circles. And we didn't think like that. So we combined all these things and thereby created a new sound."

So through Celtic Frost, mainland Europe (actually Switzerland) had its own trash thrash heroes, a band that would cause many a German to pursue the filth tones in metal, now stuck in the age of black, many going back to pay official tribute through cover versions and whole tribute albums. Not afraid to try weird covers (Wall Of Voodoo's *Mexican Radio*); long, spooky soundtrack passages; female vocals; or eccentric jazzy bits; the band was almost like this volatile entity too far outside the metal mainstream to even know what was appropriate. All of these elements, including Warrior's pre-death death vocal, have been lifted by various bands plying their trade in the death, thrash and black genres.

Celtic Frost speaks:

Tom G. Warrior on titling the Celtic Frost catalogue . . .

"TO MEGA THERION is a social statement. It means the great beast. And to us, we meant mankind. We were always of the opinion that good and evil wasn't created by religion or anything else. It's created in our heads. Everybody makes their own decision to either go down the good path or a bad one. And the way mankind has behaved on this planet, over I don't know, the last 40,000 years, it's pretty much the great beast to us. VANITY / NEMESIS was a very personal title. That reflected what the band had gone through about three years prior to that album. The absolute high with PANDEMONIUM and the absolute low with COLD LAKE, and the press reaction on both sides, and the business difficulties and everything. We just let this be reflected in the title VANITY / NEMESIS. The concept of the album was to do a straight-forward album without too many experiments, but to exploit Celtic Frost in a different kind of manner. Within in the band, we rate this one as one of the most important Frost albums. PARCHED WITH THIRST AM I AND DYING comes from a Greek Roman prayer that was discovered in a grave by archaeologists. And we just felt that the message of that prayer was just so unbelievably applicable to the very colourful career of Celtic Frost, we just had to use it. Because of course this album was a retrospective of our work and we thought it was absolutely perfect. In one place you have the whole ten years of Frost history. COLD LAKE is an air force base in Canada. It's kind of a complicated story of how we arrived at the title. But in hindsight, I don't think anything could have describe this failure of an album much better than this title. The title became much more applicable once the record was done."

Of course the band is almost more notorious for their doomed glam ploy, a Tony Platt-produced about-face into sleaze rock inexplicably called COLD LAKE. Few bothered to look past the new half-hearted glam wardrobe, the big hairdos and Tom's crooked smile to realize that the Celtic Frost sound actually hadn't changed much. Tom still croaked albeit more with a punk snivel than a textbook thrash growl; Platt managed not to produce the record; the band played like NWOBHM alcoholics; and the riffs were only a shade less sinister than previous.

In any event, after the confused revolt caused by COLD LAKE (must have been the pink logo), the band evolved and elevated into a station unbecoming of their dirt, VANITY / NEMESIS being professionally written, played and produced, Celtic Frost somehow found new ways to drive its fanbase nuts. That was it for the band, after a compilation album enigmatically called PARCHED WITH THIRST AM I AND DYING (beats "BEST OF ROCKERS 'N' BALLADS", don't it?)

So from one inky smudge of a career comes another. Celtic Frost never really mattered much in their heyday and were ridiculed in one way or another pretty much all along the line. But their eccentric, blubbery, slobbery spirit outlived their material being; their bits of black, death, thrash, anti-production and soundtracky innovations somehow leaking into a continuous flow of future genres (their presence most immediately being felt through Destruction, Sodom and Kreator and finally the new Art metal bands, the first to actually get it), resulting in a historical rewrite that finds the band hapless legends inexplicably tributized by black metal bands and fringe avant garders on the cusp of the millennium.

Discography

- APOCALYPTIC RAIDS EP (as Hellhammer) (Noise, 1984)
- MORBID TALES EP (Noise, 1985)
- TO MEGA THERION (Noise, 1985)
- TRAGIC SERENADES EP (Noise, 1986)
- EMPEROR'S RETURN EP (Noise, 1986)
- INTO THE PANDEMONIUM (Noise, 1987)
- COLD LAKE (Noise, 1989)
- VANITY / NEMESIS (Noise, 1990)
- PARCHED WITH THIRST I AM AND DYING (Noise, 1992)

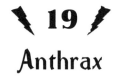

19

Anthrax

An-who? An-wah? Sadly, that's pretty much the case today after the complete critical and fan indifference to the band's last couple of records and tours, resulting in a hasty reformation of S.O.D.

But in their day, Anthrax was a pretty important piece of the metal puzzle, immediately with their first record, wedging their sneakers in the door of Bay Area thrash, giving New York its first credible act to rival the ascendancy of the California rugrats. The band's credibility was due to a spit-polished debut record called FISTFUL OF METAL, a record that sported solid production values, tight musicianship, convincing and deliberate speed metal, uncommonly clean and clear vocals from one Neil Turbin, and a prophetic song called *Metal Thrashing Mad.*

Anthrax speaks:
Charlie Benante on the state of metal . . .
"I just think that the whole thing went underground again. I mean I'm burnt out on all this other stuff that's out and I talked to a lot of other people and their burnt on it too. It just doesn't seem it's like what it was. I kind of feel unfulfilled when I listen to a lot of records out nowadays. There's nothing that I like out there. They don't excite me. It's kind of sad. I'm hoping that people just give our record a listen. There are bands that come around like White Zombie. That's a metal record, that's a metal band. So I'm hoping that people will just take the opportunity to just give this record a listen. You know with us, Metallica, Pantera and Slayer, we were always the extreme metal bands. We are what we were and we were never anything but this. So whatever this record does, maybe it's gonna take a little while for it to start because of the way it is now. So once someone hears it, it'll just be word of mouth."

Into their third and fourth records and Anthrax's competence was rewarded with a major label deal. The band made videos, moving up the press and touring hierarchy, for most of 1985 to 88, and were one of the top three or four most famous extreme metal acts, influencing an entire scene one tier down — the Metal Blade, Shrapnel and Roadrunner record labels finding themselves studded with bush league Anthrax clones.

Anthrax then proceeded to make subtle shifts in their philosophy, all having both positive and negative effects on metal and the band's own critical and fan stature within the genre. First came the band's regular cover versions, Anthrax being one of the early acts to go this novelty route (the debut sported a slick *I'm Eighteen* and later we got Kiss' *Parasite* and *Sabbath Bloody Sabbath*), widening their scope with instructive punk like the Pistols' *God Save The Queen* and Discharge's *Protest And Survive*, and lessons in obscurity with speedy Trust and Joe Jackson send-ups.

Parallel to this, the band adopted a shorts, sneakers and ball cap look, which although derided at the time, but soon came to be viewed as a mark of values — this idea that the music was tantamount and that dressing like ladies of the night was silly and rock star pretentious. In particular, grunge and hardcore would champion this point.

Anthrax also caught flak for another move which has been vindicated by history. As the band got bigger and richer, they started infusing more hardcore, more speed, more punk and increasingly simple spontaneity into their songs, eventually arriving at the landmark *Bring The Noise* rap crossover collaboration with Public Enemy and their own rap parody *I'm The Man*, building on a similar Aerosmith move with Run DMC. Ten years hence, and all of these ideas are flourishing within a myriad of hard music genres.

Anthrax speaks:
John Bush on the overlooked and under-rated STOMP 442 . . .
"I think the last record was a pretty horrible circumstance all the way around. From the beginning, the label wasn't into it and they pretty much expressed that. Granted, I don't blame them completely. They had incurred this large debt. They felt that we weren't part of their new regime and their heart wasn't into it. The problem is that people's livelihoods are on the line. We put eight or nine months of heart and soul behind it. I think the record is incredible. We already think at this point that people still don't even know the record came out. That's obviously disappointing. Whatever. That happens and it was the first time. Hopefully all the bad happened at once. We went through a bad thing with management, the label, and heavy metal period."

Enter ex-Armored Saint vocalist John Bush, and Anthrax was back to a thicker, less hysterical metal sound, perhaps reflecting the trudging levity of grunge. SOUND OF WHITE NOISE and STOMP 442 saw the band unjustly ignored, tossed off their major label, and critically quite acclaimed upon their return back to the underground.

Which is where they sit now, licking their wounds; a band from the past, but one that has done much for the current state of metal through their low hum influence spanning from about 1984 to 94. The inevitable Anthrax tribute albums will ensue, and history will find the band edging up the list of those who made a difference.

Discography
- FISTFUL OF METAL (Megaforce, 1984)
- ARMED AND DANGEROUS (Megaforce, 1985)
- SPREADING THE DISEASE (Megaforce, 1986)
- AMONG THE LIVING (Island, 1987)
- I'M THE MAN (Island, 1987)
- STATE OF EUPHORIA (Island, 1988)
- PERSISTENCE OF TIME (Island, 1990)
- ATTACK OF THE KILLER B'S (Island, 1991)
- SOUND OF WHITE NOISE (Elektra, 1993)
- ANTHRAX LIVE — THE ISLAND YEARS (Island, 1994)
- STOMP 442 (Elektra, 1995)
- VOLUME 8 — THE THREAT IS REAL (Ignition, 1998)
- ATTACK OF THE KILLER A'S (Beyond, 1999)

The 90's

Pantera

And once more, as metal's great iron wheel turns, and possibilities expand past previous frontiers, a band comes to the fore to say "Heavy? You ain't heard nothing yet." That band was Pantera.

Beginning life as an interesting sort of histrionic, detailed and technical Def Leppard experience, the band made three very indie-looking indies, before fashioning one more called POWER METAL with a new singer named Phil Anselmo. This transition album had a prophetic title, much like its bastard stepfather, Venom's BLACK METAL. For once the major label debut, COWBOYS FROM HELL, hit the streets, Pantera was the sterling definition of new power within the genre.

The innovations were many. First off, Phil had brought to metal a new aggro style which was a hardcore upratchet on the classic Hetfield croak. The look was out of hardcore also, the shorts, the tattoos, the no-shirt body slam and the eventual shaved head becoming the metal fashion within the extreme that still has yet to fade.

> Pantera speaks:
> *Vinnie Paul on crafting the band's signature sound . . .*
> "We just realized just before COWBOYS FROM HELL, that we really didn't have an identity, nothing that people could recognize us by. So when we wrote the songs we made sure they were unique and that they had their own sound. We wanted to have a special sound captured on tape. And that's really when we got the drums with a lot of attack, the guitar with a really warm bottom and a nice cut on top. And that turned into the Pantera sound and we pretty much stuck to it. Phil brought more of a hardcore side to the band that we didn't have before. And that was really good, the combination of the two makes Pantera what it is. When he came into the band the rest of us had the common things that we all liked, Judas Priest, Black Sabbath, all the stuff we grew up on. But he just had more of an underground element to him."

Then there was that drum sound, possibly less of an influence in the light of history, more like just this really cool thing, something that shows up sporadically throughout metal, especially when things get industrial. But there was no question, Vinnie Paul was this seemingly impossible marriage of the extreme with the world of exacting production values, brought more into platinum perfection through the man's obvious chops. Grooves were cold but infinitely tall —Vinnie possessed this uncanny ability to drag the rest of the band into the gaping maw of his one-man rhythm section.

Pantera speaks:

Vinnie Paul on lyrical duties . . .

"Lyrically it's as with all Pantera records. The lyrics that Philip writes are very personal. They're very true and very honest so from that aspect I'd say it's along the lines of the other albums. The lyrics have always been Phil's. All four of us write music together. He take a lot of pride in doing that, and the lyrics have pretty much been his gig from day one."

Last but most crucial in terms of influence, is the riffing and overall guitar sound of one Diamond (soon to be brought into the 90's as Dimebag) Darrell. Once more, the style was a new extreme, less about melody than rhythm, the man's machine gun attack sounds like a snare drum electrocuted with power chords. Once more, up-and-coming producer Terry Date had a lot to do with the delivery, capturing Dimebag in cold, dry precision, finding an odd gated effect that leached and beached all the warm wallow out of the band's military anthems: hot blood morphed into cold-blooded reptilian striking patterns.

The public instantly caught on and Pantera became a well-respected name in the underground, going on to become one of the top five biggest metal acts on the planet. Which brings us to another type of influence. Much like Metallica's rise, Pantera accomplished fame and fortune through sheer skill and quality, having zero radio help, buzzing through word of mouth and relentless road rat touring, eventually becoming a headline draw despite the corrupt system, not because of it. A greater construct was at work, one that simply rewards good art. Hence the influence again of inspiration, the pure ideal that if a metal band is good, an audience will follow despite active ignorance from the pop pushers at the top. What's interesting, not to mention healthy, is that while Metallica dumbed down and became a classic rock radio staple, Pantera continue to thrive ten records deep without a quarter ounce of radio support.

Pantera speaks:

Vinnie Paul on THE GREAT SOUTHERN TRENDKILL *. . .*

"Everybody brought something new to this record. Dime in particular brought a lot of new guitar sounds. And Philip too. I mean the last record was pretty much straight forward, one maybe two tracks of vocals, really dry, in your face. And on this record he definitely wanted to do some more double-tracking, different sounds, different effects with his voice that he hadn't used on previous records. The difference was with the last record, we recorded each song as we wrote it, so we were like putting it all together as we went, so we didn't really know what we had until we were done. Whereas in this record we actually did do demos, and we all knew the songs pretty well and we knew what we had before we started recording."

So Pantera showed that it could be done, and by virtue of their towering metal might, demonstrated that extreme music could matter on a commercial level. Ergo, the extreme flourished, Pantera's direct influence showing up in a number of heavy bands that blurred the line between hardcore and metal, causing better riffs and better musicality within hardcore camps, while causing a sense of moshpit mania and concrete chaos within metal camps, and having as much to do with killing the hair bands as did Nirvana.

But although there are a myriad acts borrowing from Pantera, the shoplift is scattered, scant and selective, with nobody able to really ravage this distinct Texas chemistry and live to tell about it within the critical or commercial forums. Some adopt the (non)look, one which interestingly has much of its root in Anthrax, many more adopting Phil's aggro-vocal, a few adopting those jet-engine guitar riffs, and a few more adopting Date's screeching metal-on-metal production tones. Luckily, pretty much any band deemed to be, or exposed as, a "Pantera clone" has been denigrated and discarded. Pantera's influence remains one of general heft, and the inspiring ability of that heft to sell stacks of wax.

Pantera speaks:

Vinnie Paul on the personalities within the band . . .

"I'd say that without a doubt I'm probably the balance. I pretty much handle all the business and try to keep everybody in check, even though I'm out of check sometimes (laughs.) Dime is a really great creator and performer. And the same can be said for Philip. He comes up with some stuff that nobody could dream of. It's just him, it's amazing. Everybody's got their own personality and characteristics, but he's probably the attitude of the band, that the people understand and connect with. Rex is probably also part of the balance. He holds down the low end. He's probably the most mellow dude in the band."

Discography

o METAL MAGIC (MMR, 1983)
o PROJECTS IN THE JUNGLE (MMR, 1984)
o I AM THE NIGHT (MMR, 1985)
o POWER METAL (MMR, 1988)
o COWBOYS FROM HELL (Atlantic, 1990)
o VULGAR DISPLAY OF POWER (Atlantic, 1992)
o FAR BEYOND DRIVEN (Atlantic, 1994)
o THE GREAT SOUTHERN TRENDKILL (Atlantic, 1996)
o OFFICIAL LIVE: 101 PROOF (Atlantic, 1997)
o REINVENTING THE STEEL (Atlantic, 2000)

⚡ 2 ⚡
Nirvana

I'm more or less playing into the hands of the simplistic view here. Metal sales didn't see a 50% decline (my estimate) because of Nirvana. Slightly more accurately, it's because of the handful of bands comprising the grunge scene. Even more accurately, it's because old metal fans moved on to this new genre, and younger replacement fans went straight to alternative. Possibly of utmost accuracy, is that the industry decided to push alternative and abandon budgets for metal promotion — whatever's mushed into the faces of a docile, dopey and ultimately obedient public is what they will brainlessly buy. So 1991 became known as the year punk broke in America, and in our circles, the year metal died.

But this isn't a negative discussion about who killed metal. It's a positive examination on who influenced metal and caused changes — some good, some bad. Nirvana deserves marquee placement as prime metal influence of the 90's for a couple of reasons. Number one, BLEACH was probably the best early grunge document, rivaled only by Mudhoney's debut EP, Soundgarden's debut EP and Green River's REHAB DOLL album. But BLEACH had a certain buzz to it, enveloping all that was grunge: punk, metal, stoner rock, garage rock, all the things that defined this new dangerous metal. You were scared when you heard that record, that same feeling you had when confronted with the rotting house known as RAW POWER.

Nirvana's second influence indicator was obviously their fame. NEVERMIND sold something like ten million copies, causing the corporatization of grunge (and even its fashion) and the ultimate metamorphosis of grunge into the rainbow flavours of alternative. Multi-platinum sales followed for Pearl Jam, Soundgarden and Alice In Chains (in that order), but it's Nirvana (legend status bolstered by Kurt Cobain's splashy exit) that gets one-word umbrella status for a whole genre of music.

So in terms of influence, where does this band fit? The success of NEVERMIND did, above all, cause a huge decline in the commercial prospects of the twenty or so "metal" bands going platinum every time out. No sub-genre of metal ever died completely, but many went back to the humble indie zone and many went even further underground. This one is a negative. The cart lurched and many apples spilled. Less bands were born in traditional metal genres, bigger ones broke up or, less drastically, merely sold one tenth of their previous tallies. It was a purging of pop metal, but it wasn't as if we got a healthy housecleaning. Many crap acts stayed (Great White, Def Leppard, Van Halen), and many good bands died a quick violent death (Love / Hate, Extreme, Saigon Kick), battered by bad timing, getting that deal reversed and/or revoked quicker than you could say, "where's the duct tape?"

On the positive flip however, this eye-to-eye, jeans and T-shirt, dirt rock mentality blew new life into a rebellious music that had become all about star-status, limos, excess, surgically ripped jeans and hair stylist bills that rivaled the Jack Daniels budget. These Seattle bands loved their metal, no question, but through their art school hipness had cheese detectors the size of Floyd's pig. The metal they made as a result was vital, immediate, but subtle of hook and smart of word, while cover and CD booklet layouts became just that: art, Warhol-style. And even if Nirvana were the pop punkers of the genre, the power chords were master blasters, constantly churning above Dave Grohl's post-metal grooves and Chris Novoselic's straight-edge bass drive. And Kurt's vocals also caused a bit of a double take. It was like, "Wait a minute, THAT'S metal, not that frilly guy in tights singing like a girl."

So Nirvana's influence on metal, granted, is not all positive. First, it caused a slash and burn of the genre's ranks, in generalities, a reduction in size, influence and an onslaught of critical ridicule that continues to this day (when metal is discussed at all.) Nirvana also caused the rise of alternative rock, which although the bane of metal's existence, has found a way to slide some pretty massive guitars onto the airwaves. So, on a rudimentary level, we've been hearing a lot of heavy stuff (Stone Temple Pilots, Smashing Pumpkins, I Mother Earth, Everclear, Lit, Sevendust, Coal Chamber, Danko Jones) that we've never considered metal, although when butted up against our 70's heroes, would probably blow them off the map. And note, a few bands even tried to embrace elements of the new sound, to mixed results, although let's face it, another record of the same ol' and we would only have been more disgusted. These acts include Skid Row, Warrant, Def Leppard, Dokken, Kiss, and to some extent Metallica.

So into the new millennium, there's all sorts of hard rock on the radio. Maybe it isn't metal. The guitar solos are gone and that singer sounds a little depressed and we only get guitars come chorus time. But loud alternative rock is, at least in the radar of the mainstream, the only metal that exists. In this respect, Nirvana and grunge SAVED metal, saved it from electronica and rap and swing and dance and divas and soundtrack albums and teen pop. Maybe a few limbs are missing from the metal beast you once knew, but maybe, just maybe alternative rock will one day be seen as the soft-pulsing lifeline that will link metal's past to metal's future.

Discography
- o BLEACH (Sub Pop, 1989)
- o NEVERMIND (Geffen, 1991)
- o INCESTICIDE (Geffen, 1992)
- o IN UTERO (Geffen, 1993)
- o UNPLUGGED IN NEW YORK (Geffen, 1994)
- o FROM THE MUDDY BANKS OF THE WISHKAH (Geffen, 1996)

3
Korn

As much as metal purists would like to deny it, L.A.'s metal hip-hop kings Korn have been one of the latest acts to cause a discernible kink in metal's evolution. Korn's rise to fame was not immediate. The band's debut album languished for nearly a year before the world was ready for their caustic, braying funk metal hybrid. While they waited for the record to break, the band toured with anybody that would have them, subjecting stunned crowds to Jonathan's compulsive repetition, his overflowing emotions, his bagpipes, and these large rhythmic attacks that were always more about foreign new uber-grooves than conventional songs with proper lyrics, verses and choruses.

> Korn speaks:
> *Jonathan Davis on the Korn sound . . .*
> "Our sound? Oh God . . . that's so hard. I always take the cheesy way out and call it Korn. We call it pimp rock (laughs), we have all these nicknames for it. It's just, when you hear it, you know it's us. We all get together (laughs.) All five of us go into a rehearsal studio. One of us will come up with a heavy guitar riff, and Fieldy will lay a bass line over it and David will lay down a beat and then the song starts. And then we all work together and structure the song out. Some of them come together pretty quick. We'll probably bust a song in a day. I'd say Ross got that tone that he's known for from Fieldy our bass player. Like, Ross was into the band a year before I was even into the band, when the band was called Creep. And he demoed us, he was totally into us. So we were totally the first album he had ever done. So all those tones and everything were us. All that sound was us. We came up with us. So he helped us and we helped him. So the Fieldy tone and the production thing, that's Fieldy's tone, and that's how we all sounded. And he's taken it on to do other projects, but he knows that sound though from us."

KORN, the record, was a similar, though toned-down and evenly mapped out amalgamation of exotics, from Fieldy's spider-fingered post-Primus, post-Faith No More bass lope, to the automotive shop scrape of Head's and Munky's guitar textures, to David's inventive drum battery, and finally to the package that is neurotic front man Jonathan Davis. And quite a package Jonathan was, combining a palpable fragility, that identified him closely with his Gen X fans, with a voice that was a metaphor for his persona, one that went from breathy whisper to riot-inciteful roar with the explosive sonic dynamic of his backing track. It's as if it slowly frothed to the brim then poured over the sides, then got hurled against the wall in disgust as it poured into your lap. And overseeing the whole chemical cocktail was a hot new influential producer named Ross Robinson who, after dealing with Korn and Sepultura, quickly became identified with this sound, something he doesn't seem to be bucking given a raft of similar projects on his plate for the Roadrunner label.

Korn speaks:
Jonathan Davis on LIFE IS PEACHY . . .
"This one's definitely more mature (laughs.) The last one, I just had a bunch of things I had to get out from since I was a little kid. This one's dealing more with now, all that time being on the road for a year and a half. There's some strange ones. Like *Ass Itch*, which is the last song I wrote. We wrote this whole album in a month, and I was in overload mode trying to write lyrics, and this is the last one I had to do, and I was just so pissed that I had to write another song, and it's about how I hate to write lyrics. I wait 'til the last minute. Once a song's done and all arranged, that's when I start writing lyrics for it. I just have to be alone. Like, this time I was put up in the Magic Motel in Hollywood for four or five days, and I just sat there, got a bottle of Jaegermeister, pounded half the bottle and sat there for a second and wrote five songs. They just come to me. It's weird. It's not like I have to sit there and f*** with it. It just comes out, bam! It comes in spurts and then I'm sitting there for another day and look at a piece of paper and then it's another five songs."

Korn speaks:
Jonathan Davis on his musical influences growing up . . .
"Growing up was all a mixture of new wave, Flock Of Seagulls, Missing Persons kind of thing, then onto industrial like Ministry and Skinny Puppy, then into goth music like Christian Death, and then after that I got a job as a DJ and I was totally into old school hip-hop (laughs.) And then after that I got into this band and started with the metal stuff. And now I'm back into the goth stuff."

Then there was the look — Korn's rap-derived Adidas sweat suits and sneakers fashion all but becoming the uniform of new metal, while Jonathan's multiple piercings perpetuated that trend for a couple more years.

Korn speaks:
Jonathan Davis on playing the bagpipes . . .
"That came about when I was about 17 years old in high school. I went to a school called Highland High school and I was taught by a Scotsman and I made a pipe band there. And I took lessons there, learned really how to blow on the thing there, and then I went to a real teacher, who went to Scotland and learned. He was an old highland guy, and I started competing after that, up and down the states at established gigs. But I'm a little rusty now. I have to sit down and learn all my licks again. But yeah, I used to compete. I was totally into the pipe gig, competition, everything."

So with this distinct sonic and visual package, a second album, and further perpetual touring commenced (biggest boosters: Sharon and Ozzy), culminating in the Family Values tour which further drove home the unlikely metal hip-hop marriage. Korn had begat a scene which was now spread all over one definitive CD — Incubus and Limp Bizkit comprising the core army, Ice Cube brought in for the hip-hop purists, Orgy for the techno end of the spectrum, and Rammstein . . . well, they don't quite fit with this bunch (maybe they led work-outs or something — drop and give me 300!) And the derivatives are selling records; bands like those on the disc plus Coal Chamber, Powerman 5000, Orange 9MM, and predecessors like The Deftones all garnering hit singles through relentless touring, often being added to bills with heavier traditional acts like Slayer, Pantera, Ozzy and Megadeth.

All told, that Korn sound, along with black metal and industrial marked the only brand new metal movements of the 90's. And really, only the Korn sound is initiated and invented by one band. You'd think that for this accomplishment alone, we would all stop trashing Korn as trendy posers. No?

Korn speaks:
Jonathan Davis on a career he almost had . . .
"None except for mortuary school (laughs.) You never heard about that? When I was 17 going to high school, I went to ROP which is the Regional Occupational Program. They place you at job sites. Well I worked at the Coroner's Office and started doing autopsies there. So I did autopsies for a year and when I graduated high school I went to mortuary college, came back and did an apprenticeship at a funeral and embalmer, and I worked at the Coroner's Office. So I totally had my career going before I started this band. I gave it all up to start this band. So I used to cut up dead bodies for a living."

Discography
- KORN (Sony, 1994)
- LIFE IS PEACHY (Sony, 1996)
- FOLLOW THE LEADER (Sony, 1998)
- ISSUES (Sony, 1999)

Nine Inch Nails

Much to my chagrin, industrial is a large component within hard rock today, the industrial metal hybrid accounting for a big chunk of the new bands selling lots of records right now. Folks like Marilyn Manson, Rob Zombie, Godsmack and Rammstein coming to mind (as well as the recently expired KMFDM.) And critics pretty much credit Ministry and Trent Reznor's Nine Inch Nails for this marriage between synthesized, computerized, electronic wizardry and churning metallic guitar chords. In effect, these two bands exposed the limited visual appeal of synthesizer purists, recognizing the show business realities of the live stage and reacting accordingly with a wily mix of man, machine, black leather, smoke and petulance.

Nine Inch Nails speaks:

Trent Reznor on his writing motivations . . .

"I'm not writing for anyone but myself, but I am conscious of an audience. When I sit down to write an album, my main criteria is to make it as challenging for me as I can, and to live up to the standards that I set for myself without repeating things I've done. I'm not exactly catering to anybody, but I'm trying to do the best I can and am hoping people like it. If they do great, If they don't fine. I put a substantial amount of effort into what I do. For me it's therapeutic, and for the fan that really gets it, it's therapeutic. I'm not trying to make a record that depresses people, although most of the inspiration is from depression. I relate it to when I was growing up there were records that when I was depressed, made me feel better, knowing someone else was feeling that way. I am making a conscious effort I think to shift lyrically into a different perspective which I hope will be as honest as what I've done in the past. But as a writer, with my notebook, I've been toying around with another perspective, we'll have to see what comes down. It's a hurdle for me. Musically, with THE DOWNWARD SPIRAL, I tried to open up the palette a bit in terms of what to expect. I felt that Nine Inch Nails was starting to box itself into a corner, having to be harder and faster and noisier. I tried to make a more full-range record that was going into a few different directions at once, because when I sit down to write, not everything I do sounds hard and fast and mean and angry so I'm trying to extend it that way. I'd like to do an album or a project that is more just guitar, bass, drums no obvious electronics on it other that treatments. I could make that sound unique, unlike every other guitar bass drums band, which is 99% of the bands out there."

Before NIN's second release, a half hour EP called BROKEN, and Ministry's PSALM 69, this techno-metal marriage only in less well-known works from these two bands, plus (way

back) Kraftwerk, Devo, the new romantics, and then a number of almost accidental noiseniks like Big Black, Butthole Surfers, Killdozer, Sonic Youth and Throbbing Gristle, none really deliberating upon this hybrid (and none save for Sonic Youth breaking on a commercial level.) Tying it all together was England's Killing Joke, who began as industrial metal without much truck for electronics (hence the Metallica cover), making the transition as the years went on, perhaps assembling the most complete industrial argument through their seven essential synth-metal marriages through the 80's. Unjustly ignored to this day, Killing Joke remains the dour, anti-social darklords of the genre's past.

Nine Inch Nails

But Reznor dragged the form into the mainstream after the band's much vaunted presentation at Lollapalooza 1991, and NIN became the focal point for a new, updated type of hard rock terrorism — computer technology slammed with the violence of buzz saw guitars, angst-ridden lyrical matter and a stage show that bore little resemblance to tight-top-button keyboard rock as we knew it.

> Nine Inch Nails speaks:
> *Trent Reznor on the writing process . . .*
> "The writing process is not something I do for fun, not something where I say I can't wait to sit down to write. I find it a bit painful. I don't exactly know why. But I have to have the discipline to make myself find time where I could inspire myself, just a matter of self-discipline, to have the tools around to be able to do that. I have little tricks I do. I find if I get frustrated, which I do quite often, I have a short temper. I get mad at myself. Musically if I'm stuck on a lyric or out of musical ideas, when I know that's coming up, I stop and do something else. Sometimes ten minutes of walking up the street clears that out."

BROKEN made way for the band's masterwork, THE DOWNWARD SPIRAL, which further and fervently captured the public's attention, offering more disturbing, self-flagellating lyrics, challenging futuro-metal arrangements, cool artwork and packaging, further reinforcement of the band's well-branded logo, and more hits and videos (one of which got Trent in hot water for bringing back absinthe!) that opened up a dark gothic New Orleans underworld to the mainstream.

Swirling around these releases was a spate of remixes, soundtrack tunes and rarities, Reznor unwittingly starting another trend, this whole idea of multiple versions of tracks being readied for re-release and re-possibility (think Fear Factory, Soulfly and most annoyingly Rob Zombie.) Erstwhile, the man started a label called Nothing Records which, like Madonna's Maverick, found itself with success on its hands, most notably, that of ostrich-faced protégé Marilyn Manson.

> Nine Inch Nails speaks:
> *Trent Reznor on achieving his goals . . .*
> "Well, the main goals that I set for my life, which I thought, or which I foolishly thought, would bring me some sort of satisfaction, I've achieved, being where I never thought I would be. I feel I could write and do a lot better stuff than I've done. Give me a couple more years, then I'll start dancing in traffic."

Woodstock 1994 saw further buzz around Nine Inch Nails' live show, a militaristic symphony of post-metal mayhem that hasn't been lost on German uber-metallists Rammstein and then metal's version of Devo, In Extremo. In essence, all of this helped drag metal into the computer age, proving that you could still look cool and sample. Nine Inch Nails, through the artistic bravery of shocking sounds, words and visuals, was somehow able to find commercial triumph that's an inspiration to all of those practicing the various flavours of extreme music.

Back with THE FRAGILE, Reznor has crawled deeper within a slower darker heartbeat, surprisingly building the enigma to greater heights than thought previous, basically by constructing a sprawling, often boring album that cannily contains highs between long bouts of grinding mental wear. Initially half slagged and half praised as masterpiece, THE FRAGILE is already being re-examined in only a favourable light, accomplishing what one imagines Trent would want: respect.

Nine Inch Nails speaks:
Trent Reznor on the artwork for THE DOWNWARD SPIRAL . . .
"We had met with an artist Russell Mills who had worked with Eno a lot, David Sylvain, and he had some interesting paintings so we ended up meeting, talking to him. We wanted to do an album that didn't look anything like any of the other Nine Inch Nails records. And musically I was experimenting with some textures that to me had an organic quality to them. A lot of the melody lines on DOWNWARD SPIRAL are samples of swarms of bees, insect sounds, anything we could find that had a sort of decaying, organic quality to them. I know that sounds a little ridiculous. I approached this record in terms of texture and I wanted the cover to be different. All of our covers to this point have been graphic design-oriented, sort of simple and clean."

Discography
o PRETTY HATE MACHINE (TVT, 1989)
o BROKEN (Nothing, 1992)
o FIXED (Nothing, 1992)
o THE DOWNWARD SPIRAL (Nothing, 1994)
o FURTHER DOWN THE SPIRAL (Nothing, 1995)
o THE FRAGILE (Nothing, 1999)

5
Marilyn Manson

There's more than a hint of jealously in the fact that a large chunk of the metal community wouldn't include this android androgyne with a big nose in any discussion on metal. But there's also an element of justification, Marilyn Manson being a couple layers into post-metal, layering up the attack with so much industrial and techno as to explode the definition of heaviness into little bits of meaninglessness.

But I'd say we'd have to include this band as a big influence on whatever metal is today, and this would be for a number of reasons. First, on a purely musical level, Marilyn Manson was the first to really capitalize on the industrial revolution, taking the rudimentary ideas of Ministry and Nine Inch Nails and gunking up the whole thing with the acquired knowledge of mentor Trent Reznor, on whose label, Nothing Records, the band resides.

The sound is currently even more technology-based, although the first couple albums were essentially over-produced shock rock albums, albums whose songs, when thrown

copyright Rock Classics

into the live ring, become indistinguishable from most modern metal due to the loss of subtlety inside the hockey barns of North America. It's annoying and destructive to metal that this band has found a way to rely on fuzzed-out synthesizer riffs to serve as power chords, further blurring the distinction between animal and machine. Perhaps Van Halen's *Jump* and *I'll Wait* should be called on the carpet as the culprits.

But the man does rock hard live, shaking and breaking in violent delivery of songs that you would have to admit, are (once all senses are consulted and all age barriers crumbled) intense. Which brings us to the visuals. Perhaps Marilyn Manson's greatest area of influence is that of visual impact or image. Manson is the latest in a long line of shock rockers beginning with psychedelic rock, Alice Cooper, Bowie and British glam, moving through Kiss, Mötley Crüe, WASP, Jane's Addiction, White Zombie and now, uh, this.

And because the album graphics, videos, lyrics and live shows are so disturbing, nightmarish, profane and morally destructive, Manson has constantly made the news, often within discussions of censorship and concert bannings, keeping hard music in the papers, challenging the Wal-Marts of the world with his OK-but-not-great press conference rebuttals to the hub-bub over his new mammary nubs.

Other bands haven't ignored the commercial effects of such sensationalism. Equal to Korn in influence, and more-so when we're talking about the subgenre of "spookycore" is Marilyn Manson. Even though you hear more Korn in Coal Chamber, the look is more old school Manson, something that can also be seen within the presentations of Godsmack, rappers Insane Clown Posse and newcomers Slipknot, although these boys (at least superficially) are more about gas station attendant overalls, bank robber masks and disorienting motion.

So, as with a good half of the influences in this book, the Marilyn Manson effect is a complex composite touching upon both visuals and sound, with Manson chewing up and spitting out the comfort zone in time-honoured fashion, pulling the wool over our eyes, proving the stupidity of teenkind to become excited over the same trickery time and time again, holding a mirror up to the mess that is America, then tossing it aside and cackling all the way to the bank.

Discography
- PORTRAIT OF AN AMERICAN FAMILY (Nothing / Interscope, 1994)
- ANTICHRIST SUPERSTAR (Nothing / Interscope, 1996)
- MECHANICAL ANIMALS (Nothing / Interscope, 1998)
- THE LAST TOUR ON EARTH (Nothing / Interscope, 1999)

6
Emperor

The first name in black metal, Norway's Emperor, may have been preceded by Darkthrone amongst incidental output from others, but it's this band that got a catalogue together quickly and early, one that codified and defined what state of the art would initially entail, and then as time went on, established new manifestos on which to improve.

Emperor's influence comes from many inky wells. Proving a sort of grim action-not-words code of immoral ethics, members of the band were implicated in the infamous Norwegian church-burnings, Samoth being imprisoned for the crime, while original drummer Faust went down for murdering a homosexual that made a play for him.

Musically, at barely fifteen and fourteen years of age, a young Samoth and Ihsahn fashioned together a split EP with pioneering Viking metallists Enslaved that was an early blueprint of black metal, although closer to thrash than what was to be.

IN THE NIGHTSIDE ECLIPSE was to mark the real start of the genre's next level, this layered, eerily melodic sound splashed on top with struggling keyboards. Riffs were a melted sludge of guitars and bass, drums were still more thrash than blastbeated, and the overall sound hearkened back to the echoey, bombastic strains of Viking-era Bathory.

Emperor speaks:

Ihsahn on the title, IX EQUILIBRIUM and his lyrics . . .

"An album title should reflect the contents of the whole album and the title has higher and lesser values. It's got obvious reasons; the album is released in 1999. Also coincidentally, when we mastered the album, it was the 9th of January and it took us nine hours (laughs.) But, nine, being the highest number in our number system, is a symbol of eternity. It's very much about reaching the highest bounds of things and I think it reflects a lot on the lyrical side of the album which is not as critical and rebellious towards the outside world. It's more of an overview. Some of the lyrics are critical but they might as well be interpreted as being self-critical. So in many ways I think this album is much more balanced in its contents and not so black and white."

ANTHEMS TO THE WELKIN AT DUSK has turned out to be a controversial album. Now somewhat denigrated by the band, it's an even colder and faster piece of musical wizardry, almost too layered, but one of the better examples of blastbeat perfection in black metal. It's a natural predecessor to the band's polished and proud step away from the tenets of blackness into a straight poetic, almost Libertarian prog metal extreme, a record called IX EQUILIBRIUM. This masterpiece once more raised the bar, infusing even more complexity and production accuracy, while retaining the olden Odin tones that are the signature of Emperor's frost and fire.

Emperor speaks:

Ihsahn on IX EQUILIBRIUM's blend of metals . . .

"The new album is much more direct. There's different types of music that can easily express different scenes, from very extreme death metal which is much more aggressive through the black metal parts. Because black metal is more atmospheric, at least with the kind of symphonic style. And then you have more thrash and strict heavy metal which has that nostalgic feeling that goes very deep. But that nostalgic metal feeling combined with the high-pitched screams gives it a strange, foreign feel. I think Emperor can experiment to a certain extent. We all think differently and have diverse influences. But for each new Emperor album you will still hear that it is an Emperor album and I think that is a result of the compromises that we make within the band. And I think it's unavoidable for future recordings that this compromise will colour the music. I think that being experimental for the sake of being experimental is when it's taken too far. You cannot forget the music in it. I don't think it's too hard to make something very strange and something very different but that doesn't always mean that it's good music. So I think it's important to experiment and let the music and the atmosphere come first. I mean the old composers, they had strict limits on how to build their pieces. There were strict rules but they tried to exploit the material they had available to the extreme, as far as they could and what they were allowed to do. It became very good music. I think Emperor will always use keyboards, guitars, bass, drums, and different vocal styles and we will still use the same instrumentation but we will bring in some new influences and still keep it as Emperor. If we wanted to do something else, then we would start another band (laughs.)"

In essence, Emperor's influence has been felt in their tireless quests for the next plateau. Where Emperor went, others locked up and followed while the band, like a shark through still water, silently soldiered past. From the debut, the world got thrashy black metal, poisoned by the hormonal and criminal vagaries of mid-teen madness and boredom. NIGHTSIDE ECLIPSE unleashed a primitive, cold and unholy old school black metal with a dash of the symphonic. Its follow-up brought a respectable progressive rock

Emperor speaks:

Samoth on the band's changing scope . . .

"It's really how people want to understand things. Of course that was our image in '92, but what can I say? To live a life of complete rejection is not the life I want to live. We are polite people and I think that this attitude, like if you are a Satanist, not that I label myself as a Satanist, but some people have this attitude that if you are on the darker side you have to be a bad person and I don't think that's it. I think a true Satanist should be a noble person, a person who should be a role model rather than some lunatic."

ethic, full-on production detailing, playing that was inhuman or if not at least physically daunting, all plowed under by the cryptic until it was indecipherable. Finally, the band brought us IX EQUILIBRIUM, which carries at least a couple of layers of influence. Its playing and presentation are once more a new state of the art — torrid drumming, slicing riffery, vocals of monster anguish and keyboards that add hue and dimension to a sick, sick sound. It's through this record that Emperor, along with king slayers Satyricon, have become the leaders of the purists, while Dimmu Borgir, Cradle Of Filth and worse, Children Of Bodom all take the sound more theatrical and mainstream. Emperor's measured evolution, like Metallica in the 80's and Pantera in the mid-90's, has given them that hallowed mantle of influence through inspiration, influencing a host of underground black metallers who become uneasy at the creeping cheerful metal tones threatening their atmospheric, ice-bound music.

Emperor speaks:

Samoth on spreading the band's appeal . . .

"We have a better opportunity to reach a wider audience than, let's say Darkthrone, because they are the essence of pure unholy black metal and they have a different expression. There are people who say that we sell out and I expect it more from the new album because we have better production and there will be fans that will say, 'Oh no! Emperor is like Dimmu Borgir and Cradle Of Filth and they are going for the money and blah, blah, blah . . .' Well I don't really care what these people think. And the point is that we never have spoken shit about these bands because I do not see Dimmu Borgir and Cradle Of Filth as sell-out bands. I know they work hard at what they do and they have a different expression and are more commercially-oriented than we are but they don't do it for the f***ing money. If they were doing it for the money, if they did, I don't think black metal would be the first thing that they would get into."

Discography

○ EMPEROR / ENSLAVED SPLIT CD (Candlelight, 1993)
○ IN THE NIGHTSIDE ECLIPSE (Candlelight, 1995)
○ ANTHEMS TO THE WELKIN AT DUSK (Candlelight, 1997)
○ IX EQUILIBRIUM ((Candlelight, 1999)
○ EMPERIAL LIVE CEREMONY (Candlelight, 2000)

⚡ 7 ⚡
White Zombie

Rob "Zombie" Straker's a pretty smart guy — something that comes in handy when vanquishing your competitors, or indeed your shiftless band. Emerging from the land of big city cynicism, New York City, White Zombie wrapped their stiff but powerful post-metal beats in a bit of an art concept, this whole B-movie, horror movie, road movie schtick that professed to look at the junk food culture that is America and personify its monstrous commercialism in an explosion of cartoon colour.

White Zombie

Once the band quit futzing around on Caroline, they caught the attention of two influential taste makers that don't even exist, two gaping maws stuck right in the middle of White Zombie's nihilistic message called Beavis and Butt-Head. These two mumbling MTV addicts hit the nail on the head: White Zombie's cool. And the reason they liked them is the reason we like all fast food: it looks good and it rocks.

White Zombie speaks:
Rob Zombie on the White Zombie sound . . .
"White Zombie was always a sort of a weird mixture of — I don't know how this actually mixes into our sound — Black Sabbath and Van Halen with Black Flag and the Bad Brains, and it wasn't consciously mixing sounds, it's just that those were the bands I liked. It's just kinda what came out of it. It's everything. I kinda think of the band as just one big magnet for all kinds of weird American culture. It's everything from movies to TV to books to comic books to news reports, just any kind of crazy shit."

And so we got the band's bonafide Austin Powers-worthy hit, *Thunder Kiss '65*, an influential metal groove machine that was a slightly less industrial, slightly more slurpable red-headed stepsister to Ministry's *Jesus Built My Hotrod* and any real song by the Butthole Surfers. This song poked a few different holes in metal. First of all, it followed that rap tack we had previously only fleetingly seen, say within Faith No More and the Chili Peppers. Granted, Rob attacked his rap with what was almost a shaggy death metal vocal. This track also made liberal use of sampling, albeit of the rudimentary movie type. It's also of note that White Zombie was one of the earlier pioneers in terms of scoring minor hits with their soundtrack and tribute tunes, always able to string a waiting public along with a crushing rock classic that would have likely been the standout track on any of their regular albums.

White Zombie speaks:
Rob Zombie on the influence of Black Sabbath . . .
"Everybody knows that Black Sabbath started everything and almost every single thing people are playing today has already been done by Black Sabbath. They wrote every single good riff, ever. There's one easy way to figure out how Black Sabbath has lasted. There's only certain bands that get a reaction, even though you're playing a record that's twenty years old. Sabbath are one of them."

The next record (and actually the band's last, save for the remix album, another element White Zombie brought to metal) took them further into industrial, with White Zombie becoming the most viable merger of man and machine, the one more human than human, whatever the hell that means, the one who was most plausible on stage as a flat-out old fashioned metal band.

Which was another place White Zombie's influence could be heard and emphatically seen. White Zombie, for a while there, were the biggest proponents of the big rock show, Rob quite articulately reminding everybody that Kiss shows were fun and not an embarrassment best left in the Jimmy Carter years. So we got the logical extension of the band's info-overload lyrics and cartoony booklets, pyro, lots of neon, monsters that just wanna have fun, a spectacle of a nightmarish hyper-marketed America to pounding processed beats that all sounded the same in those cold heartless hockey barns (trust me, I was there.)

So we've got a band that did a fair bit to push metal along into the 90's, bringing the industrial, the rap, the hip-hop vibe, the sampling, the remixes, bringing back the stage extravagonzo, bringing back the shock rock. Then quite abruptly, Rob fired his aimless, unproductive backing band. Really, he'd always hinted that there was friction between himself and his co-workers, so it was likely just a matter of time. Time, and the fact that his solo album was received by (and cannily delivered to) the public as essentially the next White Zombie record, resuming the sales trajectory. And Rob didn't let them down, offering the same electro-drive with screeching axes and the same house of horror cornball colours. Of course, then he remixed and repackaged the record as AMERICAN MADE MUSIC TO STRIP BY, the second time he pulled that one, furthering his morphing into Gene Simmons by becoming a little plastic action figure.

> White Zombie speaks:
> *Rob Zombie on supposed success . . .*
> "There's really not that much money to be had. It's like, the record didn't even recoup its costs until it was past gold, so now that it's past platinum, it's kinda like there's enough money that you can live, but that's about it. We chalked up so many expenses over the last two years touring that we're still paying for y'know, trucks that we rented in Germany in 1991, so maybe next year there'll be money, but we're still trying to just stay alive. Touring was really expensive, but for us, it was the only way to keep the record alive, so we toured two years straight, and it wasn't until the last few months that we were actually making a big profit, but that big profit just went to pay for all the losses."

In this guise, Rob embodies a last and lasting sphere of influence, simply the idea of being heavy, and selling a lot of records (double platinum in the states for HELLBILLY DELUXE by last count), and selling a lot of T-shirts, keeping hard music blipping on commercial radar, and doing so with lots of more human than human (there's that stupid phrase again) personal appearances, basically by touring his dreads off.

Discography
- ᴑ SOULCRUSHER (Silent Explosion, 1988)
- ᴑ MAKE THEM DIE SLOWLY (Caroline, 1989)
- ᴑ LA SEXORCISTO: DEVIL MUSIC VOL. I (Geffen, 1992)
- ᴑ ASTRO-CREEP: 2000 (Geffen, 1995)
- ᴑ SUPERSEXY SWINGIN' SOUNDS (Geffen, 1996)
- ᴑ HELLBILLY DELUXE (as Rob Zombie) (Geffen, 1998)
- ᴑ AMERICAN MADE MUSIC TO STRIP BY (as Rob Zombie) (Geffen, 1999)

Soundgarden

Alice In Chains had their guarded, self-conscious metal Jones. Mudhoney were the purer-than-thou Lyres-like garage rock professors. Pearl Jam was too busy deifying themselves unto U2. Nirvana was too cool to care. But it was Soundgarden that came to be the purified average of all of the above, adding their own Zeppified prog metal smart drugs, topping off the flaming concoction with the movement's best vocalist Chris Cornell.

As with their compatriots, plus other unique entities such as King's X and Jane's Addiction, Soundgarden's influence on metal is peripheral, abstract and complicated. In one sense, they helped kill the scene as it existed, just like Nirvana, by being too good and too smart, by pointing out the absurdity of the unit-shifting glamsters a couple o' states south, seemingly tossing off impossible songs that borrowed from rock locales obscure and familiar.

But in a positive sense (in fact more positive than that of Nirvana), Soundgarden kicked metal's cut-the-cheeks-out butt into shape, adding new hue and dimension to the form, cool innovations that were unpredictable and complex, while somehow retaining the teetering drug-addled danger of grunge, that element of spontaneous art explosion that compressed a half dozen hard rock conventions into a post-metal nail bomb that would puncture the egos of the smug hair rockers.

In this sense, Soundgarden was the band that brought metal some much-needed respect, although they (and every other metal band) would spend years denying this had anything to do with metal. Soundgarden was the art school of hard rock, blurring the lines between the blues, garage rock, grunge, Sabbath, Zeppelin and punk until the mainstream was hoodwinked into accepting their slashing chords, wailing vocals and illogical songs that ranged from painfully truncated and sparse to dopey, long and insufferable. Of course it was Cornell's ballads that really stuck, songs like *Fell On Black Days, Black Hole Sun,*

Blow Up The Outside World and *Burden In My Hand* getting the most airplay, while *Pretty Noose* and the trashy Navajo tinkle of *Spoonman* brought up the rock.

The cool thing about Soundgarden is that (save for their clumsy live shows), they rarely got a bad review. There was this rarified Zeppelin air about it — competitor, hard rock fan and critic alike all proclaiming in unison that this was something special. And there was a chemistry in the band that reminded one of Zep, four guys, all different, all masters of their trade, all writing, coming together to create this collision of dumb and smart, fast and slow, tender and noisy. And to complete the myth, the band broke up at their height, really for no apparent reason other than the fact that they were sincere and pure slaves to the muse, feeling that this configuration was exhausted of its possibility, perceptively standing ahead of the critical curve and imagining the twisted wreckage as their carriage left the road.

Discography
- SCREAMING LIFE (Sub Pop, 1987)
- FOPP (Sub Pop, 1988)
- ULTRAMEGA OK (SST, 1988)
- LOUDER THAN LOVE (A&M, 1989)
- BADMOTORFINGER (A&M, 1991)
- SUPERUNKNOWN (A&M, 1994)
- DOWN ON THE UPSIDE (A&M, 1996)
- A-SIDES (A&M, 1997)

ϟ 9 ϟ
Faith No More

Plant Faith No More in the Soundgardens of the inexplicably expired but not forgotten. Through a not-so-mere six studio records, this innovative, ironic and tragically hip hard rock phenom taught us to think again and to laugh again, re-engineering the smug sequined facade of metal much the way Nirvana did. And there's the key: Faith No More blazed a strange alternative metal track before there was any type of alt-metal, be it grunge or its rainbow of after-flavours.

Their sound was forged not with Mike Patton at the helm, but through an infectious, loud-mouthed nut case named Chuck Moseley. Chuck was wholly unmanageable, doomed to be purged from an already psychologically fragile unit. But before he left, he brought two things to metal — humour and a rap vocal style. The humour touched off a sort of California sound, a pre-grunge flutter aided and abetted by similar kin Red Hot Chili Peppers, and perhaps preceded by the whole Minutemen / Firehose phenom, Black Flag and traces of this new sound within the jiggy Run DMC / Aerosmith rejig of *Walk This Way*, the Beastie Boys' *(You Gotta) Fight For Your Right (To Party)*, and selected tracks from Living Colour's debut. Other spiritual descendants include Sublime and Sugar Ray.

The rap vocal is wrapped up in the same zone, also major credit to the Chili Peppers, and few else. It was a pre-hip-hop element that went hand-in-hand with the band's other main innovation, that of funk metal. Faith No More forged huge bass-slapped grooves

Faith No More

with their smash record THE REAL THING from 1989, addressing the masses with this hybrid of punk, metal, and black music through the *Epic* and *Falling To Pieces* hit singles. Bolstering this idea of a pre-grunge blueprint, this metamorphosis of metal into the minds of the aware, was Jane's Addiction, who mirrored Faith No More's complicated hybrid of grandiose Zep metal, subversive art, punk ethics, deconstructed songs, big bass guitars and rapid-fire vocal attacks. And ultimately, the commercial and critical success of the Peppers, Faith No More and Jane's Addiction set the ball rolling for Nirvana, Alice In Chains and Soundgarden, demonstrating what could be, and what could be heavy.

Faith No More speaks:
Mike Patton sums up the band's career . . .
"I think the reason Faith No More broke up is different for everybody in the band, but for me it was music. I didn't think that we have any gas left in the tank. At least me personally, I didn't think I had anything else to say, and I don't think the band really had much more to say after five records. We made our statement, it was good while it lasted, not too many regrets, and overall it was a good experience. It was like a decade of my life, so you have to know when to pull the plug. I think KING FOR A DAY is our best record. Most people would disagree with that. Most people say to me, 'that record is awful, what were you guys thinking?' But that's the same thing they said about ANGEL DUST when we released that. It will never cease to amaze me, people's perception of things. ANGEL DUST seemed natural at the time. All that stuff got thrown on us after it was finished, you know, from our label, our management a little bit, and from people, fans, everybody saying to us 'what the f***?!' We didn't know it was weird when we were making it. It felt natural! If you set out to make a weird record, I think you're in trouble. I don't think it's going to come off like that at all. I think it's going to come off as contrived, boring, and forced. If you just do what you do and it comes naturally, let people draw their own f***ing conclusions. On ALBUM OF THE YEAR, I think we pulled back a little bit and concentrated on a few of our strengths a little more rather than branching out the way we did on KING FOR A DAY. But I think it's a good record. I don't really think we ever made a bad record. I think each one kind of said who we were at the time. I certainly don't listen to any of them. They give me the creeps (laughs.)"

Skipping forward a few years, the direct derivatives of the Faith No More sound (as it existed and was discarded halfway through the band's remarkably experimental career) are thriving, with the earliest funk metal hybrids seen in the improbable pop metal of Extreme, followed by the flamethrown politics of Rage Against The Machine, and now filling moshzones regularly through the buzz saw attack of Korn, Limp Bizkit, Coal Chamber, Sevendust and Powerman 5000 (preceded by a brief but big buzz for Clawfinger in Europe, unnoticed stateside.) The hard rock dominance by these bands is really Faith No More's most impressive legacy, even though Patton and Co. would probably find the whole thing absurd.

And the reason the band might scoff at the whole sick fixation on their early pimp roll might have to do with the burnt match completion of the band's post-fame run. To finish the stupefied trajectory of Faith No More, after the platinum success of THE REAL THING, a kind of traumatic American junk culture psychosis set in, causing the difficult, biting, excessive and inaccessible art of 1992's ANGEL DUST (which actually sold double THE REAL THING in Europe), followed by a couple of ignored final records — 1995's KING FOR A DAY and 97's ALBUM OF THE YEAR, both musically reigned-in but lyrically arcane and accusatory. Implosion followed incompatible professed fetishes, and Patton now gets to express his fraught and fragmented mind much further to the extreme through Mr.

Bungle, Fantomas and his post-art record label, all promising to be unlistenable save only for the tin-foil tuned.

Discography
- o WE CARE A LOT (Mordam, 1985)
- o INTRODUCE YOURSELF (Slash, 1987)
- o THE REAL THING (Slash, 1989)
- o LIVE AT BRIXTON ACADEMY (Slash, 1991)
- o ANGEL DUST (Slash, 1992)
- o KING FOR A DAY (Slash, 1995)
- o ALBUM OF THE YEAR (Slash, 1997)
- o WHO CARES A LOT? THE GREATEST HITS (Slash, 1998)

⚡ 10 ⚡
Kyuss

All those press stories about jammin' generator parties out in the desert had everybody hooked on checking out the Kyuss vibe. And once they did, critic and fan alike were bowled over by the band's new bassquaked take on a sound that didn't even really have a name yet, this massive gluey update on Sabbath seen through the rosy psychedelic lenses of Califried heatstroke.

We didn't know it yet, but the band's late-fer-dinner grunge sound (see My Sister's Machine) on their debut indie WRETCH was about to be transformed by a bass-crazy Chris Goss (owner of one of the major overlooked monster records of the 80's, the self-titled debut from Masters Of Reality) into BLUES FOR THE RED SUN, the band's second record. BLUES FOR THE RED SUN had only a couple of touchstones outside of its cactus headspace, both from far away, one being Trouble and the other Cathedral. Trouble had been operating somewhat in this zone all their blessed lives, for ten years at this point to be exact. Lee Dorrian and Cathedral had only recently hit the Sabbath sludge with their pioneering SOUL SACRIFICE EP five months earlier, arriving from a different place, that of a Napalm Death-derived grindcore.

Kyuss speaks:
Scott Reeder on inspiration . . .
"There seems to be something spiritual about writing and recording in the desert. It's hard to describe it without experiencing it for yourself. There's a lot of wide open space around here; anybody from the city feels pretty overwhelmed. People come out here from the label in New York and they just freak out that we live here. The weather's nice year 'round, but in the summer it gets pretty damn hot. I'd be pretty depressed if I lived somewhere else, like in Seattle or something. Musically, we just let it flow dark and black. If we sat down and thought about it, it wouldn't have that vibe. Spontaneity is definitely one of the most important things to all of us."

But Kyuss took things much further, downtuning, cranking the bass, dishing out a constant barrage of cymbals and lacing the whole blue smoke brew with a vocal performance from John Garcia that just knew it had hit a magic mushroom groove. stoner rock was born — Kyuss' crowning contribution to metal, one that's thriving all over America, England and Sweden today. The genre has a tight range of flavours, all derived from Kyuss in some way. But by virtue of geography, Kyuss are most closely associated with the whole American junk culture crew, which includes bands like Fu Manchu, who celebrate the cheese of the 70's in skateboarded pleasure vanned ironic fashion, and the two biggest offshoot units Queens Of The Stone Age and Unida.

Elsewhere, there's the more psychedelic, science fiction-derived output from Lee Dorrian's label Rise Above (Orange Goblin, Electric Wizard, Goatlord, Newfoundland's Sheavy), plus Man's Ruin, Brainticket, MeteorCity and The Music Cartel from the US, all finding slow-brewed power chord fanatics with their own particular left turns, be they punk, grunge, alternative, psychedelia, fantasy, or authentic 70's styles, such as those tweaked by personal faves Terra Firma and Solace.

> Kyuss speaks:
> *Scott Reeder on connecting with the crowd . . .*
> "A lot of bands sound so bright and there's no bass. It just hurts your ears. Our sound just seems to pulse through your body. I'm hoping it will save my hearing. There's a concern with my hearing. I can feel it going. I've tried to play with earplugs and it doesn't work. You feel like you're underwater. It's hard for me, because I have to get into it during a show or nobody else will get into it. It's so important getting that chemistry going back and forth from the audience. If you don't hit it from the beginning, it's just not there, but when it's on, it's killer. I guess it's a sacrifice I have to take. It's not good because I come home and I have a hard time finding out what people are saying. It's going to be a big problem, but I don't see a solution besides quitting and I don't wanna!"

But basically, Kyuss started the whole thing when there was no scene to speak of (Trouble's sales couldn't be encouraging, nor could those of The Obsessed), making the band the undisputed kings of stoner rock, save for whatever one level above king is, which we must reserve for Sabbath. This status was reinforced with two more critically acclaimed records (both one notch up to Elektra) WELCOME TO SKY VALLEY from 1994 and 95's . . . AND THE CIRCUS LEAVES TOWN.

And although the band split shortly thereafter, the individual members have stuck with the genre, turning up in all sorts of quasi- and short-lived bands, the most consistent being the DESERT SESSIONS series for Man's Ruin and the most commercially successful being the aforementioned Queens Of The Stone Age, featuring guitarist Josh Homme and drummer Alfredo Hernandez. Queens Of The Stone Age have wisely lightened up on the overpowering bass that always threatened to smother Kyuss, also arriving faster with a hook and a chorus, skipping most of the long intros and swirling jams of their old band. Call it Weezer meets Kyuss.

Meanwhile vocalist John Garcia is doing his Unida thing which is much closer to the Kyuss ethic of churn and burn. All told, the former members of Kyuss are sticking around for a rainbow assortment of stoner rock sounds that have become the backbone of a thriving genre.

Discography
- o WRETCH (Dali, 1991)
- o BLUES FOR THE RED SUN (Dali / Chameleon, 1993)
- o WELCOME TO SKY VALLEY (Elektra, 1994)
- o ...AND THE CIRCUS LEAVES TOWN (Elektra, 1995)

\ 11 /
Darkthrone

Darkthrone, although not as famed as Emperor, let alone the new slick wave of black metallers like Dimmu Borgir and Cradle Of Filth, are in fact, the base material that inspired a raft of black metallers. And Darkthrone managed this simply by staying out of jail, the lock-up having hindered the development of bands like Mayhem and Burzum, and to a lesser extent, Emperor, who simply shuffled members to keep the cold blue flame alive.

Calling themselves, "true Norwegian black metal", Darkthrone began as something closer to death metal (although Fenriz' claimed influences are Slayer, Bathory, Mayhem and Snorre from Thorns), releasing SOULSIDE JOURNEY on Peaceville, both parties unaware that Norwegian metal was to take a harsh left turn. The band quite wisely had a bit of a press ban going, revealing little of their supposed fascist views, not playing live, and basically laying low while the ancient embers cooled and others from the scene received their invitations to various Norwegian jails.

Next came ABLAZE IN THE NORTHERN SKY which is widely considered the first 90's-sound black metal album. Gravely primitive, obscure, cold and unholy, it, along with its even heavier, darker, often imitated successor UNDER A FUNERAL MOON, are the early uncompromising grails of the genre, the records that many black metallers cite in interviews as the albums that made them form bands.

Darkthrone speaks:
Fenriz on the band's surprise return with a record for '99 . . .
"Oh yeah, well we've been around. And the music ain't surprising. You know it's the same-old same-old and that's very comfortable. Nocturno Culto told me that we should do another album in December and we just started working on it. It ain't hard really because we are working men and we always had jobs. We were always busy with our jobs and we did the music in our spare time. We're not like stars sitting around watching TV all the time (laughs.)"

Future product had one point of unification: severe lack of compromise, although an odd infiltration of the band's earlier death sound came back (1997's GOATLORD is even a shelved 1992 album with new vocals) along with bows to the slower pre-black metal sounds of Celtic Frost. Bad recordings were always present though, Darkthrone

stubbornly sticking to this "true" "old school" element of the sound, albums like TRANSILVANIAN HUNGER were recorded on a four-track and sound almost like double intensity Warfare.

But a survey of the catalogue would likely validate Darkthrone's claim, the band being steadfast and faithful adherents to black metal vocals, muddy blastbeats, primitive no-frills arrangements, and a craptatious racket that sounds like the cold, polar soil and rocks that it wishes to embrace. And it truly is astonishing that there were no less than six Darkthrone albums before the scene really even got off the ground. Darkthrone established through sheer volume a restricted, compressed rule book to the game that became traditional black metal.

Darkthrone speaks:
Fenriჳ on the Darkthrone approach to black metal . . .
"Well in the beginning, like all bands do, we developed and increased our playing skills but then we decided to quit the shit and start to play primitive. So that's the decision we took in 1991 and we are still sticking with that and that's why it's so easy for us to play this old school stuff. My song on RAVISHING GRIMNESS is totally old school and Nocturno Culto's songs have a lot of old school riffs combined with typical Norwegian black metal, but we just play open. We're not thrash-oriented on this album at all. Absolutely not! We're just inspired by old Bathory, Hellhammer, and the usual suspects from early Norwegian black metal. I have never been into that Sebastian Bach with fuzz sound; that's not what we've been into. But these people can do it if they want. They have a choice, you can either go old school or new school. We recorded it in the same studio as Mayhem did WOLF'S LAIR ABYSS. We had a big heavy metal band in Norway in the 80's called TNT and it's the guy's studio. It's like an old farm or some shit like that. We were booked for ten days which is mind-boggling for Darkthrone because we always did a week basically. I don't think we've ever used more than thirty hours for an album and this time we didn't either (laughs.) We were just standing there going like, 'Ten days? What the f*** are we going to do up here?' And then after three days we recorded everything. You know, me and Nocturno have been playing together since '88 so it's easy for us, and you don't have to be a rocket scientist or anything to play Darkthrone stuff (laughs.)"

Darkthrone

It is this timeless, un-evolving standard flailing away off to the side that is the band's ultimate contribution (Fenriz even takes pride in downgrading their label affiliations!), this constant reminder that there is a foundation from which all of the rapidly and increasingly unrecognizable offshoots of black metal once did flow. Back to 1999 with RAVISHING GRIMNESS, Fenriz and Nocturno Culto (Nocturno now chief songwriter and Nintendo freak) describe themselves as the "Status Quo of black metal", fiendishly and almost humourously regressing into the purest noise they can unlearn.

Darkthrone speaks:

Fenriz on the genesis of black metal . . .

"Euronymous had a huge impact because Mayhem was there all along. They are the band who should have the most credit. Euronymous and even Snorre from Thorns were the ones that created the sort of riffing that led to the typical Norwegian black metal riff. One day I should be able to show what kinds of riffs these are but there's a lot of confusion to what Norwegian black metal is. It's a style of riffing really. But Euronymous had a huge impact and I say this because he was always into the darkest stuff all the time while everyone else, and even us, were death metal kids and shit. He was the oldest dude. Black metal is not really what we're doing. Snorre told Satyr that the new Darkthrone album was cool but the drumming was so boring and my reply would be, 'hey, we're not entertainment.' I have to sacrifice because I really like to play a lot of funk and jazz, but when I play black metal, I sacrifice all that. I don't want to show any playing abilities at all and now it's even better because I don't play this style a lot. So now my drumming sounds like I just started drumming and on the new album it sounds really primitive. Maybe next time I will sound like the drummer from early Kreator, really un-tight. That would be super. Many bands want to expand the definition of black metal and that's natural for them. They never took the decision to be totally primitive. They started out at first base and went, 'Whoo-hoo!' We are still at first base, we like first base, we're really comfortable there and we have great facilities there and we have no one else to share them with, hahaha! No one is there to cramp our style.' The other guys are seemingly in this rat race but we couldn't care less."

Discography
- º SOULSIDE JOURNEY (Peaceville, 1990)
- º A BLAZE IN THE NORTHERN SKY (Peaceville, 1991)
- º UNDER A FUNERAL MOON (Peaceville, 1993)
- º TRANSILVANIAN HUNGER (Peaceville, 1994)
- º PANZERFAUST (Moonfog, 1995)
- º TOTAL DEATH (Moonfog, 1996)
- º GOATLORD (Moonfog, 1997)
- º RAVISHING GRIMNESS (Moonfog, 1999)

❱ 12 ❰
Carcass

Tough finding one act to uphold the rotting cadaver of death metal, but here's my pick — Liverpool's Carcass beats out Obituary, Deicide, Cannibal Corpse, Napalm Death, Morbid Angel, Death, Vader and Suffocation due mostly to their continuing post-death influence.

One could argue that Napalm Death was the first of the fastest and most deliberate, SCUM from 1987 having been a ludicrous landmark within grindcore. Obituary is vital but eccentric, as is Death, who, even in the beginning, were perhaps cerebrally a bit above the form. And Morbid Angel, Deicide and Cannibal Corpse, all around 1990, more or less perfected the form, establishing the restrictive death rules as they exist today.

Carcass speaks:

Michael Amott on Sabbath, Metallica and his guitar playing . . .
"Obviously Sabbath have got so many of the classic riffs. Tony Iommi is one of the riff-meisters of our time. Any of the riffs off of MASTER OF REALITY and VOL 4 are just so super-heavy. That's the basics of heavy metal. When I was 14, 15, I was really getting involved in buying music and it was Metallica, Anthrax and Exodus. They were a huge influence on me. James Hetfield was a fantastic riff-composer in his day. *Creeping Death* and stuff like that is amazing. All my music is very riff-based. I don't know how to write a song without riffs. I guess that's just from my musical background. Bands like R.E.M. don't have riffs, they have chord structures. I don't know anything about that. It's all riffs for me!"

But Carcass was equal to the above in invention, also influencing in subtler ways (for example, they were all vegans!) Everything the band did caused controversy and turned heads. The early work, REEK OF PUTREFACTION and SYMPHONIES OF SICKNESS, worked a two-fisted head-pummel with Napalm Death and Entombed as some of the earliest Earache Records madness, toiling away within an extreme post-thrash music that would be the first death metal and grindcore. Carcass underscored their barrage with early pioneering guttural vocals which, lowered and mechanized, would become a signature of the genre, as well as in selected black metal, now commonplace in many of the bands crossing over from black into mainstream metal.

Lyrically the band really cranked up the gore in death metal, something which Cannibal Corpse would champion, followed by a couple dozen tiring knock-offs. Carcass, however, wrote the dictionary on the form, churning out all manner of medical verbiage on all matters punctured, leaking and rotting, until the senses reeled in revelation of the fragile, organic, and ultimately mechanical, meat puppets housing our souls. Many third rate mid-80's bands may have flung the blood and guts first, but Carcass made an elevated impression on the death scene, even more-so once they became, along with Cathedral, one of the major label extremities due to Earache's ill-fated, short-lived liaison with Sony.

Carcass speaks:

Bill Steer, on the band's controversial SWANSONG album . . .
"Lyrically, this is different because I wrote the choruses and song titles before the lyrics. Usually I would write all these lyrics and it would be a struggle to come up with a title that would fit. What I've always wanted to do with this record was to make a more accessible Carcass record, one which might please old school Carcass fans and maybe win us some new fans as well. I got sick of the whole technical thing. This album sounds more rock 'n' roll than Carcass ever has. Most of the songs are really snide snipes at things that I see around me. They're about real, on the level things that I've experienced. It's not brutal or intense, but it's still got excitement to it and I think we've made an album which was the logical last thing to do."

This got the band exposure, but it was their last pre-Sony record, HEARTWORK, that set the stage. HEARTWORK toned down the gore (no more rotting meat for album covers), raised the production values, locked into a few grooves and even got a bit progressive at times, all making the record the band's paradigm shift masterpiece (think REIGH IN BLOOD, RUST IN PEACE, CHAOS A.D), a landmark platter of intelligent grind that injected new creative life into the cold and rigid blastbeats methodically machine-gunning their way out of Florida.

The follow-up, and final record for the band, SWANSONG, saw Michael Amott leaving for post-Trouble psychedelic doomsters Spiritual Beggars and then thinking man's thrashers Arch Enemy. More controversy ensued, fans crying sellout as the band bent their faces further into the winds of metal. Still, after the passage of three years, even SWANSONG is proving prophetic, causing first: post-Carcass reincarnation Blackstar (essentially the band without its figurehead Bill Steer), and second: this whole idea of big rawking mainstream metal with extreme vocals, which commands a range from Witchery (thrashy speed) to Children Of Bodom (black speed) to In Flames (SWANSONG!) So to sum up that Michael Amott continues to be an influential, catalytic force on the scene, first through Spiritual Beggars and now through Arch Enemy, along with earlier pre-Carcass stints with Carnage and Candlemass.

Carcass speaks:
Jeff Walker on the Carcass legacy . . .
"I always saw Carcass as post-death metal because for us members in Carcass, death metal was at the end of the 80's. We saw what we were doing as an extension of that. The great death metal period from about '84 to '89 was over. That's why we were never comfortable with being called death metal or grindcore because there was a time and a place for that. When you look back on it really, Carcass was nothing more than an extension of what had been going on musically since the early 80's: Motörhead, Venom, Slayer, Metallica. I'm sort of happy that we were a cult, underground band. Those who rise above the cult probably won't be around next year, our people won't care. It's better to have longevity. As far as Carcass goes, we had been going two or three years before we were written about in the press. I know full well you can have a band sell a few thousand albums and survive. We were never making a living, of course, but we were moderately successful as an underground band."

But despite the band's accomplishments as early death, early grind, early gore, and their moderate commercial exposure with this putrid brew, Carcass' main influence at this critical juncture has got to be their twilight crossover work, something with which Carcass purists would vehemently disagree, given their revolt over SWANSONG and Blackstar. But a quick survey at what writers are christening the future of metal would have to include bands like Witchery, Hypocrisy, Children Of Bodom, In Flames, Emperor, Arch Enemy, The Haunted, Amorphis, Rotting Christ, Old Man's Child, Dimmu Borgir, God Dethroned, Darkane, Soilwork, The Crown . . . all bands who take an extreme stance and then dress it up with mainstream enticements, from one side jerking the traditional metal fan into the hard darkness, while on the other side giving the purist this sliver of metal thrashing pleasure that their self-serious heavier-than-thou bands had never offered. Carcass took the heat and burned because of it, but their endgame has unwittingly become the spark of something fresh and productive.

Discography

o REEK OF PUTREFACTION (Earache, 1988)
o SYMPHONIES OF SICKNESS (Earache, 1989)
o NECROTISM — DESCANTING THE INSALUBRIOUS (Earache, 1991)
o TOOLS OF THE TRADE (Earache, 1992)
o HEARTWORK (Earache, 1993)
o SWANSONG (Earache, 1996)
o WAKE UP AND SMELL THE CARCASS (Earache, 1996)

13

Sepultura

Here's a band whose thumbprint is lightly pressed in a number of areas, adding up to an influence that forces us to look outside our borders for the greater good.

The Seps are first and foremost the band to which a whole continent pinned their metal hopes. Being the first metal band to break out of Brazil (finding US release with their second full-length SCHIZOPHRENIA in 1988), Sepultura spawned a thriving home country thrash scene, the next in line being the similar sounding Overdose, which has since spilled over into other South American countries (Chile's Criminal comes to mind) and upward into Mexico. Even as they transplanted to the sunny climes of Phoenix, Arizona, the band trumpeted their Brazilian heritage, most notably through the ROOTS record, which looked at the environmental damage being done to the Amazon rain forest and the indigenous peoples who inhabit it. Add to that an earlier body of political, economic and human rights-type lyrics, plus the whole soccer thing, and you have worthy metal ambassadors for the entire Latin American population.

Sepultura speaks:
Andreas Kisser on the making of ROOTS . . .
"ROOTS was a very conceptual album about Brazil. We really exploded in that direction, we really went deeper for the first time into percussion. We brought different people into the studio to work with us, like House Of Pain, Mike Patton, Korn so it's a very interesting album. A lot of people didn't like the mixture, but you can't please everybody (laughs.) Every album was very important at the time of release. We always conquer something new and something bigger. But ROOTS is an amazing record. All the experiments and all the experience we got from that album, learning all those new percussion instruments . . ."

On a purely musical level, the Seps were also something of the innovators, arriving quite early in the game (1984-85) with a harsh thrash intensity that was as much a product of the band's youth, inexperience and isolation as it was foresight. Nonetheless, early Sepultura products like MORBID VISIONS and SCHIZOPHRENIA were some of the fastest, thrashiest, most extreme barbs at the time, marrying the worlds of death, thrash, speed and punk with a cogent synthesis that was pure carnal energy. It was a much-needed

adrenaline rush dealt to the temples of a genre that was detectably cleaning up and become arty.

As the band's sales grew to match their critical stature (beginning with 1993's CHAOS A.D.), Andreas, Paulo and brothers Max and Igor became the ultimate back-up band firing up the crowds with their hard, utterly focused grooves, educating the masses on the plight of the world outside and below while snapping their necks in the mosh zone.

The album ROOTS caused another sort of innovative uproar. Producer Ross Robinson, fresh from work with a band called Korn (whose album was out but not yet a household name) was tapped to transform the Seps' sound. The result was a record that thrilled some while disgusting others. Full of buzzing bass, distorted samples, exotic percussion, tribal grooves and detectable nods to hip-hop, ROOTS expressed a second opinion on a sound which was about to explode. Korn would become the generic namesake for it, but the Ross Robinson sound would infect many bands coming out of South America, all the big Korn disciples of today (now including Machine Head) and, of course, Max Cavalera's successful breakaway band Soulfly.

Sepultura speaks:

Max Cavalera on Black Sabbath . . .

"I remember going through some of my father's things after he passed away and found the first Black Sabbath album in his collection. I was really young and I didn't know what it was, but I liked the cover. So I put in on it and I totally freaked out. I've been a Sabbath fan ever since."

With new vocalist Derrick Green, the Seps advanced multi-culturalism again, Derrick being black (and tall, busting through metal's shrimpy height barrier!) while also giving nod to the Japanese Kodo drum tradition. In a further crossover move, Derrick's heritage as a New York hardcore dude has somewhat reversed the world music trajectory of ROOTS and reminded Sepultura's fanbase of thrash's punk pedigree. And through Derrick, the flame of political activism flares brightly, Green's views and ethics meshing purposefully with those of his new mates and continuing the Seps' legacy of positive aggression, something sadly all too unique in the death-obsessed shock rock world of extreme music.

Sepultura speaks:

Andreas Kisser on the break with Max Cavalera . . .

"It was more the organization behind him, the management, Gloria. We never had a problem with Max on stage or writing music. The problem was the management. Things were not the way we wanted them to be, and we wanted to change them. She just wanted to have control of everything; she was supposed to work for the band, and not just one member. She wanted to dictate the rules, wanted Max to be the spokesperson for the band. And Max decided to stay with her. We did not want to have to managers, one for the band and one for Max. But she wasn't representing the band as four pieces, it was mainly Max. And he ended up probably taking more of the credit, when it was more for guys working together to put together the best records we could. Since he left the band, we haven't talked to him even once. He hasn't even spoken to his brother."

Discography
o BESTIAL DEVASTATION (Cogumelo, 1984)
o MORBID VISIONS (Cogumelo, 1985)
o SCHIZOPHRENIA (New Renaissance, 1988)
o BENEATH THE REMAINS (Roadrunner, 1989)
o ARISE (Roadrunner, 1991)
o CHAOS A.D. (Roadrunner, 1993)
o ROOTS (Roadrunner, 1996)
o BLOOD-ROOTED (Roadrunner, 1997)
o AGAINST (Roadrunner, 1998)

⟨ 14 ⟩
Alice In Chains

I really do believe grunge was of grave importance to the evolution of metal. In fact every and any of the rainbow of alternative tags owes much credence to the slo-mo medicine ball jolt to the temples that was the Seattle sound. Quite simply, grunge put the Doc Martens to a music that was getting bloated, vacuous, complacent, distant and way too glittery.

Therefore I've included Nirvana, Soundgarden and Alice In Chains in this discussion while omitting the saintly and creative masters of the form, Pearl Jam, simply on the grounds of their luxurious rock universality away from metal.

Of the big four however, Alice wouldn't fall far from the oak, looking like some sort of Northwest take on Anthrax — lots of long hair, long shorts, basically stoned and somewhat rural-minded casual wear metal dudes touring with the likes of a perplexed Van Halen. And if Nirvana could be said to have wrenched riff rock away from metal, causing, along with The Pixies and Husker Du, hard alternative or hard music (an industry-generated tag that has caught on and hung on beginning in late 1998), Alice could be said to have swung the pendulum back, metal as root, alternative creative spirit as blossom.

Alice In Chains speaks:
Jerry Cantrell about writing for himself . . .
"It's certainly different from a press-type situation, versus a kid sitting in his room with a record. A lot of different factors come in to how people view you, the slant they like to take on you. We've taken our shots you know, and we chose not to play the game, not to rebut against that. And that's our choice. Basically, I really don't give a rat's ass what anyone thinks about us other than the folks who get it and understand. And that's cool, and that's what it's supposed to be. And everybody's not supposed to like it either, which is also cool. It's all cool."

The Alice In Chains sound, at least early on, was emphatically riff-mad Jerry Cantrell churning forth with these down-tuned Sabbatherian dirges which were kicked out of bed by the rule-breaking complexity of progressive, arriving at logical discernible songs with their structural china cabinets rattled by Soundgarden's poltergeist. As with Cornell and crew, you could almost envisage the band huddled in the war room, under a single light bulb, pouring over blueprints, searching for ways to be heavy without losing their cool friends who wrote for The Rocket.

The exercise proved worthy, Alice first delivering FACELIFT, with the sledgehammer swagger of *Man In The Box* and the culvert-diameter cobra of *We Die Young*. DIRT followed with an ever so slight disarming of convention, resulting in the 7/4 VOL 4 of *Them Bones*, the heroin blues of *Rooster*, and even more meltdown hits in *Would?*, *Down In A Hole* and *Angry Chair*. As Layne Staley's drug albatross grew to Boeing proportions, recording and touring became sporadic, with the band eventually birthing like a kidney stone their self-titled third album. ALICE IN CHAINS proved to be a shaggy, dark smudge of harrowing squelched metal, once more the band finding the bravery to dump out their thoughts on a flatbed of metal scraps and let the criticism fall where it might.

> Alice In Chains speaks:
> *Jerry Cantrell on the Alice In Chains catalogue . . .*
> "Well, I'll just encompass them all, because it's a pretty general thing. I feel pretty much the same about them all. I'm proud of them all, and I think we and our songwriting grew with each one, and we had a hell of a lot of fun doing it. And for them to go on and be successful as they were and to have people enjoy them as much as they do, I mean, that's really all you can ask for. I'd say we surpassed any goal we might have had for ourselves early on. I really like the ALICE IN CHAINS record. It was raw, spontaneous. I thought that if there was any negativity views about the record, it's because we didn't tour on it (laughs.) That situation's been the case for awhile. I think that people haven't been able to find much weakness with the music so they try to disturb shit elsewhere. And I think that might be part of it. But I think it's one of our best records, very far-reaching and dark and heavy, and all the things I dig in an Alice in Chains record (laughs.)"

Worming its way through the catalogue was the dressed-down acoustic work of SAP, JAR OF FLIES and UNPLUGGED, establishing Alice as one of the forefront influences on acoustic metal, more pertinently the acoustic dirge, spawning bands like Days Of The New, Creed, and to some extent Bush and Silverchair.

However, all in all, there are few Alice In Chains clones of any importance, most lasting for one or two critically panned records and then scooting. The band's influence infects almost all of hard alternative, any of the early grunge clones (My Sister's Machine, Stone Temple Pilots, although for frig's sake, don't tell Dean that), and interestingly, much of the hardcore metal hybrids, who all seem to lead with hardcore, counter with a crystalline snort of Pantera, then finish with a handful of ludes (or worse) from Seattle's most famous medicine chests. If there was anything left after rattling back the pills, the lead singer would amble off with Layne's unwound nasal drone, which with a bit of hot-wiring, became a hybrid including the guy's own voice, Layne's, Eddie's, Kurt's and Weiland's.

> Alice In Chains speaks:
> *Jerry Cantrell on his country influence . . .*
> "I dig listening to all kinds of music. And I guess the last year, I've bought more country tapes than anything for awhile. I was raised on country music. My mother and father really enjoyed it. So I spent a lot of time listening to like Hank Williams, Merle Haggard and stuff, but I always do, and there's lots of AC/DC and Iron Maiden in my collection for that matter."

In any event, whether you were happy with the results or not (large armies of metal purists believe steadfastly that metal must ascribe to the five conventions of the Helloween accord and that's it), Alice's disheveled, stomach-rumbling, stoner metal lope has had a thick-as-a-brick effect on metal, arriving through a healthy (and unhealthy) creativity at an unquestionable heaviness that made loud guitar music cool again, something that was of purging importance to keeping wattage on the radio and on the charts through the tumultuous 90's.

Alice In Chains

Discography
- FACELIFT (Columbia, 1991)
- SAP (Columbia, 1992)
- DIRT (Columbia, 1992)
- JAR OF FLIES (Columbia, 1994)
- ALICE IN CHAINS (Columbia, 1995)
- UNPLUGGED (Columbia, 1996)
- NOTHING SAFE (Columbia, 1999)
- MUSIC BANK (Columbia, 1999)

\ 15 /

King's X

In considering the frustrating and frustrated problem child of influence, King's X is also some sort of all or nothing silent patriarch, kings of the under-rated, sentinel on a path to oblivion.

Fact is, it's a hard sell calling King's X an influence. On a purely imitative level, few have dared even think about lifting the unique flavours of this band for personal use. First off, the King's X sound is this euphoric amalgam of the melodic and the metallic. Oft described as Metallica meets the Beatles, expect to hear stunning, multi-part harmonies, wise but cryptic and enigmatic lyrics, progressive metal arrangements wholly without cliché, soulful, bluesy singing from Doug, pop vocals from Ty, alternative tunings, Hendrix-like axe solos, jazz chords and an odd Sabbatherian rumble, all wrapped up in a ball of wonder — smash anthem after smash anthem. 'Cept nothing ever gets to be the smash single it deserves to be, despite there being a half dozen tracks on every record that, if given the chance, would ingratiate their syrupy hooks so deep within the process centres that you'd start hating these guys as much as Green Day, Offspring or Creed.

King's X speaks:
Doug Pinnick on the band's unarguable legacy . . .
"Now, at this point in my life, I look back and I'm very proud of it. Because I'd be an idiot if I wasn't (laughs.) Friends, people in other bands, could not understand why I couldn't enjoy what I'd done. My life has been a great life. I've been playing music since I was 21, and I've made a living at it for twenty years and I haven't had to have a regular job, and you know, my life is great when it comes to that. I've made a decent living, I'm not rich, I'm not a millionaire, I'm not a rich rock star, but I made a decent living at it and I look back and I go 'wow, you did OK.' And the music that we made, I really think that us and Soundgarden really changed rock 'n' roll history for awhile there. We had the detuned groove going and we were kickin', and this was during the time of glam rock and stuff. I'm very proud of our accomplishments now, but back then I couldn't see it."

A potent chemistry, yet rarely imitated. You might see traces of the band's purifying ethic within the more experimental bits from Extreme (I could see Nuno leading this band) or within the heady harmonies of Saigon Kick. Closer to home, there's a modest Texas sound that has housed Galactic Cowboys and its one record predecessor The Awful Truth, as well as struggling band buds Atomic Opera. Outside of this close-knit group however, it gets hazier, while remaining of grave import.

King's X speaks:

Ty Tabor on fame and fortune . . .

"You know, it's really funny. I mean, over time at first, things like that are exciting and you say 'Oh great the critics love us' or whatever or other bands love us, and then after a few years you go, man, I wish we could fulfill this. You say, I wonder why we're not going platinum or gold or something. And then after a few years you suddenly don't care about it anymore at all. You don't even think about it. You're just happy to still be making records, and you just focus on making the best records you can, and not really worry about the sales. The truth of the matter is that we all make a very decent living. We're so lucky that we have this gig. I mean, it's bought my house that I have, and everything. It takes care of my family, and I'm allowed to write and make music, and do other albums with other people. And really King's X is responsible for that. So I don't really have a lot of disappointment or bitterness with that at all anymore. I started recognizing that I've really got it good, and that I'm doing all the things I ever dreamed about when I was a kid. And we still continue to be able to make records and go out and tour and stuff. So King's X is wherever it is, and it's not really up to us whether it ever becomes massive or not. It's up to us to be happy with the art we do and that's really all we think about at the moment. I mean, it could be worse, we could be a band that everybody hates and also hasn't made it big (laughs.) We're pretty honored by it that a lot of people love the band."

The reason that I've included the band is their following; through 400 or so interviews I've done with rock dudes, dozens upon dozens have spoken the mighty King's X name in hushed tones, many creative types citing the band as an influence more-so on gut emotional terms than with respect to anything they could possibly rip off. King's X just exist off to the side, the sun-dappled sword-in-stone demonstration of how much great art can come out of three guys, record after record, glorious chorus after chorus, few knowing however, that the band has around 300 more songs written that haven't even been used yet!

King's X speaks:

Doug Pinnick on the business of music . . .

It's probably a conglomerate of things. I think we got more than our fair shake, but I think we had certain people in key places who did not understand it. So it screwed us up in ways. Our ignorance in the business hampered a lot of the success we could have had. And from day one we were branded Christian, which has been a battle ever since. People always say, 'that's that God band, King's X.' That'll ruin you. People think you're Stryper or someone who's going to come out and preach at you. People don't want to hear religion in rock, and we got branded with that in the early days. So that screwed us up really bad. And even amongst the Christian world, we were embraced as a Christian band, so we got ridiculed. And even that world always hassled us, are we Christian, are we not? They're always debating who we are. They'd say like, 'well I saw Doug drinking and I saw Doug stoned and he's not a Christian,' and then somebody else would say, 'no, he would never do that, he's a Christian.' And somebody would write a letter and say that after the shows, 'how come you're not witnessing people and saving them, because they're going to go to hell and it's your responsibility.' And I'm looking at them and going, 'wait a minute! All I want to do is make music and make a living at it.' And people would write us and say 'your ministry has helped me so much,' and I say, 'this is not a ministry! There are no ministers here, we never said we were a ministry.' So that gave us a really hard time also. And I guess the fact that I'm black and that the rock world caters to white people — as much as I'd like to say the world isn't prejudiced, it is in some ways. I mean we're the most prejudiced country in the world and we're so oblivious to it we don't even know it. I do believe that me being the front man in a band was hard for the rock world to embrace. I even heard it. I heard about people sitting around with their friends and a video would come on, and they'd say 'man, I never knew the singer was black,' and there would almost be like a disappointment. And then there was the confusion of it, because people didn't know who was the lead singer of the band. Ty would be singing melodic, and I'd be singing this bluesy stuff. It was just too much ahead of its time or it was just too much for the world. I know that people are singing more bluesy and more melodic these days in heavy rock."

King's X

An argument can be made however, that King's X made alternative metal possible — some suggesting that the equally singular genetics of Soundgarden can be traced to the parallel development of King's X. In any event, as King's X quietly toiled from strength to strength, grunge devolved into the aimless punk pop of alternative. In a parallel universe, metal woke up to the alternative, but often found its constructs bland, counter to the Vais and Pearts and Tates on which they smacked their chops. And it isn't inconceivable that a few King's X records were heard along the way, pointing to this marriage of alternative, metal and progressive art that might serve as a blueprint for an alternative metal on metal's terms.

Discography
- OUT OF THE SILENT PLANET (Megaforce, 1988)
- GRETCHEN GOES TO NEBRASKA (Atlantic, 1989)
- FAITH HOPE LOVE (Atlantic, 1990)
- KING'S X (Atlantic, 1992)
- DOGMAN (Atlantic, 1994)
- EAR CANDY (Atlantic, 1996)
- BEST OF (Atlantic, 1997)
- TAPE HEAD (Metal Blade, 1998)
- PLEASE COME HOME . . . MR. BULBOUS (Metal Blade, 2000)

⚡ 16 ⚡

Biohazard

I'm not exactly "down for life", but I must say I got swept into Biohazard's fervent fan-fueled enthusiasm down at the first annual March Metal Meltdown in New Jersey (hail, Jack!) This band got one of the strongest responses of the festival with their mid-school hardcore mosh, especially whenever they did that jump up and down in one spot thing.

Biohazard speaks:
Evan Seinfeld on the band's lyrical attitude . . .
"Like we are about everything in everyday life, we fluctuate. We always shoot for the positive side of everything, you know, the positive light at the end of the negative tunnel, which is maybe unattainable at times. Like the song *Waiting To Die* is probably the most negative song on the album, because the song is about apathy, and our fight against it. There is no happy ending. It's like we're just spending our time, standing in line, waiting to die. There's other songs on the record that sing about negative things but try to rally everybody together in a positive way, this banding everybody together and saying 'f*** the rules'. And there's a lot of songs about inner strength, and looking inside yourself, or looking to your higher power for answers or for strength to rise above whatever brings you down."

Fact is, Brooklyn's Biohazard is considered the first word within a genre that is tall, wide and thriving — this whole hardcore crossover thing, the crossover being two-pronged, into the rap vocals of hip-hop and into the power-riffing of metal.

Hardcore itself has a long and distinguished history, but Biohazard was one of the early posses to drag it metal-ward. And along with da noise came the visuals; the tattooed, no shirt, big gut, short hair, shorts and ball cap look; the fat, bass-driven grooves and those dual incitements of war between Evan and Billy. The band raised the bar along the way with their rap collaborations (Onyx, Cypress Hill, Sticky Fingaz), Biohazard proposing the precept that what they were doing was really something akin to hardcore rap with metal riffs, the same urban violence, the same politics, the same "Biohazard from Brooklyn in your face!" gangsta stuff.

Biohazard speaks:
Bobby Hambel on Biohazard as therapy . . .
"I've been to a lot of funerals before I was 18. I'm lucky to be here and I don't know why. We learn from their mistakes. Before Biohazard came together, we were doing a lot of drugs, fighting and involved in a lot of bad, negative illegal shit. I literally believe that getting out of my neighbourhood and joining a band saved my life. The thing is that it was therapeutic. We began writing about things that were pissing us off, therefore our outlet was positive. Then we would get on stage and people would come down and we would say 'this is what this is about and if you have any feelings about it, let's dance and let's slam and let's let it out in a positive direction.' Sweating in a pit with a bunch of your boys, rather than going out and putting a gun to your head or putting a gun to somebody else's head. It all comes down to a positive outlet for all these negative emotions, all these negative fears, frustrations, anxieties and pains. If you can find a positive way to let it out today, then you've won the battles of that day."

And it's actually good for metal that Biohazard came along, for in their wake, we got a bunch of solid metal crossover acts that could have swung the other way into the commercial airhead punk of Offspring, Pennywise, D-Generation, Unwritten Law, Green Day, Rancid and The Descendents. Instead we got Earth Crisis, Vision Of Disorder, Downset, Stuck Mojo and Nothingface, while both Madball and Sick Of It All tasted and embraced the metal.

But Biohazard's influence really lies in their everyman ethic, their legendary live shows which find the band literally becoming the crowd and vice-versa. Through further inspiration as a rare major label signing in the world of hardcore, Biohazard also found themselves road rats preaching their grim street metal to fans of Sepultura, Pantera and Danzig (not to mention lots of curious Europeans), further spreading their violent, non-conformist but essentially moral gospel of anti-racism, tolerance and social activism.

Biohazard speaks:
Evan Seinfeld on the writing process of MATA LEAO . . .
"You know what? We were just all writing songs and we just did what we did. We did what we did. We had 28 songs for this record. Once we got in gear, the material just kept flowing and flowing. I mean, all of us can sing ten ways, you haven't heard half of it. We're just beginning to tap our resources. Billy and I are learning to complement each other. Soundwise, I'd say this record is the closest to what the band sounds like, if you just put us in a room and watched us play. Writing-wise, I'd say it's the same approach, very stripped down and raw. It's almost like a return to our most real shit. Not like we ever left, but sometimes things get lost in the hype of the whole thing. We wanted to have people hear all our moods. But guitar-wise, we don't have those big heavy metal sounds. That's the way our guitars sound live. We don't want to sound bigger than life. We're not like Pantera or Metallica, who have that big sound. So we have this sound man with us who captures those organic sounds and beams them out to where we are."

So Biohazard has paved a successful pathway, first into Warner, and then back down the ladder to Roadrunner, and now back up to Mercury (reuniting with producer Ed Stasium, yeah!), persistent and consistent, feeding off of their rabid cult following. Despite the slight pause in their inspiring career trajectory, any witness to the Biohazard philosophy in mid-mosh would admit that the band's utter focus, their limitless energy and their ability to project that energy into their fans no doubt caused future hardcore soldiers to take up the cause and get uh, "down for life."

Discography
o BIOHAZARD (Maze, 1990)
o URBAN DISCIPLINE (Roadrunner, 1992)
o STATE OF THE WORLD ADDRESS (Warner, 1994)
o MATA LEAO (Warner, 1996)
o NO HOLDS BARRED (Roadrunner, 1997)
o NEW WORLD DISORDER (Mercury, 1999)

Appendix I: Influence By Genre

One way to sort of summarize this whole mess is in a scholastic and over-medicated chart-like setting by looking at a genre of metal and seeing which long-haired no-goodniks invented the damn thing, who practiced it as a fresh construct, and then who drove it into the ground. What I've done instead is thrown out a sub-genre name and then simply listed a sampling of the bands in rough chronological order that led up to, through and past the genre's development and into decline (if we're at that stage yet.)

AOR
Styx, Journey, Kiss, Boston, Angel, Toto, Piper, Foreigner, 707, New England, Touch, Loverboy, Bon Jovi, 38 Special, Bryan Adams, Def Leppard, Night Ranger, Warrant

Bay Area Thrash (note: they don't have to be from Frisco)
Metallica, Megadeth, Exodus, Testament, Anthrax, Metal Church, Reverend, Sanctuary, Griffin, Death, Sadus, Overkill, Flotsam & Jetsam, Meliah Rage, Agent Steel, Vicious Rumors, Death Angel, The Organization, Liege Lord, Juggernaut, Mordred

Black Metal
Black Sabbath, Lucifer's Friend, Black Widow, Coven, Pentagram, Witchfinder General, Witchfynde, Angel Witch, Venom, Bathory, Slayer, Mercyful Fate, Hellhammer, Celtic Frost, Candlemass, Possessed, Death SS, Mayhem, Immortal, Darkthrone, Dissection, Emperor, Deicide, Morbid Angel, Enthroned, Burzum, Ulver, Samael, Moonspell, Rotting Christ, Judas Iscariot, Cradle Of Filth, Limbonic Art, Setherial, Satyricon, Old Funeral

Blues Metal
Cream, Yardbirds, Blue Cheer, Led Zeppelin, Edgar Winter, Mountain, Aerosmith, Bachman Turner Overdrive, Bad Company, ZZ Top, Status Quo, Foghat, Pat Travers, Mahogany Rush, Robin Trower, Molly Hatchet, Blackfoot, AC/DC, Angel City, Rose Tattoo, Vardis, Spider, Waysted, Great White, Whitesnake, The Four Horsemen, Black Crowes, Salty Dog, Junkyard, Jackyl, Quireboys, Badlands, Masters Of Reality, Gary Moore, Raging Slab, Brother Cane, Thunder, Cry Of Love, Jackyl, Loudmouth, Buckcherry

Death Metal
Slayer, Death, Sodom, Obituary, Carcass, Entombed, Napalm Death, Benediction, Sinister, Tiamat, At The Gates, Vader, Cryptopsy, Suffocation, Gorguts, Carnage, Unleashed, Dismember, Dissection, Edge Of Sanity, Hypocrisy, Morbid Angel, Grave, Gorefest, Deicide, Cannibal Corpse, Internal Bleeding, Morgoth, Broken Hope, Monstrosity, Six Feet Under, Deceased, Nile, Incantation, Arch Enemy, Hate Eternal, Amon Amarth, Bloodbath, Krisiun, Soilwork, Darkane, Angel Corpse

Doom Metal
Blue Cheer, Black Sabbath, Bang, Pentagram, Witchfinder General, Mercy, Trouble, Candlemass, Celtic Frost, Cathedral, Death SS, Memento Mori, Solitude Aeturnus, Paradise Lost, Crowbar, My Dying Bride, Anathema, Mindrot, Opeth, Today Is The Day, Morgion, Soilent Green

Funk / Rap Metal
Aerosmith, Beastie Boys, Red Hot Chili Peppers, Dan Reed Network, Living Colour, Faith No More, Fishbone, Extreme, T-Ride, Infectious Grooves, Clawfinger, Rage Against The Machine, 311, Korn, Incubus, Powerman 5000, Orange 9mm, Sugar Ray, Limp Bizkit, Godsmack, Machine Head, Slipknot, Kid Rock, P.O.D.

Glam
T. Rex, Mott The Hoople, Slade, Sweet, Queen, Alice Cooper, Kiss, Angel, Hanoi Rocks, Mötley Crüe, Wrathchild, Twisted Sister, Roxx Gang, Nitro, Poison, Cinderella, Trixter, Wildhearts, Dogs D'Amour

Gothic Metal
Black Sabbath, Joy Division, The Cure, Bauhaus, Cramps, Christian Death, Sisters Of Mercy, Nick Cave, The Mission, The Cult, My Dying Bride, Type O Negative, Paradise Lost, Anathema, Tiamat, Amorphis, Sentenced, Opeth, Dark Seed, Moonspell, The Gathering, Therion, The Tea Party, Theatre Of Tragedy, Aeturnus, Evergrey, Tristania, Katatonia, Babylon Whores

Grunge
MC5, Blue Cheer, The Stooges, The New York Dolls, Black Sabbath, Led Zeppelin, Sex Pistols, Dictators, The Damned, The Ramones, The Dead Boys, Black Flag, Angry Samoans, The Fastbacks, Dwarves, Wipers, Slow, Bullet Lavolta, Big Chief, Dinosaur Jr, Melvins, Green River, Soundgarden, Nirvana, Mother Love Bone, Sons Of Freedom, The Fluid, Swallow, Alice In Chains, Gruntruck, Temple Of The Dog, Skinyard, My Sister's Machine, Jerry Cantrell, Mad Season, Pearl Jam, Smashing Pumpkins, Stone Temple Pilots, Tool, Bush, Silverchair, Everclear, Creed, Lit

Hair Metal
Led Zeppelin, Aerosmith, Loverboy, Kiss, Def Leppard, Quiet Riot, Ratt, House Of Lords, Guns N' Roses, Warrant, Winger, Mötley Crüe, Whitesnake, Bon Jovi, David Lee Roth, Mr. Big, Dokken, Europe, Cinderella, Lita Ford, White Lion, Shark Island, Cold Sweat, Britny Fox, Thunder, XYZ, Kik Tracee, Tesla, Tora Tora, Blackeyed Susan, Tattoo Rodeo, Lillian Axe, Slaughter, Danger Danger, Tyketto

Hardcore / Punk Crossover
MC5, The Stooges, The Damned, The Drones, The Vibrators, The Dead Boys, The Ramones, The Saints, The Sex Pistols, DOA, Dead Kennedys, UK Subs, Black Flag, Misfits, Bad Brains, Husker Du, Cro-Mags, Agnostic Front, GBH, MOD, DRI, Sacred Reich, Anthrax, Rollins Band, Suicidal Tendencies, Pro-Pain, Madball, Biohazard, Earth Crisis, Downset, Vision Of Disorder, Nothingface, Stuck Mojo, Turmoil, Snapcase, Hatebreed

Industrial Metal

Killing Joke, Ministry, Nine Inch Nails, White Zombie, Skrew, Bile, Godflesh, Pitch Shifter, Prong, Monster Voodoo Machine, Stabbing Westward, Filter, Fear Factory, Sevendust, Econoline Crush, Two, Dink, Prick, Marilyn Manson, Rob Zombie, Orange 9MM, Godsmack, Static X, Dope, Apollyon Sun

NWOBHM

Quartz, Motörhead, Saxon, Tank, Iron Maiden, Girlschool, Def Leppard, Holocaust, Diamond Head, Angel Witch, Samson, Tysondog, Avenger, Battleaxe, Buffalo, Chinatown, Bitches Sin, Witchfynde, Witchfinder General, Trespass, Sweet Savage, Satan, Blitzkrieg, Venom, Raven, Tygers Of Pan Tang, More, Jaguar, Ghengis Khan, Tokyo Blade, Savage, Darkstar, White Spirit, Vardis, Gillan, Warfare, Grim Reaper, Chateaux, Fist, Gaskin, Spartan Warrior, Ethel The Frog, Wildfire, Grand Prix, Cloven Hoof, Silverwing, Spider, Black Rose, Shiva, Praying Mantis, Dedringer, Demon, Geddes Axe, Dumpy's Rusty's Nuts, Legend

Power Metal

Deep Purple, Judas Priest, Rainbow, Scorpions, Riot, Dio, Black Sabbath, Iron Maiden, Saxon, Ozzy Osbourne, Accept, Helstar, Liege Lord, Warlord, Agent Steel, Michael Schenker Group, Yngwie Malmsteen, Savatage, Helloween, Jag Panzer, Manowar, Mercyful Fate, King Diamond, Grave Digger, U.D.O., Rage, Running Wild, Sinner, Loudness, Heaven's Gate, Pink Cream 69, Virgin Steele, Riot, Artension, Iron Savior, Angel Dust, ADX, Killers, Hammerfall, In Flames, Sacred Steel, Pegazus, Nocturnal Rites, Steel Prophet, Pain Of Salvation, Eidolon, Mob Rules, Gothic Knights, Labyrinth, Demons & Wizards, D.C. Cooper, Jacobs Dream, Millenium

Progressive Metal

Led Zeppelin, Rush, Kansas, Jethro Tull, Uriah Heep, Triumph, Queensryche, Nightwing, Marillion, Pallas, Fates Warning, Warlord, Savatage, King's X, Saigon Kick, Voivod, Watchtower, Atheist, Angra, Blind Guardian, Stratovarius, Iced Earth, Nevermore, Virgin Steele, King Diamond, Morgana Lefay, Tad Morose, Meshuggah, Shadow Gallery, Magellan, Artension, Royal Hunt, Platypus, Tiles, Elegy, Kamelot, Ice Age, Destiny's End, Spock's Beard, Narnia, Under The Sun, Pain Of Salvation, Vanden Plas, Mastermind, Digital Ruin

70's Metal

Black Sabbath, Led Zeppelin, Deep Purple, The Stooges, Uriah Heep, New Trolls, RDM, Strawberry Path, Head Machine, Troika, Buffalo, November, German Oak, Andromeda, Human Beast, God Bless, Blue Cheer, Sir Lord Baltimore, Bang, Budgie, Hawkwind, Pink Fairies, Queen, Thin Lizzy, Montrose, Judas Priest, UFO, Mahogany Rush, Pat Travers, Aerosmith, Kiss, Nazareth, Status Quo, Scorpions, Rex, Rush, Sweet, Runaways, Rainbow, Ted Nugent, Angel, Starz, Riot, Legs Diamond, Y&T, Ram Jam, Triumph, Moxy, Goddo, Teaze, Van Halen

Shock Rock

Little Richard, Arthur Brown, Screaming Lord Sutch, Coven, Alice Cooper, Kiss, Mötley Crüe, WASP, Ozzy Osbourne, Iron Maiden, Twisted Sister, White Zombie, Gwar, Marilyn Manson, Coal Chamber, In Extremo, Rammstein, Rob Zombie, Slipknot

Sleaze Metal
The Stooges, Aerosmith, New York Dolls, Mötley Crüe, Hanoi Rocks, Wrathchild, Guns N' Roses, L.A. Guns, Cinderella, Keel, Seahags, Vain, Bang Tango, Skid Row, Love / Hate, Buckcherry

Speed Metal
Judas Priest, Motörhead, Metallica, Slayer, Iron Maiden, Grave Digger, Helloween, Coroner, Rage, Annihilator, Exciter, Virgin Steele, At The Gates, Witchery, Angra, Gamma Ray, Blind Guardian, Stratovarius, Hammerfall, Primal Fear

Stoner Rock
Blue Cheer, MC5, Black Sabbath, Bang, Hawkwind, Witchfinder General, Trouble, Black Flag, Cathedral, The Obsessed, Pentagram, Saint Vitus, Count Raven, Kyuss, Crowbar, Eyehategod, Fu Manchu, Acrimony, Monster Magnet, Lake Of Tears, Sleep, Tiamat, The Gathering, Sons Of Otis, Queens Of The Stone Age, Sheavy, Orange Goblin, Transport League, Spiritual Beggars, Spirit Caravan, Terra Firma, Roadsaw, Mammoth

Thrash
Venom, Warfare, Metallica, Slayer, Exodus, Sadus, Heathen, Testament, Exciter, Annihilator, Anvil, Voivod, Grave Digger, Running Wild, Pile Driver, Possessed, Destruction, Sodom, Kreator, Sepultura, Coroner, Deathrow, Tankard, At The Gates, Napalm Death

White Metal
Trouble, Petra, Stryper, Stryken, Salem Travellers, Mass, Fierce Heart, AD, Guardian, Tempest, Whitecross, Force Three, Neon Cross, Rosanna's Raiders, King's X, Jerusalem, Barren Cross, Mortification, Tourniquet, Paramecium, Narnia, P.O.D.

Appendix II: 15 Amazing Bands Too Unique To Make The List

Here's a list devised and deviated simply to give large hails to some great bands that were just too singular, complicated, strange and genius to cause trends or individual imitators. Basically at the top nubbin of the "don't try this at home" concept, the following folk burned any bridges behind their butts by being too good and too unique. Note: this is not to say bands that made the cut were not equally unique (Led Zeppelin and Sabbath are good examples of this.) But for a band to make the cut, they had to cause some sort of large direct result through something they did, even if it was throwing TVs out of hotel windows or punching each other black and blue on stage. The bands listed below just "exist", causing few and even no clones or sounds in their wake, no school, no genre, no offspring. And for that reason, they're all among my favourites of all time.

Budgie

The band's 1971 debut is very early, very heavy metal, a type of thick ostrich-skulled throb that's as absurdist as it is Sabbatherian. Many classics along the way, but too looped for anyone to ever follow. Great, but of no direct influence, save for those famous Metallica covers, and their mild, passing importance to purveyors of the NWOBHM.

Status Quo

Quo influenced Vardis and Spider, but this whole thousand ways to boogie thing was just too weird. Outside of these bands, it's addressed only vaguely within the hallowed warm beer canon of AC/DC. It was a considerable hard rock assortment by the mid-70's however, which then descended into double and triple parody, irony and novelty.

Uriah Heep

Their 1970 debut beats the metal quo of Sabbath I, but not that of Paranoid. A strange proggy metal band who embraced and then discarded so many styles that nobody could or would dare to follow the instructions. Often deemed a poor man's Purple for their axe and keyboard alloys, Heep trundle on to this day, led by the enthusiasm of vocalist Bernie Shaw and the sagey, new agey pubbiness of one irrepressible Mick Box.

Foghat

Like Quo, Foghat was a spiffy boogie band that crossed over into metal. Few followed their path, especially come their pop boogie coffin nails of the early 80's. Note: Feb. 2000 and leading light Dave Peverett is now deceased from cancer. Sadly missed, for no-one could brighten an already bright summer day like Foghat with a full head of steam.

Nazareth

Of grave metal influence with their third, fourth, fifth and sixth records, Nazareth decided to pass on Roger Glover's advice and pursue a non-metal muse, casting them into an obscurity that exists to this day. Likely over with, as the business brains behind the band, Darrell Sweet, is now deceased.

Max Webster
One of my favourite bands ever, Max Webster was a prog pop metal legend from Toronto with smart, smarmy and wise lyrics from non-performing band member Pye Dubios and slinky ironic post-metal leads from my second fave guitarist of all time, Kim Mitchell. Considered a poor man's Rush with a Zappa cackle and a big beefy Beefheart. Kim Mitchell's solo material is hit-and-miss due to large stylistic swings, but Pye's lyrics, although toned down, are on most of it and Kim's solos are as graceful, composed and fatherly as ever.

Blue Öyster Cult
My favourite lyrics of all time and a plethora of intelligent, intellectual styles. With warm, traditional axework from Buck and smooth harmonies, it's the best pop metal in the biz. The riff rockers rule too. One of my top four or five fave acts ever.

Manowar
Here's another band nobody dared to follow. Manowar constructed their own recording techniques, arrangements, even their own metaller-than-thou language. Viking themes, biker themes, you name it, Manowar did it first and best. Hammerfall and Virgin Steele sorta carry the torch, but with thinner arms.

Love / Hate
Mensa-like sleaze metal if you can believe it, especially on their second album WASTED IN AMERICA. History will slot these guys up the pay scale, you just watch. As my buddy Michael Hannon puts it: Jizzy Pearl is Jim Morrison.

Pearl Jam
Responsible for my fave album of the 90's (VS.), Pearl Jam are the most talented of the grungsters, but just a bit too unique and a bit too non-metal to make the grade. They do have many imitators, but none of them are really metal either. It goes Beatles, Zeppelin, U2, Pearl Jam. Really.

Corrosion Of Conformity
A unique and potent brew that's equal parts Sabbath, Metallica and grunge with a buckshot of the south's nasty Nola anti-sound. Pepper and Co. are responsible for two of my favourite albums of the 90's, DELIVERANCE and WISEBLOOD, and for that I thank their way-too-cool-for-metal metal hearts.

Therion
Another well-regarded stand-alone type band — dark, gothic metal mixed with classical music and opera. Just don't call it Wagnerian. Christofer was always a weirdo, but the earlier stuff is a little blacker and deathier compared to his truly committed strings, woodwinds and brass conundrums of new.

My Dying Bride
Actually quite influential really, My Dying Bride are pioneers in slow, crushing gothic depression, not to mention the use of violins and female vocals. Yet to put out a bum album, Aaron and Co. have slipped from the limelight, only to abstractly climb the rungs of critical acclaim.

Amorphis
One of my current faves, Amorphis come from fantasia-like Finnish death metal but now play a kind of imaginative snow-smothered prog metal that can only hail from the gray North.

Hypocrisy
Probably my favourite band right now, Hypocrisy started mixed up in death, thrash and black, but as of late are building songs that are dirty, powerful, extreme but at the heart, strangely old-school. Peter Tagtgren is of course now more known for his prolific production credits amongst the pantheon of black and post-black metallists.

Appendix III: 25 "Almosts"

Here's a roughly chronological list of 20 bands that made my short list, with a few comments on why they matter plus, on occasion, a few comments on why they didn't matter enough to make the grade. Just wanted you to know I was paying attention, agonizing over who to write up in full and distressed at who I had to drop. Consider this a hail to the 51st through 70th most influential metal bands of all time.

Blue Cheer
Probably the apex of the "almosts", Blue Cheer didn't make it because of their casual, stumbling, accidental discovery of metal. But hot damn, they were heavy, and heavy very early, cranking out no less that four hot slabs by early 1970. I also didn't include them because they were sadly quite overlooked, really not influencing many in great drabs, although their presence within metal, grunge, punk and stoner music is palpable, at least among the true scholars deep inside the genres. Kind of a thickening of The Who or at least the idea of Keith Moon.

MC5
Three records, with only the first, KICK OUT THE JAMS mattering a whole lot. Heavy and heavy early, this live firecracker is a chilling look at the 60's gone dark and violent, and a cornerstone of a regional (Detroit) scene which produced much lysergic power chord drip-droppings.

The Runaways
They sucked, but they were the first properly heavy girl band. So I was going to do this whole girl power essay around 'em, but there just wasn't enough substance there, nor in the band's derivatives Pat Benatar, Joan Jett, Girlschool, Rock Goddess, L7 or Hole. Kittie just might save the day though.

Sex Pistols
NEVER MIND THE BOLLOCKS is the best punk album ever, one that had an effect on many metal bands, evidenced by all the novelty covers throughout the years. But one record wasn't enough to stick 'em in, especially when it wasn't a metal record as such.

Ramones
The Ramones were the Motörhead of punk, churning out a constant, even-keeled wave of power chords record after dead identical record, and for that they must be hailed. Many a metal dude was inspired by the band because of their unswerving belief in tuneful but heavy punk pop. And indeed they were the first heavy US punk band, quickly followed by the Dead Boys.

Riot
Riot rocked hard and early, best loved for 1979's NARITA and 1981's FIRE DOWN UNDER. But then there were the bluesy Rhett years, the experimental CBS years, and now Riot is one of the more prolific, though still only moderately enjoyed, power / speed / prog metal acts. The crucial influence however, remains with the early work, and although important, Riot wasn't one of the biggies.

Anvil
Definitely an influence on the whole thrash / speed metal scene, Anvil actually had a big effect on both Metallica and Pantera. But their influence was split among home country brethren Exciter and Razor plus the entire NWOBHM. And then quickly thereafter there were the big four who continued the damage wrought by Lips and Co.

Saxon
Here's another band that was close but no cigar, Saxon being this moderately revered band with a spotty catalogue. The classics are WHEELS OF STEEL and POWER & THE GLORY, but much of the rest eroded their place high up the chart. Just kind of there, Saxon are seeing a revival among the 80's power metal gang with fetchingly competent albums in the late 90's.

Fate's Warning
In the prog world, there was Rush and then for the longest time, pretty much Queensryche and Fate's Warning. But although there is a mountain of high-minded prog metal mania here, sadly few cite the band as a big influence.

Accept
Accept almost slid in on the robe-tails of Ozzy and Dio, being somewhat that kind of traditional power metal influence. But they just weren't big enough for long enough. U.D.O. owns the other half of the Accept catalogue, so in essence, there is much by-the-book material when you combine the two riff-grooved bodies of work.

Mötley Crüe
Not saying they're smart or anything, but these accidental lobotomies almost fit on the "too unique" list, with very few following their drippy, clogged thunk metal sound, more a casual mix of glam and black leather. But you gotta call them an inspiration, especially with their semi-thriving presence and good records late into the 90's. Drop-dead fun, fun, fun live too.

Trouble
One of my fave acts of all time, Trouble was the best stoner / doom rockers on the planet. But their schtick was too intense to cause much imitation. Today's stoner rockers are more into the Sabbath via Cathedral thing, something which another close "almost" dug under more studiously, those Swede caveboys, Candlemass.

Megadeth
Almost made the top 50, until I realized that few ever followed that closely any component of the Megadeth sound, although RUST IN PEACE is a huge milestone in Bay Area thrash. The early sound was just weird. And the later sound was so unique to the band that Megadeth's main influence comes from their fame, the fact that CRYPTIC WRITINGS was one of metal's surprise best sellers in the late 90's, and the more tuneful and mainstream RISK from 1999 also pushed brisk sales.

Voivod
Christofer from Therion worships them, so they gotta be good, as does Jason from Metallica who squeezes in recording time with Michel whenever he's allowed. Rural Quebec's Voivod have long been lauded as thinking man's thrashers, injecting high science into both their music and their word. To my mind, this is the predecessor of both Hypocrisy and Satyricon, even if, incredibly, Peter Tagtgren doesn't know 'em.

Napalm Death
Along with Carcass and Entombed, Napalm Death were the fathers of grindcore, a big part of death metal, and early on, casual proponents of Relapse-style white noise. But the later material is too unique to the band, influencing no one, indeed kind of reviled, revered and, through the ironic fault of too much good product, ignored.

Dream Theater
And after Rush, Queensryche and Fate's Warning came Dream Theater. So you see the problem. We're already four deep into the genre, although Dream Theater are certainly the modern elders of prog metal, really the closest thing to the European sound that exists today. These guys are a pretty strong "almost", given their increasingly regal stature after ten years at the prog tailpipe.

Death
Chuck Schuldiner and crew are pretty important (I now liken their legacy to that of At The Gates and Carcass), but it's an underground thing, and one that fragments to all sorts of influences, maybe the biggest umbrella being Slayer.

At The Gates
History is re-writing these speedsters into the pantheon of the greats affecting much of what we hear as the Gothenburg sound and beyond. At The Gates was essentially the Soundgarden of Swedish death, throwing in meaningful chunks of prog, speed, death and black to create a brew that's hip today.

Entombed
The original monsters of "death rock", Entombed was the ones who injected a bit of groove into death metal, inventing an extremely volatile mixture that unknowingly captured the magic of heavy grunge. Plus before this WOLVERINE BLUES sound, they were a large part of the invention of pure Swedish death.

Dismember
While Entombed wandered, Dismember were quietly (and to little acclaim) flying the flag of gutted, brutal Swedish death, building a catalogue that's now central to the story, despite derision along the way as a baby Entombed. 1999's HATE CAMPAIGN demonstrates that the band's deafeningly clanky metal magic was no fluke.

Monster Magnet
Dave Wyndorf and crew get a mighty hail for being stoner rock when it wasn't cool, finally breaking in a big way with 1998's POWERTRIP, becoming the object of jealousies within the form because of it, and finding themselves dropped from most stoner rock discussions while a younger generation sets in.

The Gathering
Influential as one of the first to go mellow, electronic and trip-hoppy, as well as one of the first to feature female vocals prominently under the dreamy doom death blanket of metal. Next up: Theatre Of Tragedy.

Cradle Of Filth
Place with Dimmu Borgir and Children Of Bodom as the flash within black metal, the palatable derivatives of the first wave, any one of the three possibly breaking on a moderate level. Imperious imp Dani is starting to get on everyone's nerves though, even if I think he's pretty funny. Nick don't think so. Anyway, Satyricon deserves to trounce all these studied fashion plates.

Hammerfall
Basically the first name in modern power metal, Hammerfall is the closest thing to a straight 80's retro band we've got, especially when looking at fame, exposure, and pancakes sold. Too much the novelty act for my liking, grumbles are starting to be uttered, along with similar derision for Primal Fear.

Coal Chamber
Too early to tell, but Coal Chamber are probably some sort of leaders or influencers, combining this Korn sound with Manson theatrics into a thing called spookycore. Slipknot usurped them in 1999 as the big nutters to watch, but Coal Chamber, in the hyper-compressed culture-watch of the internet age, are already being seen as wise forefathers of the scene.

Appendix IV: Heavy Metal's Top 100 Most Influential Albums Of All Time

It's no surprise you'll see the top bands represented in spades. But this serves two purposes. First, you'll see the classic albums within those bands that lit the fire of the larger abstraction. And second, you'll see a few albums that meant something by bands who didn't kick up enough leather-booted fuss to make the hallowed cut. Another funny thing is that in doing this gosh-forsaken exercise, I found that there are influential bands that have their importance spread over two or three platters; for example, acts like Candlemass, Carcass, Cathedral, Enslaved, Entombed, Helloween, Hypocrisy, Iced Earth, Judas Priest, Kyuss, Overkill, Savatage, Testament and Trouble, some of which tip to inclusion on the master list, some of which don't. I've left this chronological (as opposed to ranked) for the following reasons: 1) the smaller the artistic entity examined, the bigger the opportunity for bias. It's like ranking songs, or your children for that matter. 2) As a chronology, you get a nice survey of highlights as they occur in time. Anyway, come an' get all misty-eyed with me . . .

The 70's
- Blue Cheer — VINCEBUS ERUPTUM (1967)
- MC5 — KICK OUT THE JAMS (1968)
- The Stooges — THE STOOGES (1969)
- Led Zeppelin — I (1969)
- Led Zeppelin — II (1969)
- Black Sabbath — BLACK SABBATH (1970)
- Uriah Heep — VERY 'EAVY VERY 'UMBLE (1970)
- Deep Purple — IN ROCK (1970)
- Led Zeppelin — IV (1970)
- Black Sabbath — PARANOID (1970)
- Nazareth — RAZAMANAZ (1972)
- Deep Purple — MACHINE HEAD (1972)
- Alice Cooper — SCHOOL'S OUT (1972)
- Iggy And The Stooges — RAW POWER (1973)
- Queen — QUEEN (1973)
- Montrose — MONTROSE (1973)
- The Sweet — DESOLATION ANGELS (1975)
- Kiss — ALIVE! (1975)
- Aerosmith — ROCKS (1976)
- Rush — 2112 (1976)
- Rainbow — RISING (1976)
- Kiss — DESTROYER (1976)
- Thin Lizzy — JAILBREAK (1976)

o Judas Priest — SAD WINGS OF DESTINY (1976)
o Ted Nugent — FREE FOR ALL (1976)
o Sex Pistols — NEVER MIND THE BOLLOCKS (1977)
o UFO — LIGHTS OUT (1977)
o Judas Priest — SIN AFTER SIN (1977)
o Scorpions — TAKEN BY FORCE (1978)
o Judas Priest — STAINED CLASS (1978)
o AC/DC — HIGHWAY TO HELL (1978)
o Van Halen — VAN HALEN (1978)

The 80's
o Iron Maiden — IRON MAIDEN (1980)
o AC/DC — BACK IN BLACK (1980)
o Angel Witch — ANGEL WITCH (1980)
o Motörhead — ACE OF SPADES (1980)
o Judas Priest — BRITISH STEEL (1980)
o Ozzy Osbourne — DIARY OF A MADMAN (1981)
o Rush — MOVING PICTURES (1981)
o Anvil — METAL ON METAL (1982)
o Venom — BLACK METAL (1982)
o Scorpions — BLACKOUT (1982)
o Iron Maiden — NUMBER OF THE BEAST (1982)
o Accept — RESTLESS & WILD (1983)
o Mercyful Fate — MELISSA (1983)
o Slayer — SHOW NO MERCY (1983)
o Savatage — SIRENS (1983)
o Metallica — KILL 'EM ALL (1983)
o Mötley Crüe — SHOUT AT THE DEVIL (1983)
o Def Leppard — PYROMANIA (1983)
o Van Halen — 1984 (1983)
o Metallica — RIDE THE LIGHTNING (1984)
o Exciter — VIOLENCE & FORCE (1984)
o Celtic Frost — TO MEGA THERION (1985)
o Stormtroopers Of Death — SPEAK ENGLISH OR DIE (1985)
o Yngwie Malmsteen's Rising Force — MARCHING OUT (1985)
o Exodus — BONDED BY BLOOD (1985)
o Slayer — REIGN IN BLOOD (1986)
o Guns N' Roses — APPETITE FOR DESTRUCTION (1988)
o Queensryche — OPERATION: MINDCRIME (1988)
o Jane's Addiction — NOTHING'S SHOCKING (1988)
o Faith No More — THE REAL THING (1989)

The 90's

- ° Pantera — COWBOYS FROM HELL (1990)
- ° Megadeth — RUST IN PEACE (1990)
- ° Obituary — CAUSE OF DEATH (1990)
- ° Nirvana — NEVERMIND (1991)
- ° Savatage — STREETS: A ROCK OPERA (1991)
- ° Ministry — PSALM 69 (1992)
- ° Nine Inch Nails — BROKEN (1992)
- ° Dream Theater — IMAGES AND WORDS (1992)
- ° Biohazard — URBAN DISCIPLINE (1992)
- ° Alice In Chains — DIRT (1992)
- ° Kyuss — BLUES FOR THE RED SUN (1992)
- ° Stone Temple Pilots — CORE (1992)
- ° Rage Against The Machine — RAGE AGAINST THE MACHINE (1992)
- ° White Zombie — LA SEXORCISTO: DEVIL MUSIC VOL. I (1992)
- ° Tool — UNDERTOW (1993)
- ° Cathedral — THE ETHEREAL MIRROR (1993)
- ° Entombed — WOLVERINE BLUES (1993)
- ° Sepultura — CHAOS A.D. (1993)
- ° My Dying Bride — TURN LOOSE THE SWANS (1993)
- ° Korn — KORN (1994)
- ° Mayhem — DE MYSTERIIS DOM SATHANAS (1994)
- ° Burzum — DET SOM ENGANG VAR (1994)
- ° Meshuggah — NONE (1994)
- ° Cannibal Corpse — THE BLEEDING (1994)
- ° Opeth — ORCHID (1995)
- ° Emperor — IN THE NIGHTSIDE ECLIPSE (1995)
- ° Dissection — STORM OF THE LIGHT'S BANE (1995)
- ° The Gathering — MANDYLION (1995)
- ° Arcturus — ASPERA HIEMS SYMFONIA (1996)
- ° Therion — THELI (1996)
- ° In Flames — THE JESTER RACE (1996)
- ° Marilyn Manson — ANTICHRIST SUPERSTAR (1996)
- ° Coal Chamber — COAL CHAMBER (1997)
- ° Hammerfall — GLORY TO THE BRAVE (1997)
- ° Children Of Bodom — SOMETHING WILD (1998)
- ° Monster Magnet — POWERTRIP (1998)
- ° Witchery — RESTLESS & DEAD (1998)
- ° Slipknot — SLIPKNOT (1999)

Appendix V: Who Influenced The Influencers? – The Pre-History Of Metal

You can be really crazy about this and go back to the birth of music. You could cite the ominous tones of Gregorian chanting. You could take the lead from Ritchie and Yngwie and go back to Bach, Beethoven, or Paganini (the original crossroads guy who apparently sold his soul to the devil for talent.)

Then there's the birth of the blues and blues guitar, the biggest guy mentioned being Robert Johnson, the man in the middle of the most enduring Faustian rock and roll tale. Johnson reputedly met the devil down at the crossroads and worked out a pact for fortune and fame. Other's that led to Zeppelin include John Lee Hooker, Elmore James, and of course, Howlin' Wolf.

Skip forward, and you've got smatterings of 50's influences, the main ones mentioned being Chuck Berry, Eddie Cochran, Link Wray and Buddy Holly's *Not Fade Away*, while the idea of Elvis and his pelvis brought sexual tension back into the fraught fray.

Into the 60's and you've got the very idea of The Beatles, the first earth-shattering fanatical rock and roll extravaganza, one of the biggest, if not the biggest, influence on future musicians in any genre (more on these guys later.) Next up would be the smattering of fledgling riff rockers: *My Generation* and *I Can't Explain* from The Who, *You Really Got Me* and *All Day And All Of The Night* from The Kinks, plus *Satisfaction* and *Paint It Black* from The Rolling Stones. Then there's the seminal garage chord progressions which would come from *Wild Thing* and *Louie Louie*. But remember The Beatles? My vote goes to them for the first "modern" heavy metal song of all time, *Helter Skelter*, with its Sabbatherian plod, its reduced reliance on the blues, its dive-bombing licks, and its new brash guitar sound. That record ("The White Album") also had semi-heavies *Back In The USSR* and *Everybody's Got Something To Hide Except Me And My Monkey*.

But by then the hippie revolution had taken hold, beginning in San Francisco and spreading to influential rock zones like Detroit and then fab London. One of the first and most metallic of the bunch was Jimi Hendrix (a Seattle native who had relocated to London), who is perhaps the biggest guitar influence of all time. Jimi smashed the rule books and harnessed the potential of electrics, letting out like a yowling cat and mesmerizing with his inverted, left-handed flying fretwork. The focal point here was *Purple Haze*, secondary status ascribed to *Foxy Lady*.

Cream was a logical extension, the power trio, although the band's hard rock was still a dated fog built of hippie conventions chafed against the blues, amps turned up but no really new ideas (*Spoonful, Strange Brew, White Room, Sunshine Of Your Love, Tales Of Brave Ulysses*: yawn.) Elsewhere, we had The Yardbirds, Vanilla Fudge, Dutchmen Golden

Earring (who reach back to 1965!), and Iron Butterfly, who fall within that whole crossover thing called "heavy psyche" (ergo, Sandy Pearlman even associates the idea of metal with The Byrds, not to mention the medieval philosophical art of alchemy!) So in the late 60's, you get a real blurring of loud, untold, unharnessed abrasion within this psyche genre, as well as that whole "heavy blues" mudhole that began in earnest with the British Invasion, and its late trinity of guitarists: Beck, Clapton and Page, who together spawned the idea of guitar heroes.

It's of note that the term "heavy metal" is something attributed to beat author William Burroughs, or to Steppenwolf's *Born To Be Wild* ("Heavy metal thunder" referring to the roar of motorcycles), or to noted deceased rock critic Lester Bangs ascribing the Burroughs term to his favourite new music.

Finally, before we really kick into it, you've got Blue Cheer, MC5 and The Stooges, all doing their business around 1968 and 69, three that really made a pre-difference. Other early fringe practitioners we've left out of the Top 50 list would include Ted's old fruitcakes the Amboy Dukes, Psyche Alice, Purple and Quo, Ten Years After, Troika, Necromandis (produced by Tony Iommi), RDM, Human Beast, Andromeda, Clear Blue Sky, Head Machine, Dschinn, Stray, Groundhogs, German Oak, Hell Preachers Inc., Iron Maiden (different band), Spirit Of Christmas (Rush-type prog metal before Rush), God Bless (from Indonesia), Strawberry Path, Murasaki (competent Deep Purple clones from Japan), Tea, Mountain, Atomic Rooster, Grand Funk Railroad, Brownsville Station, Third World War, Free, Mountain, Bloodrock, Germany's Tiger B. Smith, Lucifer's Friend, Buddy Guy, Tear Gas, Germany's Birth Control, Black Oak Arkansas, ZZ Top, Stone The Crows, The Who, Rory Gallagher's Taste (and mid to late Rory for that matter), Pot Liquor, Wild Turkey, Juicy Lucy, Australia's Buffalo and Buster Brown, Bull Angus, Cactus, Savoy Brown, Three Man Army, Thundermug, Skin Alley, Spooky Tooth, Steamhammer, Budgie, Edgar Winter, Mott The Hoople, Bang, Sir Lord Baltimore, April Wine, Bachman Turner Overdrive, Brave Belt and the occasional Guess Who, Tempest, Captain Beyond and Dust.

But keeping it in perspective, and focusing on the crucial and substantial, the real history of metal begins with Sabbath, Purple's IN ROCK and maybe the first Heep; stateside, Stooges and The MC5. Next question?

Appendix VI: Influence Equals Tribute – The Top 15 Tribute Albums Of All Time

Well, I really don't know how you measure something like this. There's the obvious situation where a crappy band plays it straight, plowing through the track with little imagination or variation, and is unarguably deficient, bad vocals, bad production, etc. Enough of these, and you just have a bad tribute record. But then personal taste kicks in. Some find a complete deconstruction of a song blasphemy. Others find it refreshing and innovative. Others claim to be able to spot seasoned pros merely sleepwalking through the job, a touchy area where the artistry or lack thereof becomes subjective. Others want to hear something as uncannily close to the original as possible, like it's some sort of archaeological reconstruction. Others are just listening to the wrong band doing it, the wrong band being tributized, or a track that is just too over-exposed, all turn-offs which happen likely for the wrong reasons. I guess one of my favourite things is when a band can repossess the track and make it sound like one of their own signature tunes. Oh, whatever, here's some good ones anyway, in chronological order.

By the way, just a few trivia notes. The Venom Tribute, IN THE NAME OF SATAN, is another highly regarded album, featuring the likes of Forbidden, Skyclad and Voivod. High up the tribute list are Motörhead and Maiden, with about six each as of late 1999 (including a Korean look at Metallica!) Other interesting tribute ideas include Yngwie Malmsteen's Inspiration album of covers, Tom Angelripper's beer drinking songs album, Metallica's GARAGE DAYS and GARAGE INC. covers albums (probably the biggest selling tribute work of all time), the rare FUNKY JUNCTION TRIBUTE TO DEEP PURPLE done by Thin Lizzy guys in the early 70's, live Zep tributes by both Great White and Bonzo's son Jason, shredder Paul Gilbert's Hendrix tribute, and Helloween's METAL JUKEBOX, which is a similar idea to Yngwie's INSPIRATION. Folks are also raving about a Maiden spread including DiAnno and a bunch of NWOBHM folk.

Honourable mentions: A BLACK MARK TRIBUTE VOL. II (more of the same weird song choices), BLACK NIGHT: DEEP PURPLE TRIBUTE ACCORDING TO NEW YORK (gets the funk out!) and an early Dwell Records tribute, before they became an assembly line, their first of two Maiden tributes thus far, entitled A CALL TO IRONS (featuring Morgion, Steel Prophet, Angel Corpse, Absu and the greatest new band in all the lands, Opeth.) So right, here you go . . .

○ **MASTERS OF MISERY - BLACK SABBATH: THE EARACHE TRIBUTE** (1992)
Certainly one of the earliest metal tribute albums, this one gathers all the shaggy Earache noiseniks and gives them good songs to scar up. Highlights: Cathedral, Sleep, Brutal Truth, Iron Monkey, and of course Ultraviolence doing a techno-panik version of *Paranoid* and Pitch Shifter sending *N.I.B.* to the Ministry.

o NATIVITY IN BLACK: A TRIBUTE TO BLACK SABBATH (1994)
One of the early big budget, big shot tribute albums, NATIVITY IN BLACK featured many of the bands in this book — influences in their own right. Top of the bill would be White Zombie's horrifically heavy *Children Of The Grave*, Megadeth's tight 'n' taut *Paranoid* and Sepultura's steely-eyed and groovy *Symptom Of The Universe*. The promo-only version of this disc was a two CD package with all the originals on one CD (Old Testament) and the covers on the second (New Testament.) Note: a major label (EMI) follow-up came out in mid-2000 featuring a bunch of googly nu-metallers.

o SMOKE ON THE WATER: A TRIBUTE (Deep Purple) (1994)
Shrapnel's SMOKE ON THE WATER: A TRIBUTE was created in the spirit these possessed by tribute albums in the early days when they were an event rather than a quick buck-maker. Consequently, it's crammed full of shred kings and vocal technicians, any one of which from either discipline, could have deserved the Purple gig. The idea here was a crack band, fronted by various singers and axemen, a laundry list including the likes of Kelly Keeling, Yngwie, Kip Winger, Tony MacAlpine, Glenn Hughes, John Norum, Ritchie Kotzen, Joe Lynn Turner, Paul Gilbert, Robert Mason, Don Dokken, Reb Beach, Jeff Scott Soto and Tony Harnell. The band is a bit of a mean, median, average blend, but the names are also shiny: Deen Castronovo, Jens Johansson, Todd Jensen and Russ Parish.

o ENCOMIUM: A TRIBUTE TO LED ZEPPELIN (1995)
This is big alternative acts of the day being way artsy and imaginative. Of most lasting importance is Stone Temple Pilots' acoustic version of *Dancing Days* (great Weiland vocal), Blind Melon's hippie-tripped *Out On The Tiles*, complete with mostly new chords, Cracker's snotty *Good Times Bad Times* and *Four Sticks* from the Rollins Band, which actually finds Henry attempting singing.

o NORDIC METAL: A TRIBUTE TO EURONYMOUS (1995)
An astonishing blister-pak of the genre's early best in dark hails the early dead king of black metal, the man who drove the scene through his store, label and questionable business practices. This is a cool way to gather subtle interpretations of music that's a chorus of sledgehammers, and it was also a way of demonstrating the close, closed and incestuous nature of this creepy scene.

o APOCALYPTICA: PLAYS METALLICA BY FOUR CELLOS (1996)
A novel idea. Sold like crazy, as did the band's second, which widened its scope to include bands like Sepultura, Faith No More and Pantera, along with more Metallica and some originals. If you don't know already, this is a bunch of Finns playing cellos, making Metallica sound like the buzzing locusts from that under-rated second Exorcist movie.

o **WORKING MAN** (Rush) (1996)
Like the Purple tribute, this is prog's and power's best. Great performances, great production, and given its conception by progressive rock label Magna Carta, a scourge of their marquee individuals, folks that form the backbone of America's progressive rock resurgence. These versions don't stray greatly, but then again, how could they?

o **LEGENDS OF METAL: A TRIBUTE TO JUDAS PRIEST** (1996)
A stunning array of top-notch metal acts making these songs their own. The European version of this was 2 CDs, 2 LPs (just like the Dio), but we still got Mercyful Fate's hair-whitening take on *The Ripper*, Gamma Ray crunching through *Victim Of Changes* and Testament's thrashy bloody-fisted *Rapid Fire*. Practically all big power metal names, past and present.

o **DRAGON ATTACK: A TRIBUTE TO QUEEN** (1997)
Part of the high quality DeRock spate of these at the time, this one's got an all-star cast per usual. But unlike the Aerosmith tribute with a similar ilk of people, this one highlights vocalists and guitarists equally. Big shots on board: Chris Impellitteri, James LaBrie (man he makes *Sheer Heart Attack* sound, well, refreshing), Marty Friedman, Jeff Scott Soto, Mark Boals, Yngwie, John Bush, Lemmy, Ted Nugent, John Petrucci, man, and on and on it goes. Highlight: more or less Anthrax firing up one of the band's under-rated gems, *It's Late*.

o **A BLACK MARK TRIBUTE** (various) (1997)
A scintillating and largely humourous idea: Black Mark's high quality and under-rated acts playing obscure metal and non-metal treasures. Fun times include Memento Mori doing Nazareth obscurity *Sold My Soul*, Tad Morose's blaze up in and through Savatage's crushing *Power Of The Night*, Divine Sin doing long-lost Picture classic *Eternal Dark* and Edge Of Sanity's sparkly take on The Police's *Invisible Sun*. A pleasure through and through.

o **THUNDERBOLT: A TRIBUTE TO AC/DC** (1997)
An insane army of 80's hair metal royalty (although that doesn't always result in quality.) Still, look at this list of lead vocalists: Kevin Dubrow, Sebastian Bach, Joe Lynn Turner, Whitfield Crane, Jack Russell, John Corabi, Stephen Pearcy (wanker), Dave Meniketti, Dee Snider and Mr. Showbiz hisself Lemmy. Musically there's a knawing ordinariness to the thing, but as soon as all those pipes open up, man oh man.

o NOT THE SAME OLD SONG AND DANCE: TRIBUTE TO AEROSMITH (1999)
This is a surprisingly high watermark offering from Deadline, who, as of 2000, had
been punishing the world with full-on techno tribute albums to the likes of Van
Halen, Zeppelin and the Gunners, as well as the slightly more palatable prospect of
bands re-recording their old hits. It's a curious mix of Aerosmith's disciples and
contemporaries, with a few non-metal icons thrown in for good measure. Get a load
of this roll call: Ted Nugent, Vinnie Colaiuta, Derek Sherinian, Vince Neil, Blues
Saraceno, Earl Slick, Tommy Shaw, Jack Blades, Mike Inez, Randy Castillo, Ronnie James
Dio, Yngwie, Fee Waybill, Steve Lukather, Tim Bogert, Tommy Aldridge, Tony Levin and
Eric Singer.

o A TRIBUTE TO ACCEPT (1999)
This one wins the day simply because of the power metal elite that have assembled
for the cause, fully fourteen power metal acts and a few oddities (Therion, Dimmu
Borgir) bouncing and grooving their way through expertly executed versions of the
hits and beyond. Highlights: (surprisingly) Tankard, Primal Fear, Grave Digger,
newcomers Metalium and of course Dimmu Borgir, who creep out the attic with
their chilly *Metal Heart.*

o CATCH THE RAINBOW: A TRIBUTE TO RAINBOW (1999)
Fierce, heartfelt, maniacally meticulous renditions by an army of power metal's elite,
core city-state being Gamma Ray, Helloween and Primal Fear dudes, along with
biggest contributor, keyboardist about town, Ferdy Doernberg. Amazing songs
tightened, pan-seared, power-charged and sung their asses off. Basically any album
with *Lost In Hollywood* and *Eyes Of The World* on it, well, you rule.

o SLAVE TO THE POWER: THE IRON MAIDEN TRIBUTE (1999)
This one wins by cheating, i.e. by offering two CDs of bewildering variety, from
Sebastian Bach and Crowbar to new power metal types like Iron Savior and Holy
Mother, to obscure stoner rock acts like Archie Bunker, Tchort and Las Cruces. 26
tracks in all, this covers most of the bases with a number of Bruce-worthy vocals to
boot. Granted, lots of filler, but just lots.

Appendix VII: The Most Influential Bands In Metal: The Future Five

Here's where we all get to look back at the author in ten years and laugh our baggy pants off. I wish somebody would write a book of predictions within the music biz gone terribly wrong. Hey, I'd buy it. Anyway, here's some brave and gullible shots at who I think will, can, or should (there's a protective blanket, eh?) steer metal's next decade. See you in 2010.

Slipknot
OK, kind of already has happened, at least in terms of the band possessing a huge buzz. But one can see those twist on the "bounce" band theme causing more just like them, even if their visuals are too unique to even attempt replicating. The sound is an agitated upratchet on the whole Korn, Coal Chamber thing, and one can imagine at least another dozen who go there soon.

In Flames
Already kinda big in our geeky circles, these guys are the unswerved middle of the Gothenburg, Sweden death metal sound, the accessible heart of it, doing well through melody, Maiden-isms and large production values. Many are already pouring through in their wake, some, interestingly, already rebelling and going heavier (Darkane, Soilwork.)

Witchery
Once more, a band combining the harsh stuff from black and death and pouring in a little rock and roll hipshake. Few so far have tried to follow the band, most opting for more complicated forms of thrash. But given the band's effusively received records and live shows, one can imagine a few alcohol-fueled retro-thrash culture-jammers to attempt this vibe.

Satyricon
Currently leading the pack blazed by a cherry-picking of Emperor's, Old Man Child's, Borknagar's and Voivod's most acidic thought processes, Satyr and his collective are rightfully touted as the next level of black metal provocation. And if rumour comes true, they may get on Pantera's European tour, marking the first time a black metal band has crossed over into the squinty harsh light of a commercially viable world populated by regular folks.

Iron Maiden
Hey, as we sit waiting for the new record with Bruce to drop, could Maiden fulfill the empty promises of Kalodner's Ratt and Great White ruses and actually drag metal back to the fore? It just might work. Obviously, as you read this, you'll know how they did.

And as a side note, Mötley Crüe doesn't seem to be going away and Megadeth is still thriving and AC/DC is causing big frothy pre-waves with STIFF UPPER LIP. Now get out there and buy the stuff! Oh yeah, and see picture below for the band that should have been the next (and first) Metallica, after a monsterpiece in 1983 called ALL FOR ONE.

RAVEN

copyright 1982 Phil Anderson / KAOS2000 Magazine

A GUIDE TO THE ARTISTS WHO MADE THE CENTURY'S GREATEST ROCK MUSIC

20th CENTURY ROCK AND ROLL

A COLLECTOR'S GUIDE PUBLISHING SERIES

Psychedelia   ISBN 1-896522-40-8
Alternative Music   ISBN 1-896522-19-X
Progressive Rock   ISBN 1-896522-20-3
Pop Music   ISBN 1-896522-25-4
Punk Rock   ISBN 1-896522-27-0
Glam Rock   ISBN 1-896522-26-2
Women In Rock   ISBN 1-896522-29-7

The Collector's Guide To Heavy Metal
by Martin Popoff

... for who can resist the unswerving majesty of the power chord? Read about, it as we batter, praise and otherwise penetrate the essence of over 3,700 bruising records comprising a large wedge of the world's Most Powerful Music.

Designed to guide the discerning fan through the jungle of releases competing for your CD dollar.

Hard Rock, Heavy Metal, Grunge, Thrash, Funk Metal, Black Metal, Death Metal, Euro Metal, Prog Metal, Punk, et. etv.

Includes: CD sampler with nineteen Heavy Metal Bands.

ISBN 1-896522-32-7

$19.95 USA
$26.95 Canada
£15.95 UK

554 pages

Jimi Hendrix: Experience The Music
by Belmo and Steve Loveless

This exhaustive work provides fans and collectors with the complete details of all of Jimi Hendrix's musical output and is the most comprehensive guide yet written on the recordings and films of Jimi.

Nearly 650 titles (singles, LP's, compact discs, promotional releases and bootlegs) are included in the discography — from the first studio recordings in 1963 to the last recorded jam session in 1970.

Every song EVER recorded is listed and abalyzed in the Song Index which includes over 4,000 entries!

ISBN 1-896522-45-9

$15.95 USA
$18.95 Canada
£11.95 UK

504 pages